REEF
CREATURE
Identification

FLORIDA CARIBBEAN BAHAMAS

PAUL HUMANN

EDITED BY
NED DELOACH

NEW WORLD PUBLICATIONS, INC.

Printed by
Paramount Miller Graphics, Inc.
Jacksonville, Florida

Acknowledgments

This book was the result of considerable encouragement, help, and advice from many friends and acquaintances. It became a much larger undertaking and involved many more people than ever expected. I wish to express my sincere gratitude to everyone involved. Naturally, the names of a few who played especially significant roles come to mind.

Copy editor, friend and confidante, Patricia Reilly-Collins, spent untold hours making sure the text was phrased in comprehensible English. Mary DeLoach and Fred McConnaughey also gave valuable assistance in the editing process. Joe Gies and Michael O'Connell were most helpful with advice and assistance in design, layout, typesetting and production. Finally, I must mention editor, friend and business partner Ned DeLoach, without whose help this project would never have been completed.

Wonderful friends, John and Marion Bacon gave generously of their time, assistance, and boat, helping me photograph and collect marine invertebrates of Florida. Professional marine life photographers Mike Bacon, Marjorie Bank, Doug Perrine and Fred McConnaughey assisted by providing their knowledge of abundance, distribution, habitat and behavior of many species. Helping collect photographed specimens for scientific examination: Mike Bacon; Captains Graeme Teague, Louis Usie and Clay Weismen of the Aggressor Fleet; Phil Bush, Asst. Scientific Officer, and Michael Grundy, Marine Parks Officer, Cayman Islands Natural Resources Laboratory; Nick DeLoach.

PHOTO CREDITS

Mike Bacon 119c, 125c, 153b, 165c, 169a, 195c, 201c, 203a, 205c, 211a, 213b, 215c, 249a&c, 251a, 253a, 273a&b; *Marjorie Bank* 77b, 83a, 127a, 173b, 181b, 183b, 207c, 217b, 219c, 223c, 239a; *Cathy Church* 165b; *Ned DeLoach* 107c, 175b; *Denise Feingold* 259c; *Josh Feingold* 97b, 151a, 185c, 251b, 289a; *Dr. John Forsythe* 260c, 261a; *Dr. David Hall* 279c; *Jeff Hamann* 217c, 219a&b, 221c, 223b, 225a&c, 227c, 229ab&c, 231ab&c, 235a&b, 237b&c, 239c, 240, 241ab&c, 243c, 244ab&c, 247a; *Dr. Roger Hanlon* 263b, 263c; *Dr. Linda Harrison* 205b; *Larry Lipsky* 175c, 181c; *Fred McConnaughey* 113a, 159b, 177a; *Geri Murphy* 299c; *Doug Perrine* 225b, 261c, 285a; *John Rhodes* 147a; *Jeff Rotman* 285b; *Dr. Gus Schwartz* 85b; *Walter Stearns* 275c, 279a; *Graeme Teague* 121b, 233a, 279b, 283c; *Louis Usie* 121a, 243a; *Bryan Willy* 261b, 275b; *Jeannie Wiseman* 5; all other pictures were taken by the author, *Paul Humann.*

CREDITS

Editor: Ned DeLoach
Copy Editor: Patricia Reilly-Collins
Layout & Design: Paul Humann & Ned DeLoach
Art Direction & Drawings: Joe Gies
Art Direction & Typography: Michael O'Connell
Color Separations: Lithographic Services Inc., Inc. Jacksonville, FL
Printed by: Paramount Miller Graphics, Inc., Jacksonville, FL
First Printing: 1992
Second Printing: 1993
Third Printing: 1994
Fourth Printing: 1996; Fifth Printing: 1999
ISBN 1-878348-01-9
Library of Congress #91-067361
Copyright: ©1992 by Paul Humann
Published and Distributed by New World Publications, Inc., 1861 Cornell Road, Jacksonville, FL 32207, Phone (904) 737-6558

Scientific Acknowledgments

Special tribute must be given to the numerous scientists who gave freely of their time, advice and knowledge. Without this most generous assistance, the book could have never been published. Every attempt was made to keep this text and the identifications as accurate as possible; however, I'm sure a few errors crept in, and they are my sole responsibility.

The invaluable assistance of Dr. Walter Goldberg, of Florida International University, deserves special mention. He undertook the Herculean task of principal scientific adviser, and coordinator for this project.

Following are the scientists who assisted with identifications and other information. Their specialty and institution are also listed. Those taking the time and effort to make laboratory examinations of photographed and collected specimens are specially noted with an asterisk.

SPONGES
Dr. Shirley Pomponi, Harbor Branch Oceanographic Institute, Ft. Pierce, FL

HYDROIDS
Dr. Dale Calder, Royal Ontario Museum, Toronto, Canada

SIPHONOPHORES
Dr. Phil Pugh, Institute of Oceanographic Sciences, Surrey, England

TRUE JELLYFISH, COMB JELLIES
Dr. Ronald Larson, Harbor Branch Oceanographic Institute, Ft. Pierce, FL

ANEMONES, ZOANTHIDS, CORALLIMORPHS
Dr. Charles E. Cutress, University of Puerto Rico, Mayaguez, PR
Dr. Daphnie Fautin, Snow Museum, University Of Kansas, Lawrence, KS
Dr. Richard Mariscal, Florida State University, Tallahassee, FL

COMB JELLIES
Dr. George I. Matsumoto, Monterey Bay Aquarium Research Institute, Pacific Grove, CA

FLATWORMS
Dr. Stephen Prudhoe, British Museum of Natural History, London, England

SEGMENTED WORMS
Thomas H. Perkins, Florida Marine Research Institute, St. Petersburg, FL

SCALE WORMS
Dr. Marian H. Pettiebone, National Museum Of Natural History, Smithsonian Institution, Washington, DC

SHRIMP, LOBSTERS, HERMIT CRABS, CRABS
Dr. Robert H. Gore, BIO-ECON, Inc., Naples, FL
Dr. Mary K. Wicksten, Texas A & M University, College Station, TX

MANTIS SHRIMP
Dr. Raymond B. Manning, National Museum Of Natural History, Smithsonian Institution, Washington, DC

HERMIT CRABS, BARNACLES
Dr. Patsy A. McLaughlin, Shannon Point Marine Center, Western Washington University, Anacortes, WA

BRYOZOANS
Dr. Judith E. Winston, American Museum of Natural History, New York, NY

SNAILS, BIVALVES, CHITONS
Dr. Ken Grange, Department of Scientific Research, Wellington, New Zealand
Mike Bacon, North Palm Beach, FL

SHELL-LESS SNAILS
Jeff Hamann, El Cajon, CA
Dr. Kerry B. Clark, Florida Institute of Technology, Melbourne, FL

SQUID, OCTOPUSES
John W. Forsythe, Marine Biomedical Institute, University of Texas, Galveston, TX
Dr. Roger T. Hanlon, Marine Biomedical Institute, University of Texas, Galveston, TX
Dr. Nancy Voss, Rosenstiel School Of Marine Sciences, University of Miami, FL

CRINOIDS, SEA STARS, URCHINS
Dr. Charles G. Messing, NOVA University Oceanographic Center, Dania, FL

SEA STARS, BRITTLE STARS
Dr. Gordon L. Hendler, Natural History Museum of L.A., Los Angeles, CA

SEA CUCUMBERS
Dr. David L. Pawson, National Museum of Natural History, Smithsonian Institution, Washington, DC

TUNICATES
Dr. Ivan Goodbody, The University Of The West Indies, Kingston, Jamaica
Dr. Francoise Monniot, Museum National d'Histoire Naturelle, Paris, France

GENERAL ASSISTANCE
Dr. Hazel A. Oxenford, Bellairs Research Institute, Holetown, St. James, Barbados, W.I.
Josh Feingold, Rosenstiel School of Marine Sciences, Miami University, FL
Phil Bush, Natural Resources Laboratory, Georgetown, Cayman Islands
Dr. Louise Bush, Gray Museum, Marine Biological Laboratory, Woods Hole, MA
Dr. D.I. Gibson, British Museum of Natural History, London, England

Laymen find it difficult to pronounce Latinized scientific names and as a consequence rarely use them. In an attempt to help solve this problem we went to Dr. Shaila Van Sickle, a specialist in phonetics, at Ft. Lewis State College, Durango, Colorado. For this project, she developed a unique system of phonetic spellings of the Phyla and their major subdivisions that makes their proper pronunciation much easier.

Editor's Note

Life began in the sea. Today, warm tropical waters still provide the quintessential environment for life on earth. Here tiny coral polyps have proliferated, forming limestone structures that provide habitat for a biological diversity of exotic and colorful species that can only be rivaled by the world's great rain forests.

When a diver swims over a coral garden, the abundance of life creates a spectacle difficult to imagine. First to attract the eye are the many dazzling fishes that move by with endless energy; but, when the sunlit crest is left behind and the reef's craggy surface is explored, a new realm is discovered — this is the domain of the marine invertebrate, where many of our earth's most beautiful and bizarre creatures make their home.

Reef Creature Identification is a comprehensive, pictorial guide for the visual identification of marine invertebrates that live in, on, and around the reefs of Florida, the Caribbean and Bahamas. It is a companion text to *Reef Fish Identification*, first published in 1989, and the second of a three volume set that will include *Reef Coral Identification*.

In the past, the underwater naturalist's enthusiasm was too often tempered by the inability to identify or locate information about the many strange creatures encountered on the reef. This frustrating situation stemmed from the fact that scientific identifications, the majority completed well before the advent of SCUBA, relied on laboratory examinations of preserved specimens. These studies were unable to take into account visual clues such as colors, patterns, and behavioral traits exhibited by the creatures in the wild. Underwater identification has, unfortunately, been limited to those species known by characteristics of their external anatomy; for those requiring dissection and/or microscopic examinations, there was no established method for recognizing the species in their natural habitat.

As divers are becoming more conscious of the reefs' natural history, marine biologists are also spending more research time underwater; both groups understand the importance of bridging the gap between laboratory taxonomy and visual identification. *Reef Creature Identification* represents a cooperative and productive collaboration between the scientific community and author/ photographer Paul Humann. Over thirty biologists,specialists in their fields, contributed information, advice and lab time to this project. This process, requiring complicated photographic/ collection dives, careful packaging and shipping of specimens, lab examinations and documentation has, for the first time, made it possible to identify many invertebrates by visual characteristics alone.

Underwater identification plays a significant role in the protection of our coral reef systems by functioning as a catalyst for environmental awareness. When we learn to recognize a new species, we immediately begin to become familiar with the creature's patterns of behavior; and, when we begin to understand the nature of an animal, a concern for its welfare always follows. It is our hope that *Reef Creature Identification* and its companion volumes will add a new dimension to your underwater exploration, and with each personal discovery deepen your resolve to help save our seas.

About The Author

Paul Humann took his first underwater photograph in 1964. What began as a hobby turned into a full-time enterprise seven years later when he left his established law practice in Wichita, Kansas, to become captain/owner of the diving cruiser *MV/Cayman Diver*, the Carribean's first live aboard. For the next eight years he spent thousands of hours underwater documenting the rich biological diversity of coral reefs in the Caribbean.

Paul soon discovered that many of his passengers shared his interest in the reefs' natural history. Evening hours always found a group gathered in the ship's salon sharing diving experiences and attempting to identify the many fish and invertebrates sighted during the day. To satisfy his growing curiosity and as a service to guests, Paul began to study marine biology. As his knowledge grew he organized his underwater slides into a series of identification presentations called "Sea Talks". These enjoyable evening programs quickly became a featured part of every trip.

In 1979 he sold the *Cayman Diver* to travel, photograph and write full time. His photographs and articles have appeared in nearly every major diving and wildlife publication. He has produced nine books, including *Cayman Seascapes, Galapagos, and Guide to Corals*. His 1989 publication, *Reef Fish Identification — Florida, Caribbean, Bahamas* quickly became the most popular fish reference for divers. This comprehensive text, which includes 345 color photographs, revolutionized fishwatching. It is presently used by hundreds of diving retailers and resorts as the text for a popular fish identification specialty diving course based on his "Sea Talks". *Reef Creature Identification*, the companion volume to *Reef Fish Identification*, is a continuing effort to help the underwater naturalist learn about and enjoy the reefs they dive.

Today, Paul spends much of his time leading diving tours and presenting his ever-popular "Sea Talks" for live-aboard cruisers throughout the world. He continues to study marine biology, write, photograph, and collaborate with scientists on methods to visually identify marine life species in their natural habitat.

Contents

How To Use This Book

Ten Identification Groups
Common & Proper Phylum Names

1. Sponges – Porifera   14-61

Typical Shapes of Sponges

2. Cnidarians – Cnidaria   62-107

Hydroid

Hydromedusa

Siphonophores

True Jellyfish

Box Jellies

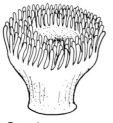

Sea Anemones

Zoanthids

Corallimorphs

Tube-Dwelling Anemones

3. Comb Jellies – Ctenophora   108-115

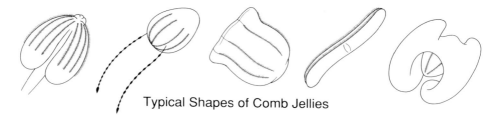

Typical Shapes of Comb Jellies

4. Flatworms – Platyhelminthes   116-121
Ribbon Worms – Rhynchocoela

Flatworms

Ribbon Worms

5. Segmented Worms – Annelida   122-141

Fire Worms

Fan Worms

Calcareous Tube Worms

Spaghetti Worms

6. Crustaceans – Arthropoda 142-185

Shrimp

Lobsters

True Crabs

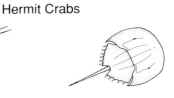

Hermit Crabs

Barnacles

Mantis Shrimp

Horseshoe Crab

7. Bryozoans – Ectoprocta 186-195

Typical Shapes of Bryozoan Colonies

8. Mollusks – Mollusca 196-263

Snails

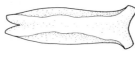

Headshield Slugs

Sea Hares

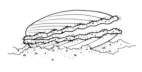

Sidegill Slugs

Sea Slugs

Nudibranchs

Bivalves

Chitons

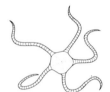

Squid

Octopuses

9. Echinoderms – Echinodermata   264-299

Feather Stars

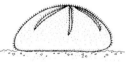

Sea Stars

Brittle Stars

Basket Stars

Sea Urchins

Heart Urchins

Sand Dollars

Sea Cucumbers

10. Tunicates – Chordata   300-320

Typical Shapes of Tunicate Colonies

Pelagic
Tunicates

Overview

Over one million species of animals have been described in the Animal Kingdom. Of these, approximately seven percent are single-celled animals. The rest are multicellular animals that fall into two general groups: the vertebrates — animals with backbones, and the invertebrates — animals without backbones. Vertebrates make up only four or five percent of the multicellular species total but, in the sea, they include some rather important animals such as fishes, dolphins, whales, seals and, of course, sport divers. The remaining and overwhelming majority (about 88 percent) are invertebrates. In the sea they include many commonly known groups such as sponges, jellyfishes, corals, shrimp, crabs, snails, octopuses, sea stars and sea urchins. This book deals with the identification of marine invertebrates that live on or near the reefs of Florida, the Caribbean and Bahamas. Those included are the species most likely to be encountered by divers, with the exception of the invertebrates commonly called corals, which are identified in a separate volume.

How To Use This Book

The hundreds of marine invertebrates that inhabit reefs and their adjacent habitats are divided into eleven major scientific classification groups called phyla. The members of each phylum are presented together in one of ten Identification Groups. This format varies only in ID Group 4, Flatworms and Ribbonworms, where two small phyla are included together. The ID Groups/Phyla appear in the order of general anatomical complexity, from the simplest — sponges, to the most complex — tunicates. A brief explanation of the predominant anatomical features that distinguish each phylum is given in the ID Groups' introduction. It is important to note that although animals within a phylum share basic anatomical similarities, some appear distinctly different from their relatives within these broad scientific classifications.

The animals in a phylum are classified further into class, order, family, genus and species. In some cases, even these classifications are subdivided further. Similar appearing invertebrates commonly recognized by the public as a group, such as jellyfish, crabs, sea stars, etc., usually fall completely within one of the lower classifications. These **Commonly Recognized Groups** are important reference keys for using this text. Each of the 50 groups are summarized in their corresponding ID Group/Phyla introduction. They are also listed with a visual reference diagram under their associated phylum in the content pages; in the master index on the inside front and back covers; at the top of the left page where their members are described in the text; and in bold type next to the identification photograph. It is important, as a first step in invertebrate identification, to become familiar with these groups and their locations within the text.

Names

Information about each species begins with the animal's common name (that used by the general public). In the past, using common names for identification was impractical because several species were known by more than one name.

For example, the Giant Anemone is often improperly known as the Pink Tipped Anemone. The common names used in this text are based on previously published names, and the standardized common names published by The American Fisheries Society. Many species included have never had a common name published. In these instances, a name was selected that describes a distinctive feature that can be used for visual identification. In this book, common species names are capitalized to help set them apart, although this practice is not considered grammatically correct.

Below the common name, in italics, is the two-part scientific name. The first word (always capitalized) is the genus. The genus name is given to a group of animals with very similar physiological characteristics. The second word (never capitalized) is the species. A species includes only animals that are sexually compatible and produce fertile offspring. Occasionally "sp." appears in the place of a species name. This means the species is not known; "spp." means it is one of two known species. Continuing below genus and species, in descending order, is a list of classification categories to which the genus and species belong. This scientific nomenclature, rooted in Latin (L.) and Greek (Gr.), is used by scientists throughout the world.

Size

The size range of the species that divers are most likely to observe. This is followed by a maximum species' size when appropriate. Occasionally, the length of tentacles, spines, etc. is also given if this information is useful in making a visual identification.

Depth

The average depth range at which divers are most likely to sight a species, although species are occasionally found outside this range. Depths below the recommended safe diving limit of 130 feet are not given even if the species regularly inhabits these waters. Species that live exclusively below 130 feet are not included in this book.

Visual ID

Colors, markings and anatomical differences that distinguish the species from similar appearing species. In most cases, these features are readily apparent to divers, but occasionally they are quite subtle. The features listed first are considered the most distinctive visual characteristics of the species.

Abundance & Distribution

Abundance refers to a diver's likelihood of observing a species in its normal habitat and depth range on any given dive. This is not always indicative of the actual population. Definitions are as follows:

Abundant – At least several sightings can be expected on nearly every dive.
Common – Sightings are frequent, but not necessarily to be expected on every dive.
Occasional – Sightings are not unusual, but are not to be expected on a regular basis.
Uncommon – Sightings are unusual.
Rare – Sightings are exceptional.

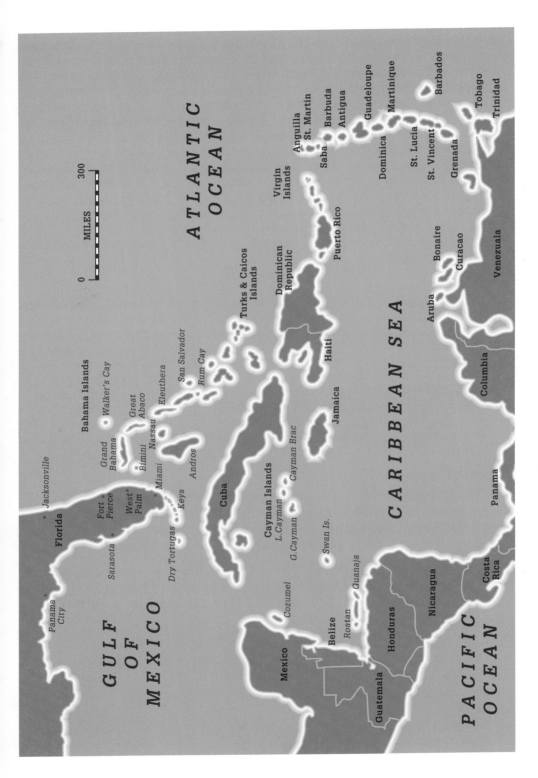

Distribution describes where the species may be found geographically within the range of the map on the opposite page. The Turks and Caicos Islands, an extension of the Bahama Islands' chain, are also included. Described species may also be found in areas such as Bermuda, Brazil, etc., but no attempt has been made to include this specific information, although additional data has occasionally been included. In many cases the extent of a species' geographical range is not yet known; consequently, species may occasionally be found in areas not listed. If sightings are made that do not correspond with the geographic information provided, the publisher is interested in obtaining details for updating future editions.

Habitat & Behavior

Habitat is the type of underwater terrain or associated organism where a particular species is likely to be found. Only habitats frequented by divers, such as natural and artificial reefs, adjacent areas of sand and rubble, sea grass beds and walls are emphasized.

Behavior is the animal's normal activities that can be observed by a diver and help in identification.

Effect On Divers

If a species is known to have a negative effect on divers, it is listed. The agent of the injury, how it might occur, symptoms, and recommended treatment are included where appropriate.

Reaction To Divers

Relates to the species' normal reaction to divers, if any, and describes tactics a diver can use to make a closer observation.

Similar Species

Occasionally there are similar appearing species that are not pictured. Usually they are invertebrates that are rarely observed by divers. Characteristics and information are given that distinguish them from the species pictured.

Note

Additional information that may help in the visual identification process such as: recent changes in classification, other common names also used for the same species, or details relating to the method used to identify the photographed specimen.

Phylum Porifera

(Por-IF-er-uh / L. hole-bearing)

Sponges

Sponges are the simplest of the multicellular animals. The individual cells display a considerable degree of independence, and form no true tissue layers or organs. Depending upon a cell's location within the sponge, they do, however, perform somewhat specialized functions. A sponge's surface is perforated with numerous small holes called **incurrent pores** or ostia. Water is drawn into the sponge through these pores and pumped through the interior by the beating of whip-like extensions on the cells called flagella. As water passes through the sponge, food and oxygen are filtered out. The water exits into the body's interior cavity and out the animal's one or more large **excurrent openings** or oscula.

Sponges come in many sizes, colors and shapes. Some are quite small, less than half an inch across, while the Giant Barrel Sponge may attain a height of over six feet. Their colors range from drab grays and browns to bright reds, oranges, yellows, greens, and violets. The shape of what can be considered a typical sponge resembles a vase. However, growth patterns vary tremendously. Those with one large body opening form bowls, barrels and tubes. Sponges with multiple body openings may form irregular masses, or shapes like ropes, candles, branching horns or, in the case of encrusting sponges, take the shapes of what they overgrow.

Although sponges come in many forms, they can usually be recognized as a group by their excurrent openings that are generally large and distinct. Another key is their lack of any evident movement. Nearly all animals react with an obvious protective movement when approached or touched, but sponges show no reaction when disturbed. Sponges may occasionally be confused with tunicates (Identification Group 10), which often have similar-appearing body openings and grow in comparable patterns, shapes and colors. Tunicates, however, are highly evolved animals, having a nervous system and relatively complex muscles that can rapidly close their body openings.

While sponges are easy to recognize as a group, many individual species are difficult to identify. This is because the same species may grow in different shapes and patterns, which is the consequence of several factors, including age, location, depth and water movement. Color is often another poor clue to identification. Variations of color within the same species may result from the water chemistry, depth, light conditions and the presence of algae living in symbiosis with the sponge. For these reasons, correct identification of many species can only be made in the laboratory, by microscopic examination of the tissue or the shape of tiny structural elements called spicules. Fortunately, a number of the more common sponges found on reefs grow in relatively consistent patterns, shapes and colors, making visual identification possible.

For the convenience of visual reference this Identification Group is arranged by shape rather than scientific classification. The order of these shape/categories is: tubes, vases and barrels, balls, irregular masses, ropes, encrusting, boring, and finally, the calcareous sponges.

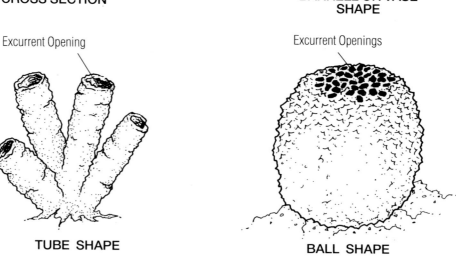

Excurrent Openings

Sponge Wall

Water Flow

Incurrent Pore

**TYPICAL SPONGE
CROSS SECTION**

Excurrent Opening

**BARRELL OR VASE
SHAPE**

Excurrent Opening

TUBE SHAPE

Excurrent Openings

BALL SHAPE

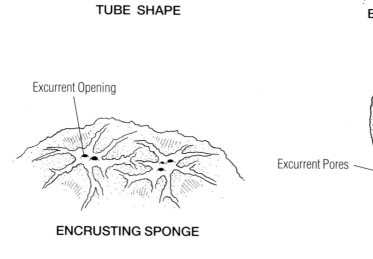

Excurrent Opening

ENCRUSTING SPONGE

Excurrent Pores

ROPE SPONGE

VISUAL ID: Cluster of numerous tubes extend and branch from a base mass. Profusion of small bumps on exterior gives these sponges a stippled texture. Interiors of openings are shades of yellow. Exterior color variable, including yellow, purple, orange and olive green.

ABUNDANCE & DISTRIBUTION: Abundant Caribbean; common Bahamas; occasional South Florida.

HABITAT & BEHAVIOR: Inhabit coral reefs, often grow on walls.

NOTE: Visual identifications confirmed by microscopic examination of small samples collected from pictured specimens.

Purple Variety

Orange Variety

BRANCHING TUBE SPONGE

Pseudoceratina crassa

CLASS:
Sponges
Demospongiae

SIZE: 6 - 18 in.
DEPTH: 20 - 80 ft.

Yellow Variety
Note the bright red
Erect Rope Sponge
[pg.43].

Olive Variety

17

VISUAL ID: Large, thick-walled tube with rough exterior and numerous small finger-like projections. Lip of tube opening is thin and protrudes from mass of sponge. Usually covered with a variety of algal growth and sediment. Color variable due to encrusting organisms, but sponge itself is dark gray to black. Grows as a solitary tube.

ABUNDANCE & DISTRIBUTION: Occasional Caribbean, Bahamas; rare Florida.

HABITAT & BEHAVIOR: Inhabit drop-off areas. Usually hang from walls, under ledges or in other protected areas.

NOTE: Visual identification confirmed by microscopic examination of small sample collected from pictured specimen.

VISUAL ID: Tubes are long, slender, thin, and soft-walled. Exterior, shades of lavender [opposite], shades of gray [below] or brown [below right]. Tubes' interiors often cream colored, but may be lighter shade of exterior color. Grow as solitary specimens or in clusters.

ABUNDANCE & DISTRIBUTION: Common Caribbean; occasional Bahamas.

HABITAT & BEHAVIOR: Inhabit deeper reefs, often grow on walls.

Gray Variety

ROUGH TUBE SPONGE
Oceanapia bartschi
CLASS:
Sponges
Demospongiae

SIZE: 1 $\frac{1}{2}$ - 4 ft.
DEPTH: 60 - 130 ft.

STOVE-PIPE SPONGE
Aplysina archeri
CLASS:
Sponges
Demospongiae

SIZE: 2 - 6 ft.
DEPTH: 50 - 100 ft.

Brown Variety

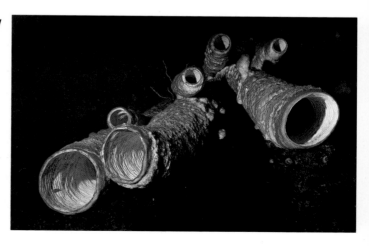

VISUAL ID: Tubes are yellow to orange, and soft-walled. Usually in clusters joined at the base. In shallow water, clusters tend to be shorter with antler-like growths extending from around the openings [opposite]. In deeper water, especially along walls, tubes tend to be longer and without antler-like growths [below]. In natural light, especially in deeper water, appear to be yellow-green. Retain yellow-green color even at great depth, probably the result of fluorescent pigments.

ABUNDANCE & DISTRIBUTION: Abundant Caribbean; common Bahamas; occasional Florida.

HABITAT & BEHAVIOR: Inhabit coral reefs, especially in open water areas and on walls. Gobies and cardinal fish often live inside the tubes.

NOTE: If squeezed, secrete a purple dye that will stain skin for several days.

VISUAL ID: Massive, thick-walled barrels or tubes. Deeply convoluted and pitted exteriors. Ridges dark green to yellowish-green, valleys and pits yellow-green to yellow. Interior walls have yellow excurrent pores. Grow solitary or in small groups.

ABUNDANCE & DISTRIBUTION: Occasional Bahamas, Caribbean.

HABITAT & BEHAVIOR: Inhabit coral reefs and walls. May attach to solid substrate and grow upright like barrels, or attach to walls and extend outward as massive tubes. Often have sediment, algae and various organisms on surface.

YELLOW TUBE SPONGE

Aplysina fistularis

CLASS:
Sponges
Demospongiae

SIZE: 2 - 4 ft.
DEPTH: 15 - 100 ft.

CONVOLUTED BARREL SPONGE

Aplysina lacunosa

CLASS:
Sponges
Demospongiae

SIZE: 1 - 3 ft.
DEPTH: 60 - 130 ft.

VISUAL ID: Soft-walled tubes are medium brown to tan to grayish-brown with lighter interiors. Although the exterior can be somewhat lumpy or pitted, the surface texture tends to be quite smooth (compare with similar growth patterns of Brown Encrusting Octopus Sponge [pg. 37] distinguished by a felt-like surface texture). Grow in clusters joined at the base [opposite], but occasionally form shapes like moose antlers [below, right page], octopus arms [below right], or trumpets [below left].

ABUNDANCE & DISTRIBUTION: Common Bahamas, Caribbean; occasional Florida.

HABITAT & BEHAVIOR: Inhabit reefs and walls, especially in more protected areas such as in canyons, crevices and other large recesses. Golden Zoanthids [pg. 99 and opposite] or Maroon Sponge Zoanthids, [pg. 99 and below right page], may grow on the surface.

VISUAL ID: Cluster of smooth, small brown tubes grows from a common basal mass. Tube openings are often irregular and may appear pinched in.

ABUNDANCE & DISTRIBUTION: Occasional Florida, Bahamas, Caribbean.

HABITAT & BEHAVIOR: Inhabit reef tops. Often grow around the bases of coral heads.

NOTE: Visual identification confirmed by microscopic examination of small sample collected from pictured specimen.

BROWN TUBE SPONGE
Agelas conifera
CLASS:
Sponges
Demospongiae

SIZE: 1 - 3 ft.
DEPTH: 35 - 130 ft.

Growth Patterns

BROWN CLUSTERED TUBE SPONGE
Agelas wiedenmyeri
CLASS:
Sponges
Demospongiae

SIZE: Tubes 1 - 3 in.
DEPTH: 15 - 75 ft.

VISUAL ID: Thin, stiff-walled tubes. Outer walls commonly have many irregular conical projections. Usually in clusters, ranging from a few to 20 or 30 tubes. Vary from lavender [opposite] to brownish-gray [below] to greenish-gray [below right] and occasionally light tan. When growing in areas of strong current and/or sedimentation, they form vases and fans [below right].

ABUNDANCE & DISTRIBUTION: Common South Florida, Bahamas, Caribbean.

HABITAT & BEHAVIOR: Inhabit shallow and mid-range coral reefs, walls, and rocky areas. Exterior surface frequently covered with Sponge Zoanthids [pg. 99], and often have associated Sponge Brittle Stars [pg. 281].

Brownish-Gray Variety
Note sponge,
zoanthids and
Sponge Brittle Stars.

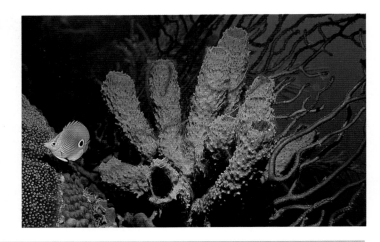

VISUAL ID: Pink to purple and fluoresces light blue, vase-like sponge. Exterior elaborately sculptured with numerous convoluted ridges and valleys. Grow solitary or in groups of two or three. On rare occasions, apparently when colony is dying, pale yellow to gold.

ABUNDANCE & DISTRIBUTION: Common to occasional Caribbean; occasional South Florida, Bahamas.

HABITAT & BEHAVIOR: Inhabit coral reefs, most commonly grow on walls. Often have associated Sponge Brittle Stars [pg. 281].

BRANCHING VASE SPONGE
Callyspongia vaginalis
CLASS:
Sponges
Demospongiae

SIZE: 6 - 36 in.
DEPTH: 6 - 65 ft.

Fan Shaped, Greenish-Gray Variety

AZURE VASE SPONGE
Callyspongia plicifera
CLASS:
Sponges
Demospongiae

SIZE: 6 - 18 in.
DEPTH: 20 - 75 ft.

VISUAL ID: Brilliant shades of red and orange. Vase- or cup-like with rough-textured exterior. Usually in a cluster of several joined individuals, but may be solitary. Appear dark burgundy at depth without artificial light.

ABUNDANCE & DISTRIBUTION: Occasional Florida Keys, Bahamas, Caribbean.

HABITAT & BEHAVIOR: Inhabit coral reefs, most commonly grow on walls. Attach to solid substrate, branches of Black Coral trees [pictured] and occasionally stalks of dead gorgonians. Often have associated Sponge Brittle Stars [pg. 281].

VISUAL ID: Pink, lavender, blue, greenish-gray or gray. Usually vase- or bowl-shaped. Edge of opening bordered with a nearly transparent membrane.

ABUNDANCE & DISTRIBUTION: Occasional South Florida, Bahamas, Caribbean.

HABITAT & BEHAVIOR: Inhabit coral reefs. Exterior surface frequently covered with Sponge Zoanthids [pg. 99]. Often have associated Sponge Brittle Stars [pg. 281].

VISUAL ID: Brown to reddish-brown. Stiff, usually bowl-shaped. Bowls often have an irregular or incomplete shape and may encrust small areas around base. Surface has sandpaper-like texture.

ABUNDANCE & DISTRIBUTION: Occasional South Florida, Bahamas, Caribbean.

HABITAT & BEHAVIOR: Inhabit coral reefs, often in rubble areas between reefs, or on walls.

STRAWBERRY VASE SPONGE

Mycale laxissima

CLASS:
Sponges
Demospongiae

SIZE: 3 - 12 in.
DEPTH: 35 - 130 ft.

PINK VASE SPONGE

Niphates digitalis

CLASS:
Sponges
Demospongiae

SIZE: 4 - 12 in.
DEPTH: 25 - 75 ft.

BROWN BOWL SPONGE

Cribrochalina vasculum

CLASS:
Sponges
Demospongiae

SIZE: 8 - 18 in.
DEPTH: 35 - 100 ft.

VISUAL ID: Large barrel-shape, diameter about half its height. Exterior has distinctive, raised, net-like texture and appears rubbery. Dark green, olive, yellow-green, yellow-brown or green-brown. Smooth interior walls are often a lighter yellowish color and pitted with numerous, round excurrent pores.

ABUNDANCE & DISTRIBUTION: Occasional Bahamas, Caribbean; rare Florida.

HABITAT & BEHAVIOR: Inhabit exposed areas of moderate to deep clear water reefs. Several species of fish and possibly turtles occasionally bite this sponge, leaving bright yellow pits.

VISUAL ID: Huge barrel-shape with rough, often jagged, stone-hard exterior. Shades of gray, brown, or red-brown. Generally solitary, but one or two smaller individuals occasionally grow around base.

ABUNDANCE & DISTRIBUTION: Common Bahamas, Caribbean; occasional Florida.

HABITAT & BEHAVIOR: Inhabit mid-range to deep coral reefs. Often abundant on steep slopes.

NOTE: The size of these sponges often tempts divers to climb inside. This practice is discouraged because the lip breaks easily, disrupting the pumping action of the sponge and allowing the entry of organisms that may cause the colony's death. A sponge large enough to hold a diver may be over 100 years old, as they grow only about one-half inch a year!

VISUAL ID: Squatty barrel-shape with thick, hard, leathery walls. Exterior often heavily pitted. Shades of brown and gray.

ABUNDANCE & DISTRIBUTION: Common Florida Keys, Bahamas, Caribbean.

HABITAT & BEHAVIOR: Inhabit coral reefs. Usually covered with sediment and algal growth. The pictured sponge is "smoking," which is a release of sperm cells, one way in which some species of sponges reproduce.

NOTE: Visual identification confirmed by microscopic examination of small sample collected from pictured specimen

NETTED BARREL SPONGE
Verongula gigantea
CLASS:
Sponges
Demospongiae

SIZE: 2 - 5 ft.
DEPTH: 35 - 130 ft.

GIANT BARREL SPONGE
Xestospongia muta
CLASS:
Sponges
Demospongiae

SIZE: 2 - 6 ft.
DEPTH: 50 - 130 ft.

LEATHERY BARREL SPONGE
Geodia neptuni
CLASS:
Sponges
Demospongiae

SIZE: 1¹/₂ - 2¹/₂ ft.
DEPTH: 40 - 100 ft.

VISUAL ID: Squatty barrel-shape with flattened top. Central depression has numerous excurrent openings. Hard, leathery, convoluted surface. Exterior shades of gray to dark brown, central depression dark brown to black.

ABUNDANCE & DISTRIBUTION: Common Florida, Bahamas, Caribbean.

HABITAT & BEHAVIOR: Found in a variety of habitats, including shallow patch reefs and areas of sedimentation. Surface often covered with sediment and algal growth. Frequently host a large number of symbiotic shrimp that live in its canals.

VISUAL ID: Ball- or cake-shaped, occasionally with lobes. One or more slight depressions with clusters of excurrent openings. Soft external surface covered with conical knobs. Black to gray overall, knobs are whitish with fine radiating lines.

ABUNDANCE & DISTRIBUTION: Common to occasional Florida, Bahamas, Caribbean. May be locally abundant.

HABITAT & BEHAVIOR: Inhabit shallow to mid-range coral reefs. Prefer brightly lit areas.

VISUAL ID: Single, black excurrent openings scattered over surface. Light gray or light brown with hexagonal design of low, white knobs, often with interconnecting lines. Shape varies, though most commonly encrusting lobes.

ABUNDANCE & DISTRIBUTION: Abundant to common Florida, Bahamas, Caribbean.

HABITAT & BEHAVIOR: Inhabit shallow to mid-range reefs, often grow near living coral.

NOTE: Common name derives from its foul odor when removed from the water.

LOGGERHEAD SPONGE
*Spheciospongia
vesparium*
CLASS:
Sponges
Demospongiae

SIZE: 1½ - 5 ft.
DEPTH: 15 - 60 ft.

BLACK-BALL SPONGE
Ircinia strobilina
CLASS:
Sponges
Demospongiae

SIZE: 1 - 1½ ft.
DEPTH: 15 - 75 ft.

STINKER SPONGE
Ircinia felix
CLASS:
Sponges
Demospongiae

SIZE: 6 - 12 in.
DEPTH: 5 - 65 ft

VISUAL ID: Orange, ball-shaped sponge, pitted with excurrent openings.

ABUNDANCE & DISTRIBUTION: Common South Florida, Bahamas, Caribbean.

HABITAT & BEHAVIOR: Inhabit protected areas of coral reef, especially under ledges and in caves. Often covered with growths of algae and sediment.

NOTE: There are two similar appearing Orange Ball Sponges: *Cinachyra alloclada* is more common; *C. kuekenthali* is known primarily from deeper reefs. Because they are difficult to distinguish visually, microscopic examination of specimens is required for positive identification.

VISUAL ID: Dark reddish-brown to black, soft, irregular mass. Smooth-textured surface with scattered excurrent openings that form volcano-like projections.

ABUNDANCE & DISTRIBUTION: Occasional Caribbean; rare Florida, Bahamas. Common in some locations.

HABITAT & BEHAVIOR: Inhabit reefs, especially small patch reefs in exposed areas. Maroon Sponge Zoanthids [pg. 99] may grow on the surface.

NOTE: Visual identification confirmed by microscopic examination of small sample collected from pictured specimen.

VISUAL ID: Brown to tan encrusting lobes with numerous pits and ridges over surface. Excurrent openings not grouped and often lighter in color with tints of yellow.

ABUNDANCE & DISTRIBUTION: Occasional Florida Keys, Bahamas, Caribbean.

HABITAT & BEHAVIOR: Inhabit coral reefs.

ORANGE BALL SPONGE
Cinachyra sp.
CLASS:
Sponges
Demospongiae

SIZE: 4 ½ - 6 ½ in.
DEPTH: 15 - 100 ft.

DARK VOLCANO SPONGE
Calyx podatypa
CLASS:
Sponges
Demospongiae

SIZE: 1 - 3 ft.
DEPTH: 30 - 90 ft.

PITTED SPONGE
Verongula rigida
CLASS:
Sponges
Demospongiae

SIZE: 6 - 14 in.
DEPTH: 20 - 80 ft.

VISUAL ID: Pink, lumpy mass, with numerous short, cone-like and knob-like projections. Red, vein-like canals radiate and meander from excurrent openings.

ABUNDANCE & DISTRIBUTION: Common South Florida; occasional to uncommon Bahamas, Caribbean.

HABITAT & BEHAVIOR: Found in a variety of habitats, including reefs.

NOTE: Visual identification confirmed by microscopic examination of small sample collected from pictured specimen.

VISUAL ID: Pinkish to lavender-gray, lumpy mass. Often form rope-like appearance by overgrowing gorgonians and using stalks as support.

ABUNDANCE & DISTRIBUTION: Common Florida, Bahamas, Caribbean.

HABITAT & BEHAVIOR: Found in a variety of habitats, including reefs.

NOTE: Identification made by microscopic examination of small sample collected from pictured specimen.

SIMILAR SPECIES: *Desmapsamma anchorata*, can only be distinguished by microscopic examination.

VISUAL ID: Orange to red, irregular mass with scattered excurrent openings that often form volcano-like projections.

ABUNDANCE & DISTRIBUTION: Common Florida, Bahamas, Caribbean.

HABITAT & BEHAVIOR: Inhabit bays, lagoons, turtle grass beds and rubble areas around shallow patch reefs.

EFFECT ON DIVERS: Contact with bare skin can result in a severe irritating reaction, including burning pain, numbness, swelling and rash that may last several days. Treat with vinegar, followed by a sprinkling of meat tenderizer; rinse and soothe with hydrocortisone ointment.

PINK LUMPY SPONGE
Monanchora unguifera
CLASS:
Sponges
Demospongiae

SIZE: 4 - 16 in.
DEPTH: 30 - 100 ft.

LUMPY OVERGROWING SPONGE
Holopsamma helwigi
CLASS:
Sponges
Demospongiae

SIZE: 4 - 16 in.
DEPTH: 15 - 75 ft.

FIRE SPONGE
Tedania ignis
CLASS:
Sponges
Demospongiae

SIZE: 4 - 12 in.
DEPTH: 1 - 35 ft.

VISUAL ID: Massive, dark brown, lumpy surface has a felt-like texture. Grows in a wide variety of irregular patterns. Large, uneven excurrent openings. Interior surface is covered with white specks that are actually tiny polychaete Sponge Worms [pg. 127].

ABUNDANCE & DISTRIBUTION: Abundant to occasional Florida, Bahamas, Caribbean.

HABITAT & BEHAVIOR: Found in a variety of habitats, from shallow inshore reefs and adjacent areas of rubble to deep fore reefs. A number of animals live in association with this sponge, including Touch-Me-Not Fan Worm [pg. 139], Sponge Brittle Star [pg. 281], tube-worm snails [pg. 217], Yellowline Goby, *Gobiosoma horsti*, and Shortstripe Goby, *G. chancei*.

EFFECT ON DIVERS: Contact with bare skin can result in a severe allergic reaction, including pain, numbness, swelling and rash that may last several days. Treat with vinegar, followed by a sprinkling of meat tenderizer; rinse and soothe with hydrocortisone ointment. Severe reactions may include difficulty in breathing, requiring oral antihistamine and medical attention. Interestingly, the species' Latin name, *nolitangere*, means "do-not-touch."

VISUAL ID: Shades of reddish-brown to brown with numerous raised excurrent openings ringed with a lighter colored lip. Lumpy, with felt-like surface texture. Encrusts dead areas of reef [opposite], and overgrows gorgonian stalks, may extend long arms that resemble octopus tentacles [below] (compare similar growth patterns of Brown Tube Sponge [pg. 23] distinguished by smooth surface texture).

ABUNDANCE & DISTRIBUTION: Common Caribbean, Bahamas; occasional Florida Keys.

HABITAT & BEHAVIOR: Inhabit reefs and adjacent areas. Often grow over coral rubble and dead areas of reef.

NOTE: Visual identification confirmed by microscopic examination of small sample collected from pictured specimens, opposite and below right. Encrusting variety also commonly known as "Brown Volcano Sponge."

TOUCH-ME-NOT SPONGE

Neofibularia nolitangere

CLASS:
Sponges
Demospongiae

SIZE: 1 - 4 ft.
DEPTH: 10 - 130 ft.

BROWN ENCRUSTING OCTOPUS SPONGE

Ectyoplasia ferox

CLASS:
Sponges
Demospongiae

SIZE: 6 - 16 in.
DEPTH: 40 - 75 ft.

Growth Patterns

VISUAL ID: Shades of lavender, occasionally somewhat pinkish. Long and rope-like with porous, somewhat rough texture. Often in tangled masses.

ABUNDANCE & DISTRIBUTION: Scattered distribution, but can be locally common in South Florida, Bahamas, Caribbean.

HABITAT & BEHAVIOR: Inhabit reefs and frequently walls. Often hang from ledges and other outcroppings. Usually covered with Sponge Zoanthids [pg. 99] and Sponge Brittle Stars [pg. 281].

VISUAL ID: Excurrent openings form long rows [see below] (compare similar Scattered Pore Rope Sponge [next]). These openings have thin, protruding lips, often of lighter color. Surface texture is not porous (compare similar Erect Rope Sponge [pg. 43]). Long, branching and rope-like; generally hang downward with last few inches curving upward. Color highly variable and not distinctive, and include among others red [right], purple [below right], lavender [below].

ABUNDANCE & DISTRIBUTION: Common Bahamas, Caribbean; occasional South Florida.

HABITAT & BEHAVIOR: Inhabit deep sloping reefs and walls.

Lavender Variety
Note rows of excurrent openings.

LAVENDER ROPE SPONGE

Niphates erecta

CLASS:
Sponges
Demospongiae

SIZE: 3 - 6 ft.
DEPTH: 40 - 100 ft.

ROW PORE ROPE SPONGE

Aplysina cauliformis

CLASS:
Sponges
Demospongiae

SIZE: 4 - 8 ft.
DEPTH: 40 - 130 ft.

Purple Variety

VISUAL ID: Excurrent openings are scattered [see below] (compare similar Row Pore Rope Sponge [previous]). These openings have thin, protruding lips, often of lighter color. Surface texture is not porous (compare similar Erect Rope Sponge [pg. 43]). Long, branching and rope-like; generally hang downward with last few inches curving upward. Color highly variable and not distinctive, and include amoung others tan [opposite], yellow-green [below right], brown and purple [below].

ABUNDANCE & DISTRIBUTION: Common Bahamas, Caribbean; occasional South Florida.

HABITAT & BEHAVIOR: Inhabit deep sloping reefs and walls.

NOTE: Visual identification confirmed by microscopic examination of small sample collected from pictured specimens below and below right.

Brown and Lavender Varieties

Note scattered excurrent openings. Red is Erect Rope Sponge [pg. 43], note porous texture.

VISUAL ID: Thin, rope-like, often in tangled masses. Shades of red to pink.

ABUNDANCE & DISTRIBUTION: Common South Florida, Bahamas, Caribbean.

HABITAT & BEHAVIOR: Inhabit coral reefs and frequently walls. Often covered with winding chains of Golden Zoanthids [pg. 99 and opposite].

NOTE: Visual identification confirmed by microscopic examination of small sample collected from pictured specimens. Formerly classified in the genus *Thalysias*.

SCATTERED PORE ROPE SPONGE
Aplysina fulva
CLASS:
Sponges
Demospongiae

SIZE: 4 - 8 ft.
DEPTH: 10 - 130 ft.

Yellow-Green Variety

THIN ROPE SPONGE
Rhaphidophlus juniperinus
CLASS:
Sponges
Demospongiae

SIZE: 1 - 5 ft.
DEPTH: 20 - 100 ft.

VISUAL ID: Numerous finger-like branches mottled in shades of green. May grow erect, in tangled masses or hang from outcroppings.

ABUNDANCE & DISTRIBUTION: Common South Florida, Bahamas, Caribbean.

HABITAT & BEHAVIOR: Inhabit coral reefs and walls. Frequently covered with winding chains of Golden Zoanthids [pg. 99].

NOTE: If squeezed, secrete a black dye.

VISUAL ID: Rope-like, usually branched structure grows upward from substrate. Smooth, but surface is porous (compare with Row Pore Rope Sponge [pg. 39] and Scattered Pore Rope Sponge [pg. 40]). Usually brilliant red, but can be burgundy or maroon. Excurrent openings are scattered and do not have thin, light-colored lips.

ABUNDANCE & DISTRIBUTION: Common Florida, Bahamas, Caribbean.

HABITAT & BEHAVIOR: Inhabit coral reef tops, occasionally walls. On walls may closely resemble Row Pore Rope Sponge or Scattered Pore Rope Sponge, but their characteristic upward growth pattern remains distinctive.

VISUAL ID: Red to orange, branched, rope-like structure grows upward from substrate. Surface texture is rough.

ABUNDANCE & DISTRIBUTION: Uncommon Caribbean, Bahamas; rare Florida.

HABITAT & BEHAVIOR: Inhabit coral reef tops, often near drop-offs.

NOTE: The similarity in appearance between three species, *Ptilocaulis gracilis*, *P. walpersi*, and *P. spiculifera* requires microscopic examination for positive species identification.

GREEN FINGER SPONGE
Iotrochota birotulata
CLASS:
Sponges
Demospongiae

SIZE: 1 - 3 ft.
DEPTH: 15 - 60 ft.

ERECT ROPE SPONGE
Amphimedon compressa
CLASS:
Sponges
Demospongiae

SIZE: 2 - 3 ½ ft.
DEPTH: 35 - 70 ft.

RED-ORANGE BRANCHING SPONGES
Ptilocaulis sp.
CLASS:
Sponges
Demospongiae

SIZE: 8 - 15 in.
DEPTH: 40 - 80 ft.

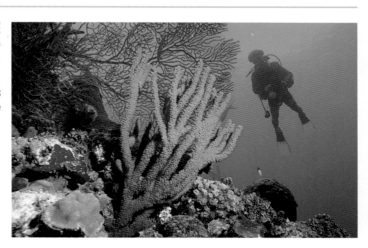

VISUAL ID: White, lumpy encrusting sponge with scattered, large excurrent openings. Often has light shadings of gold or pink.

ABUNDANCE & DISTRIBUTION: Common South Florida.

HABITAT & BEHAVIOR: Encrust dead areas of reef and shipwrecks.

NOTE: Identification of genus by microscopic examination of small sample collected from pictured specimen. Possibly an undescribed species.

VISUAL ID: Smooth, encrusting mass is speckled pink and/or red.

ABUNDANCE & DISTRIBUTION: Occasional Florida, Bahamas, Caribbean.

HABITAT & BEHAVIOR: Inhabit reefs and walls. Prefer shaded, protected areas; encrust around undercut bases of coral heads, in recesses, and wall faces under ledge overhangs.

NOTE: Visual identification confirmed by microscopic examination of small sample collected from pictured specimen.

VISUAL ID: Bright red encrusting sponge with circular, raised, sieve-like areas of tightly packed, tiny incurrent pores that surround small, protruding excurrent openings. (Note different appearance of meandering, sieve-like areas of Orange Sieve Encrusting Sponge [next]).

ABUNDANCE & DISTRIBUTION: Occasional Caribbean.

HABITAT & BEHAVIOR: Inhabit reefs and walls. Prefer shaded, protected areas; encrust around undercut bases of coral heads, in recesses, and wall faces under ledge overhangs.

REACTION TO DIVERS: One of the few sponges that reacts to being touched; it slowly closes its openings and pores.

NOTE: Visual identification confirmed by microscopic examination of small sample collected from pictured specimen.

WHITE LUMPY ENCRUSTING SPONGE
Strongylacidon sp.
CLASS:
Sponges
Demospongiae

SIZE: 8 - 15 in.
DEPTH: 40 - 80 ft.

PINK & RED ENCRUSTING SPONGE
Spirastrella coccinea
CLASS:
Sponges
Demospongiae

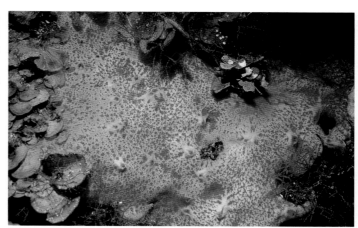

SIZE: 1 - 3 ft.
DEPTH: 30 - 100 ft.

RED SIEVE ENCRUSTING SPONGE
Phorbas amaranthus
CLASS:
Sponges
Demospongiae

SIZE: 6 - 18 in.
DEPTH: 20 - 100 ft.

VISUAL ID: Red-orange encrusting sponge with raised, often meandering, sieve-like areas of tightly packed incurrent pores that surround large, protruding, excurrent openings. (Note different appearance of circular, sieve-like areas of Red Sieve Encrusting Sponge [previous]).

ABUNDANCE & DISTRIBUTION: Occasional Caribbean.

HABITAT & BEHAVIOR: Inhabit reefs and walls. Prefer shaded, protected areas; encrust around undercut bases of coral heads, in recesses, and wall faces under ledge overhangs.

NOTE: Identification of genus determined by microscopic examination of small sample collected from pictured specimen. Possibly an undescribed species.

VISUAL ID: Red-orange, thin, encrusting sponge. Several root-like canals radiate from the slightly raised excurrent openings. These canals often intertwine and connect with canals radiating from other excurrent openings. (Note, areas between canals do not have scattered white spots like Red Encrusting Sponge [next].)

ABUNDANCE & DISTRIBUTION: Common Caribbean; occasional South Florida, Bahamas.

HABITAT & BEHAVIOR: Inhabit coral reefs, prefer shaded areas. Often encrust under ledge overhangs, in recesses and caves.

NOTE: Visual identification confirmed by microscopic examination of small sample collected from pictured specimen.

VISUAL ID: Brilliant red, thin, encrusting sponge. Several root-like canals radiate from the slightly raised excurrent openings. These canals often intertwine and connect with canals radiating from other excurrent openings. Areas between canals have scattered white spots; occasionally this area appears pink.

ABUNDANCE & DISTRIBUTION: Common Caribbean; occasional South Florida, Bahamas.

HABITAT & BEHAVIOR: Encrust dead areas of reefs, especially around the bases of living coral heads.

NOTE: Visual identification confirmed by microscopic examination of small sample collected from pictured specimen.

ORANGE SIEVE ENCRUSTING SPONGE
Diplastrella sp.

CLASS:
Sponges
Demospongiae

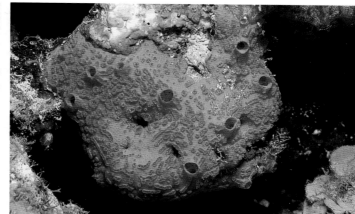

SIZE: 6 - 18 in.
DEPTH: 20 - 75 ft.

RED-ORANGE ENCRUSTING SPONGE
Diplastrella megastellata

CLASS:
Sponges
Demospongiae

SIZE: 4 - 10 in.
DEPTH: 25 - 75 ft.

RED ENCRUSTING SPONGE
Monanchora barbadensis

CLASS:
Sponges
Demospongiae

SIZE: 4 - 10 in.
DEPTH: 25 - 75 ft.

VISUAL ID: Peach-colored, thin, encrusting sponge. Several root-like canals radiate from the slightly raised excurrent openings. These canals often intertwine and connect with canals radiating from other excurrent openings. Numerous large incurrent pores distinguish this species.

ABUNDANCE & DISTRIBUTION: Common Caribbean; occasional South Florida, Bahamas.

HABITAT & BEHAVIOR: Encrust dead areas of reefs and walls, especially under ledges, in recesses and other protected areas.

NOTE: Identification of genus confirmed by microscopic examination of small sample collected from pictured specimen. Possibly an undescribed species.

VISUAL ID: This thin, encrusting sponge is distinguished by several canals that radiate in a star-shaped pattern from small groups of pitted excurrent openings. These "stars" are well separated. Unlike several similar appearing sponges, the canals are only occasionally branched, and do no intertwine or interconnect. See "NOTE" regarding color.

ABUNDANCE & DISTRIBUTION: Occasional Florida, Bahamas, Caribbean.

HABITAT & BEHAVIOR: Encrust dead areas of reefs and walls, especially under ledges, in recesses and other protected areas.

NOTE: Identification of genus confirmed by microscopic examination of small sample collected from pictured specimen [opposite]. Possibly an undescribed species that apparently comes in a variety of colors [below and below right].

PEACH
ENCRUSTING SPONGE
Clathria sp.
CLASS:
Sponges
Demospongiae

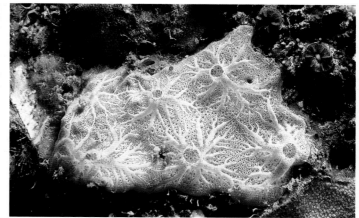

SIZE: 4 - 10 in.
DEPTH: 25 - 75 ft.

STAR
ENCRUSTING SPONGE
Halisarca sp.
CLASS:
Sponges
Demospongiae

SIZE: 3 - 10 in.
DEPTH: 25 - 100 ft.

Color Varieties

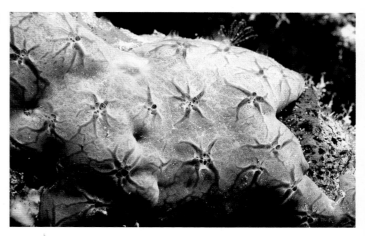

VISUAL ID: Orange encrusting sponge. Numerous vein-like canals radiate from protruding excurrent openings. These canals often intertwine and connect with canals radiating from other excurrent openings. Areas between canals often lighter color. Relatively large incurrent pores scaterred over surface.

ABUNDANCE & DISTRIBUTION: Occasional Florida, Bahamas, Caribbean.

HABITAT & BEHAVIOR: Encrust dead areas of reefs and walls, especially under ledges, in recesses, caves and other protected areas.

NOTE: Visual identification confirmed by microscopic examination of small sample collected from pictured specimen.

VISUAL ID: Bright orange encrusting sponge with large, white to transparent, projecting excurrent openings. Encrust edges and under margins of coral plates and ledges. Modify growth of coral around excurrent openings, causing the margins of coral plates to have a scalloped pattern.

ABUNDANCE & DISTRIBUTION: Abundant to common Florida, Bahamas, Caribbean.

HABITAT & BEHAVIOR: Grow in association with a variety of living hard coral species, protecting the coral from bioerosion by boring sponges.

VISUAL ID: Orange, rough-textured, soft, encrusting sponge. Excurrent openings blend into texture of sponge (similar species, Orange Icing Sponge [previous], has protruding white to transparent excurrent openings).

ABUNDANCE & DISTRIBUTION: Common Florida, Bahamas, Caribbean.

HABITAT & BEHAVIOR: Found in a wide variety of habitats, from roots of mangroves to areas of reef rubble and living reefs. Encrust dead areas of substrate, often around edges of living coral.

SIMILAR SPECIES: Orange, thin encrusting sponge, *Ulosa hispida*, commonly grows on mangrove roots.

ORANGE VEINED ENCRUSTING SPONGE

Rhaphidophlus venosus

CLASS:
Sponges
Demospongiae

SIZE: 4 - 12 in.
DEPTH: 25 - 100 ft.

ORANGE ICING SPONGE

Mycale laevis

CLASS:
Sponges
Demospongiae

SIZE: 4 - 18 in.
DEPTH: 20 - 100 ft.

ORANGE LUMPY ENCRUSTING SPONGE

Ulosa ruetzleri

CLASS:
Sponges
Demospongiae

SIZE: 4 - 12 in.
DEPTH: 15 - 75 ft.

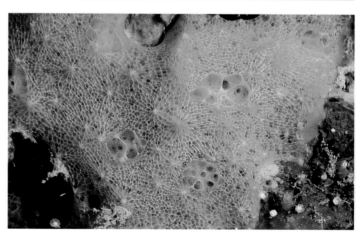

VISUAL ID: Massive, orange encrusting sponge. Convoluted surface, consisting of ridges and valleys, forms a maze-like pattern. Scattered excurrent openings raised slightly. Often has algal growth and sediment on surface.

ABUNDANCE & DISTRIBUTION: Occasional Caribbean, Bahamas. Can be common in some locations.

HABITAT & BEHAVIOR: Inhabit caves and undercuts on drop-off walls and other moderate to deep reef areas. Prefer protected locations with little current.

EFFECT ON DIVERS: Contact with bare skin can result in a severe irritating reaction, including burning pain, numbness, swelling and rash that may last several days. Treat with vinegar, followed by a sprinkling of meat tenderizer; rinse and soothe with hydrocortisone ointment.

NOTE: Identification made by microscopic examination of small sample collected from pictured specimen. Another sponge, *Didiscus oxeatus*, looks identical; positive identification requires microscopic examination of spicules.

VISUAL ID: Massive, thick, rubbery, orange sponge, with pitted and convoluted surface texture. Grow in a variety of irregular masses and patterns. Often form huge mounds and/or encrust large areas of reef. Occasionally extend from walls in large, flat, mat-like formations that sometimes resemble large ears.

ABUNDANCE & DISTRIBUTION: Common to occasional Florida, Bahamas, Caribbean. Can be abundant in some locations.

HABITAT & BEHAVIOR: Inhabit reefs and walls, prefer areas with some water movement. Often compound tunicates, hydroids and a variety of other organisms grow on their surface.

CONVOLUTED ORANGE SPONGE
Myrmekioderma styx
CLASS:
Sponges
Demospongiae

SIZE: ¹/₂ - 3 ft.
DEPTH: 40 - 130 ft.

ORANGE ELEPHANT EAR SPONGE
Agelas clathrodes
CLASS:
Sponges
Demospongiae

SIZE: 2 - 6 ft.
DEPTH: 35 - 130 ft.

Growth Patterns

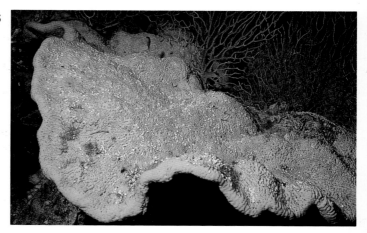

VISUAL ID: Brown encrusting sponge; appearance often resembles a flow of viscous material. Smooth surface with occasional excurrent openings.

ABUNDANCE & DISTRIBUTION: Common Florida, Bahamas, Caribbean.

HABITAT & BEHAVIOR: Inhabit reefs and walls. Often grow on faces of undercuts, walls of canyons, and in caves.

VISUAL ID: Tan to brown, irregular-shaped sponge that appears to encrust the substrate. May have irregular structures and excurrent openings protruding prominently. There is also a massive variety that grows on the substrate, see below.

ABUNDANCE & DISTRIBUTION: Common to uncommon Florida, Bahamas, Caribbean.

HABITAT & BEHAVIOR: Bore into solid substrate of deeper reefs by secreting minute amounts of acid. There appears to be little or no visible damage; however, the base rock of the reef may be riddled with tunnels and chambers.

VISUAL ID: Tan to brown, massive, lumpy, irregular sponge. Excurrent openings of lighter color protrude prominently.

HABITAT & BEHAVIOR: Inhabit shallow fringing and patch reefs, areas of coral rubble, and grass flats.

VISCOUS SPONGE
Plakortis angulospiculatus
CLASS:
Sponges
Demospongiae

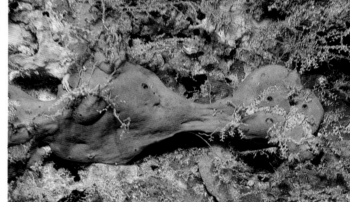

SIZE: 3 - 12 in.
DEPTH: 30 - 100 ft.

BROWN VARIABLE SPONGE
Encrusting/Boring Variety
Anthosigmella varians
CLASS:
Sponges
Demospongiae

SIZE: 6 - 18 in.
DEPTH: 10 - 100 ft.

Massive Variety

VISUAL ID: Tan to yellow-brown, irregular, massive sponge. Often forms hollow, antler-like structures above the substrate.

ABUNDANCE & DISTRIBUTION: Uncommon Caribbean; rare Bahamas.

HABITAT & BEHAVIOR: Variety of habitats, most often in dead areas of coral rubble and sand, between and around reefs.

VISUAL ID: Olive to dull brown, thin encrusting and boring sponge. Numerous tiny excurrent openings. Overgrows and bores into living coral heads.

ABUNDANCE & DISTRIBUTION: Common to occasional Caribbean; rare Florida, Bahamas.

HABITAT & BEHAVIOR: Inhabit coral reefs. Overgrow and bore into living coral, taking on the pattern of the underlying structure. Note small gray patch of remaining living coral in photograph.

NOTE: Identification confirmed by microscopic examination of small sample collected from pictured specimen. Another species, *C. aprica*, looks identical; positive identification requires microscopic examination.

VISUAL ID: Red to red-orange sponge that appears to encrust, but actually bores into coral heads. Numerous low wart-like spots on surface, with excurrent openings that protrude prominently.

ABUNDANCE & DISTRIBUTION: Occasional South Florida, Bahamas, Caribbean.

HABITAT & BEHAVIOR: Bore into coral heads by secreting minute amounts of acid. From the exterior there is usually no visible damage. However, the corals' interiors may be riddled with tunnels and chambers that may eventually cause their structures to disintegrate. Sponge Zoanthids [pg. 99] and Sponge Brittle Stars [pg. 281] often live in association with this species.

ANTLER SPONGE
Spheciospongia
cuspidifera
CLASS:
Sponges
Demospongiae

SIZE: 6 - 24 in.
DEPTH: 10 - 100 ft.

CORAL ENCRUSTING SPONGE
Cliona langae
CLASS:
Sponges
Demospongiae

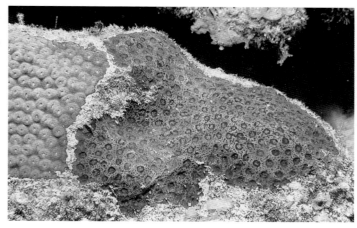

SIZE: 6 - 36 in.
DEPTH: 15 - 100 ft.

RED BORING SPONGE
Cliona delitrix
CLASS:
Sponges
Demospongiae

SIZE: 6 - 12 in.
DEPTH: 15 - 100 ft.

VISUAL ID: Sulfur- to lemon-yellow, occasionally white, deep boring sponge. Grow in a wide variety of patterns: appear as an encrusting sponge [right]; vase-like tubes extending from coral heads [below left]; finger-like branches extending from coral [below right]; tiny tubes extending from dead coral areas [below right page].

ABUNDANCE & DISTRIBUTION: Common Caribbean, Bahamas; occasional to rare Florida.

HABITAT & BEHAVIOR: Inhabit coral reefs and drop-off walls. Bore into coral by secreting minute amounts of acid. From the exterior there is usually little or no visible damage; however, these sponges bore large, fist-sized holes in coral heads.

NOTE: Pictured specimens below were identified visually. Visual identification of pictured specimens opposite and below right were confirmed by microscopic examination of small collected samples.

VISUAL ID: Small, white tube-like or vase-like structures. Occasionally have light pink, gold or green shading. May be solitary or grow in small clusters.

ABUNDANCE & DISTRIBUTION: Common Caribbean; rare Bahamas, Florida.

HABITAT & BEHAVIOR: Inhabit the ceilings of caves and deep-undercuts, especially along drop-off walls. Prefer areas protected from current and water motion.

VARIABLE BORING SPONGE
Siphonodictyon coralliphagum
CLASS:
Sponges
Demospongiae

SIZE: 2 - 4 in.
DEPTH: 30 - 130 ft.

Growth Patterns

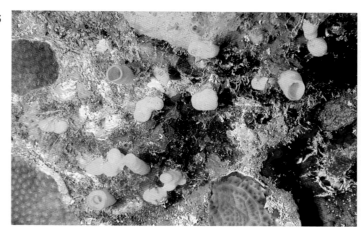

WHITE CRYPTIC SPONGE
Leucandra aspera
CLASS:
Calcareous Sponges
Calcarea

SIZE: 2 - 12 in.
DEPTH: 50 - 130 ft.

VISUAL ID: Bright yellow, small intertwined tubes. Soft and quite fragile.

ABUNDANCE & DISTRIBUTION: Occasional to rare Florida, Bahamas, Caribbean.

HABITAT & BEHAVIOR: Inhabit the ceilings of caves, deep-undercuts, and other dark protected recesses.

NOTE: Visual identification was confirmed by microscopic examination of small sample collected from pictured specimen.

VISUAL ID: White, small intertwined tubes. Skeletal network of calcareous spicules can be seen. Soft and quite fragile.

ABUNDANCE & DISTRIBUTION: Occasional to rare Florida, Bahamas, Caribbean.

HABITAT & BEHAVIOR: Inhabit the ceilings of caves, deep-undercuts, and other dark, protected recesses.

VISUAL ID: Tiny white ball with single excurrent opening and numerous needle-like spines protruding from surface. May have some algal growth and debris on spines.

ABUNDANCE & DISTRIBUTION: Common to rare Caribbean; rare Florida, Bahamas.

HABITAT & BEHAVIOR: Inhabit dark, protected areas of the reef, especially caves.

YELLOW CALCAREOUS SPONGE
Clathrina canariensis
CLASS:
Calcareous Sponges
Calcarea

SIZE: 2 - 4 in.
DEPTH: 25 - 75 ft.

WHITE CALCAREOUS SPONGE

CLASS:
Calcareous Sponges
Calcarea

SIZE: 2 - 4 in.
DEPTH: 25 - 75 ft.

SPINY BALL SPONGE
Leucetta barbata
CLASS:
Calcareous Sponges
Calcarea

SIZE: $^1/_2$ - $^3/_4$ in.
DEPTH: 25 - 130 ft.

Phylum Cnidaria

(Nigh-DARE-ee-uh / L. a nettle)

Hydroids, Jellyfish & Anemones

Most cnidarians are tiny individual animals that group together, by the thousands, to form colonies, such as, corals and hydroids. These colonies, that vary greatly in size and shape, attach to substrate or living organisms to form most of a coral reef's hard and soft structure. A few species, such as jellyfish and anemones, are not colonial and live as individuals.

Animals in this phylum have a simple structure consisting of a cup-shaped body, a central, single opening that functions both as a **mouth** and **anus**, and a number of **tentacles** that encircle the mouth. When the animal is attached, it is called a **polyp**; if it is unattached and free-swimming, it is called a **medusa**. A unique characteristic shared by all cnidarians is numerous stinging capsules, called **nematocysts**, which is the origin of the phylum's Latin name. These minute capsules, located primarily on the tentacles, are used for both capturing prey and defense.

The stings of most cnidarians have no harmful effect on divers, but a few are quite toxic and should be avoided. In the event of a sting, never rub the affected area or wash with fresh water or soap. Both actions can cause additional nematocysts to discharge. Saturating the area with vinegar will immobilize unspent nematocysts; a sprinkling of meat tenderizer may help to alleviate the symptoms.

The phylum is divided into three classes that include hydroids, jellyfish, anemones and their relatives. Corals (fire, lace, soft, hard and black) and gorgonians are also classified in this phylum; however, they are identified in a separate volume.

HYDROIDS

Class Hydrozoa (High-druh-ZO-uh / Gr. water animal)
Order Hydroida (High-DROY-duh / Gr. water form)

Hydroids are usually colonial, and have a branched skeleton that generally grows in patterns resembling feathers or ferns. Individual polyps are attached to this structure. The arrangement of the **stalk, branches** and attached **polyps** is usually the key to visual identification. Most species are whitish or neutral shades, ranging from brown to gray or black and rarely display vibrant colors.

Most hydroids have a complex life cycle. The polyps in an adult colony are specialized for either feeding or reproduction. The reproductive polyps give rise to buds that form free-swimming medusae. This stage, often small in size and short-lived, is only occasionally observable by divers. When in these reproductive stages, called **hydromedusae**, they can be distinguished from similar-appearing "true" jellyfish by the margin of their **dome**, which turns inward, forming a "shelf" called a **velum**. Radial

canals run from the **mouth** to the margin of the velum. The velum is absent in jellyfish. Varying numbers of **tentacles** with stinging nematocysts hang from the dome's margin. The hydromedusa is the dominant stage in a few species.

The stinging nematocysts of several hydroids are toxic enough to cause a painful burning sensation that may produce a visible rash, redness or even welts. Fire and lace corals are also members of this class, but classified in different orders.

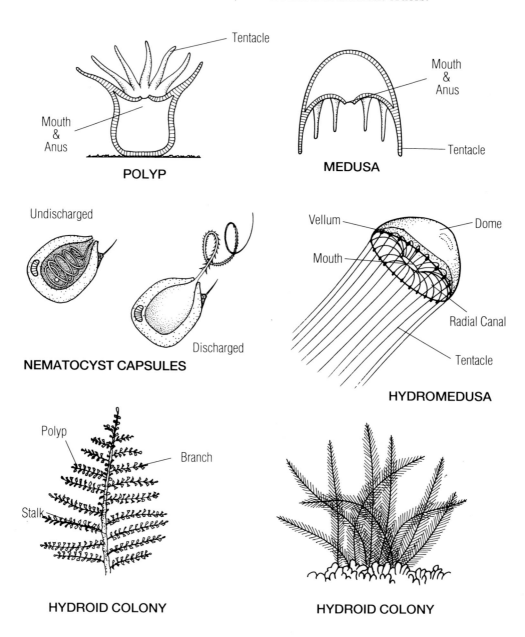

POLYP

MEDUSA

NEMATOCYST CAPSULES

HYDROMEDUSA

HYDROID COLONY

HYDROID COLONY

SIPHONOPHORES

CLASS Hydrozoa
ORDER Siphonophora (Sigh-fawn-NOFF-or-uh / Gr. to have hollow tubes)

Siphonophores are a complex form of unattached hydroid colonies that float by means of a **gas-filled float**. Below the float hang numerous nematocyst-bearing **tentacles** that can be contracted close to the float, or relaxed to extend to great lengths. The best known example is the **Portuguese Man-Of-War**, which floats on the surface and moves by turning its float to the wind. These unique animals are capable of stinging a diver so severely that medical attention is required. Unlike the Portuguese Man-Of-War, most siphonophores float below the surface in open water, controlling their depth by regulating the gas content of the sack. They move about by pulsating modified medusae, called **swimming bells**, that are just below the gas float. Their sting is not a threat to divers, but can be felt for a short time.

TRUE JELLYFISH

Class Scyphozoa (Sky-fuh-ZO-uh / Gr. cup-shaped animal)

True jellyfish are translucent, unattached medusae that swim in open water. All have a prominent **dome** which varies in shape from a shallow saucer to a deep bell. Hanging from the margin of the dome are nematocyst-bearing **tentacles**, the number and length of which vary greatly from species to species. Occasionally the margin is scalloped, forming lobes called **lappets**. The mouth is at the end of a **feeding tube** that extends from the center of the dome's underside. In some species, four frilly **oral arms** hang to considerable length from the feeding tube. Both the feeding tube and oral arms carry stinging nematocysts. Many species are large, long-lived and quite colorful.

Jellyfish move through the water by pulsating contractions of the dome. Although only a few jellyfish are toxic, caution should be taken with all members of the class.

BOX JELLIES

Class Scyphozoa
Subclass Cubomedusae (Cue-BO-muh-due-see / L. cube-shaped medusa)

Box jellies, also commonly called sea wasps, can be identified by their distinctive **cuboidal dome**. One or more nematocyst-bearing **tentacles** hang from each of the four corners of the open end of the cube. Additional tentacles are absent from the remaining margin. The sting of many box jellies can be severe, occasionally requiring medical attention. Many zoologists believe box jellies are only distantly related to scyphozoans and place them in their own class, the Cubozoa.

GORGONIANS, CORALS, ANEMONES

Class Anthozoa (An-thuh-ZO-uh / L. flower-like animal)

The class Anthozoa contains many familiar marine invertebrates, including hard and soft corals, black corals and sea anemones. All have only the polyp stage in their life cycles. There are two major sub-classes: Octocorallia, animals with eight tentacles, which include sea fans, sea whips and soft corals (not included in this volume); and Hexacorallia, animals with tentacles in multiples of six, which include hard and black corals (also not included in this volume), sea anemones, zoanthids, corallimorphs and tube-dwelling anemones.

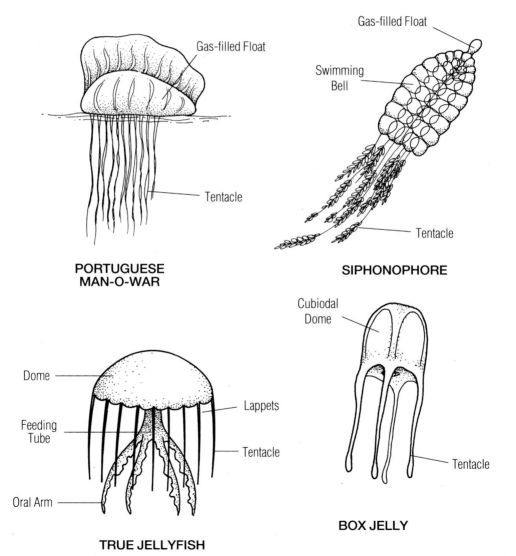

PORTUGUESE
MAN-O-WAR

SIPHONOPHORE

TRUE JELLYFISH

BOX JELLY

SEA ANEMONES

Class Anthozoa
Subclass Hexacorallia (Hex-uh-core-AL-ee-uh / Gr. & L. six and coral animal)
Order Actiniaria (Ack-TIN-ee-AIR-ee-uh / L. a ray)

Sea anemones are solitary polyps that attach to the bottom. They lack any hard skeletal parts and are generally quite large compared to the polyps of other cnidarians. Their bodies range from a few inches to over a foot across. The **tentacles**, which vary in length, shape, color and number, are often keys to identification. The pattern of tentacles often appears random, although some species exhibit distinct rings.

Stinging nematocysts on the tentacles rarely affect divers, but are toxic enough to paralyze small fish and invertebrates that stray into their reach. The immobilized prey is drawn by the tentacles into a **slit-like mouth** in the center of the **oral disc**. Living in association with many anemones are certain species of fish, shrimp and crab that are not affected by the nematocysts. Anemones rarely move, but can relocate in a slow, snail-like manner. They prefer secluded areas of the reef where they often lodge in crevices with only their tentacles exposed. If disturbed they can contract their tentacles for protection.

ZOANTHIDS

Class Anthozoa, Subclass Hexacorallia
Order Zoanthidea (Zo-an-THID-ee-uh / Gr. animal flower)

Zoanthids appear similar to anemones, but are considerably smaller, usually no larger than a half inch, and are generally colonial or live in close proximity to one another. The **oral disc** is without tentacles except for **two rings of tentacles** around the outer edge, which visually distinguish them from other anemone-like animals. Some species live in association with sponges, hydroids and other invertebrates.

CORALLIMORPHS

Class Anthozoa, Subclass Hexacorallia
Order Corallimorpharia (Core-AL-uh-more-FAIR-ee-uh / Gr. & L. coral-like)

Corallimorphs are easily confused with anemones. The best visual clue to the order's identity is the arrangement of the tentacles, which form two geometric patterns concurrently. **Tentacles radiate out** from the center of the **oral disc**, like spokes, and form **concentric circles** which progressively increase in diameter from the center. These patterns, however, are often obscure. The tentacles in most species are short and stubby, resembling nubs or warts. Generally, the oral disc is quite flat, and the **mouth protrudes** noticeably. They are occasionally called false corals because their polyps' structure is much like those of hard corals, except they secrete no calcareous skeleton. Corallimorphs may be solitary, but also live in close association, occasionally crowding together so closely that the individual polyps are difficult to distinguish from one another.

TUBE-DWELLING ANEMONES

Class Anthozoa, Subclass Hexacorallia
Order Ceriantharia (Sair-ee-an-THAIR-ee-uh / L. & Gr. wax flower)

These anemones live inside **tubes** buried in mud, sand or fine gravel. Their oral disc and crown of tentacles nearly always remain hidden during the day, only extending at night when the animals feed. They can be distinguished from other anemone-like animals by the arrangement of their tentacles. Several rings of long, **pointed outer tentacles** extend from the edge of the **oral disc**, and at the center is a **tuft of shorter tentacles** that often hide the mouth.

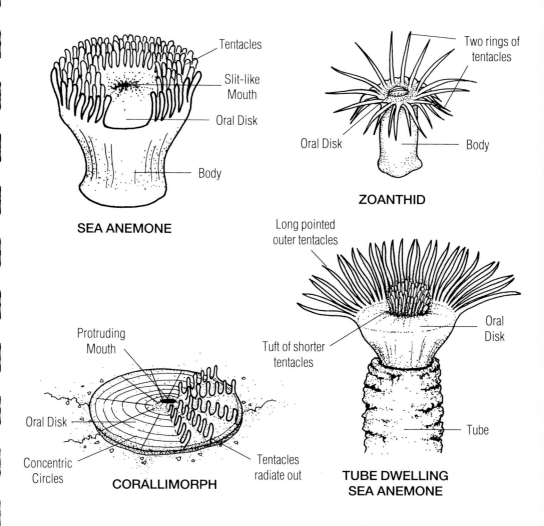

Tentacles

Slit-like Mouth

Oral Disk

Body

SEA ANEMONE

Two rings of tentacles

Oral Disk

Body

ZOANTHID

Protruding Mouth

Oral Disk

Concentric Circles

Tentacles radiate out

CORALLIMORPH

Long pointed outer tentacles

Tuft of shorter tentacles

Oral Disk

Tube

TUBE DWELLING SEA ANEMONE

Hydroids

VISUAL ID: Thin, tightly spaced, whitish branches extend alternately in a single plane from a brown central stalk. Tiny white polyps lining the branches are visible. Usually grow in clusters. Compare with similar Slender Feather Hydroid [next].

ABUNDANCE & DISTRIBUTION: Common to occasional Caribbean.

HABITAT & BEHAVIOR: Inhabit reef tops. Prefer clear water and some current.

EFFECT ON DIVERS: Toxic; sting bare skin.

VISUAL ID: Thin, tightly spaced branches extend alternately in a single plane from a dark central stalk. Compared to similar Feather Hydroid [previous], branches tend to be shorter, giving colony an overall thinner appearance. Usually grow in clusters.

ABUNDANCE & DISTRIBUTION: Common to occasional Southeast Florida, Bahamas, Caribbean.

HABITAT & BEHAVIOR: Inhabit reef tops. Prefer clear water and some current.

EFFECT ON DIVERS: Toxic; sting bare skin.

NOTE: Visual identification confirmed by microscopic examination of collected specimen matched with photograph.

VISUAL ID: Branches extend alternately on a single plane from stout, brownish central stalk. Obvious white polyps attached, alternately, to the top and bottom of branches. May grow solitary, but more commonly in clusters.

ABUNDANCE & DISTRIBUTION: Occasional Central to North Florida.

HABITAT & BEHAVIOR: Most commonly inhabit floats of pelagic *Sargassum*; also attach to hard bottom substrates.

EFFECT ON DIVERS: Slightly toxic; produce sting to sensitive skin.

FEATHER HYDROID
Gymnangium
longicauda
ORDER:
Hydroids
Hydroida

SIZE: 3$\frac{1}{2}$ - 5$\frac{1}{2}$ in.,
12 in. max.
DEPTH: 25 - 100 ft.

SLENDER FEATHER HYDROID
Gymnangium speciosum
ORDER:
Hydroids
Hydroida

SIZE: 2$\frac{1}{2}$ - 5 in.,
12 in. max.
DEPTH: 20 - 100 ft.

FEATHER PLUME HYDROID
Aglaophenia
latecarinata
ORDER:
Hydroids
Hydroida

SIZE: 1 - 3 in.
DEPTH: 0 - 120 ft.

VISUAL ID: Branches extend alternately on a single plane from stout, brownish central stalk. Obvious white polyps attached, alternately, to the top and bottom of branches. Grow solitary or in small clusters.

ABUNDANCE & DISTRIBUTION: Common to occasional Florida, Bahamas, Caribbean.

HABITAT & BEHAVIOR: Inhabit all areas on reef, especially around recesses. Often on shipwrecks. Prefer areas with some water movement.

EFFECT ON DIVERS: Slightly toxic; produce sting to sensitive skin.

VISUAL ID: Branches extend alternately on a single plane from stout, brown central stalk. A single white, obvious polyp at tip of branches and stalk. Additional polyps grow along branches. Hair-like tentacles which extend from the polyp may be discernible. Usually grow in small clusters.

ABUNDANCE & DISTRIBUTION: Common to occasional Florida, Bahamas, Caribbean.

HABITAT & BEHAVIOR: Inhabit all areas on reef. Often found attached to dead gorgonians and hard corals, sponge colonies and shipwrecks. Prefer areas with current.

EFFECT ON DIVERS: Slightly toxic; produce sting to sensitive skin.

VISUAL ID: A few heavy branches on a stout central stalk support visible alternating polyps. Colony grows on a single plane. Generally grow in clumps, often partially covered with algae.

ABUNDANCE & DISTRIBUTION: Common to occasional Florida, Bahamas, Caribbean.

HABITAT & BEHAVIOR: Inhabit all areas of reef and, often, shipwrecks.

EFFECT ON DIVERS: Slightly toxic; may produce mild sting to sensitive skin.

BRANCHING HYDROID
Sertularella speciosa
ORDER:
Hydroids
Hydroida

SIZE: 3 - 5½ in.
DEPTH: 30 - 100 ft.

CHRISTMAS TREE HYDROID
Halocordyle disticha
ORDER:
Hydroids
Hydroida

SIZE: 1½ - 3½ in.
DEPTH: 10 - 60 ft.

ALGAE HYDROID
Thyroscyphus ramosus
ORDER:
Hydroids
Hydroida

SIZE: 2 - 5 in.
DEPTH: 5 - 130 ft.

Hydroids

VISUAL ID: Heavy, unbranched stalk supports visible alternating polyps. Generally grow in clusters, often partially covered with algae.

ABUNDANCE & DISTRIBUTION: Common to occasional Florida, Bahamas, Caribbean.

HABITAT & BEHAVIOR: Inhabit all areas of reef, especially dead gorgonians and hard corals. Often grow on shipwrecks.

EFFECT ON DIVERS: Slightly toxic; may produce mild sting to sensitive skin.

VISUAL ID: Bush-like colony of stout central stalks and numerous angular primary branches and sub-branches. Primary branches and sub-branches lined with fine, tightly spaced, polyp-bearing secondary branches. Colonies usually have Hydroid Zoanthids [pg. 97] growing on their branches.

ABUNDANCE & DISTRIBUTION: Occasional to common Florida, Bahamas, Caribbean.

HABITAT & BEHAVIOR: Inhabit reef tops, outcroppings along walls and hard flat substrates, especially in areas with current. Grow with the plane of the colony perpendicular to the current.

EFFECT ON DIVERS: Toxic; sting bare skin.

NOTE: Visual identification confirmed by microscopic examination of collected specimen matched with photograph.

VISUAL ID: Heavy central stalk supports a few primary branches of similar size. Thin, tightly spaced, polyp-bearing secondary branches extend from stalk and primary branches. Tiny white polyps are barely visible. All branches are on same plane.

ABUNDANCE & DISTRIBUTION: Occasional Florida, Bahamas, Caribbean.

HABITAT & BEHAVIOR: Inhabit all areas on reef.

EFFECT ON DIVERS: Toxic; sting bare skin.

UNBRANCHED HYDROID
Cnidoscyphus marginatus
ORDER:
Hydroids
Hydroida

SIZE: 2¹/₂ - 3¹/₂ in.
DEPTH: 5 - 130 ft.

FEATHER BUSH HYDROID
Dentitheca dendritica
ORDER:
Hydroids
Hydroida

SIZE: 8 - 12 in.
DEPTH: 30 - 130 ft.

STINGING HYDROID
Macrorhynchia allmani
ORDER:
Hydroids
Hydroida

SIZE: 1¹/₂ - 3 in.
DEPTH: 30 - 100 ft.

Hydroids

VISUAL ID: Dark stalk with numerous primary branches and sub-branches, all lined with fine, tightly spaced, polyp-bearing secondary branches. Colonies usually grow in clusters.

ABUNDANCE & DISTRIBUTION: Occasional Southeast Florida, Bahamas, Caribbean.

HABITAT & BEHAVIOR: Inhabit all areas on and around reef.

EFFECT ON DIVERS: Toxic; sting bare skin.

NOTE: Visual identification confirmed by microscopic examination of collected specimen matched with photograph.

VISUAL ID: Long, thin central stalk lined with short, alternating, polyp-bearing side branches. Grow in clusters.

ABUNDANCE & DISTRIBUTION: Common to occasional Southeast Florida, Bahamas, Caribbean.

HABITAT & BEHAVIOR: Inhabit all areas on reef.

EFFECT ON DIVERS: Mildly toxic; sting sensitive bare skin.

NOTE: Visual identification confirmed by microscopic examination of collected specimen matched with photograph.

VISUAL ID: Reddish to purple stalk is heavily branched and lined with thin, short, polyp-bearing, whitish branches, all on a single plane.

ABUNDANCE & DISTRIBUTION: Uncommon South Florida, Bahamas and Caribbean.

HABITAT & BEHAVIOR: Attach to rocky outcroppings in areas of surge or current. Prefer clear water.

EFFECT ON DIVERS: Slightly toxic; may produce mild sting to sensitive skin.

STINGING BUSH HYDROID

Macrorhynchia robusta

ORDER:
Hydroids
Hydroida

SIZE: 4 - 8 in.,
12 in. max.
DEPTH: 20 - 100 ft.

THREAD HYDROID

Halopteris carinata

ORDER:
Hydroids
Hydroida

SIZE: 2 - 4 in.,
6 in. max.
DEPTH: 20 - 100 ft.

SEAFAN HYDROID

Solanderia gracilis

ORDER:
Hydroids
Hydroida

SIZE: 6 - 18 in.
DEPTH: 15 - 80 ft.

VISUAL ID: Large, white, solitary polyp with long, thin, translucent tentacles. Attach to tips of gorgonian branches, especially sea plumes, *Pseudo-pterogorgia sp.* Outstretched tentacles often curl at tip.

ABUNDANCE & DISTRIBUTION: Occasional to rare Caribbean, Bahamas.

HABITAT & BEHAVIOR: Inhabit reefs where sea plumes and other gorgonians grow. Several may grow from the same sea plume, but never more than one per branch tip. Outstretched tentacles curl if disturbed.

EFFECT ON DIVERS: Toxic; sting bare skin.

NOTE: Visual identification confirmed by microscopic examination of collected specimen matched with photograph.

VISUAL ID: Large, pinkish, solitary polyp with long, thin, translucent tentacles. Attach to sponges. Outstretched tentacles do not tend to curl at tips as similar species, Solitary Gorgonian Hydroid [previous].

ABUNDANCE & DISTRIBUTION: Occasional Florida, Bahamas, Caribbean.

HABITAT & BEHAVIOR: Inhabit reefs where sponges grow. Attach to a wide variety of sponge species, usually in clusters of several individuals. Outstretched tentacles curl if disturbed.

EFFECT ON DIVERS: Toxic; sting bare skin.

VISUAL ID: Transparent hemispherical dome. Distinctive club-shaped organ at the base of each tentacle where it attaches to margin of bell. Few radial canals are visible on velum.

ABUNDANCE & DISTRIBUTION: Occasional Florida, Bahamas, Caribbean.

HABITAT & BEHAVIOR: Float near surface of open water, often in large aggregations.

EFFECT ON DIVERS: Slightly toxic; may produce mild sting to sensitive skin.

NOTE: The hydromedusae stage is the dominant life phase of this species.

SOLITARY GORGONIAN HYDROID

Ralpharia gorgoniae

ORDER:
Hydroids
Hydroida

SIZE: ¹/₂ - 1 in.
DEPTH: 15 - 65 ft.

SOLITARY SPONGE HYDROID

Zyzzyzus warreni

ORDER:
Hydroids
Hydroida

SIZE: ¹/₂ - 1 in.
DEPTH: 20 - 100 ft.

CLUB HYDROMEDUSA

Orchistoma pileus

ORDER:
Hydroids
Hydroida

SIZE: 1 in.
DEPTH: 0 - 15 feet.

VISUAL ID: Translucent hemispherical dome of thick jelly, with numerous long tentacles attached to margin of bell. Numerous radial canals are visible on velum.

ABUNDANCE & DISTRIBUTION: Occasional to uncommon Florida, Bahamas, Caribbean.

HABITAT & BEHAVIOR: Float near surface of open water.

EFFECT ON DIVERS: Slightly toxic; may produce mild sting to sensitive skin.

NOTE: The hydromedusae stage is the dominant life phase of this species.

VISUAL ID: Pink to purple, translucent, gas-filled float with numerous long, thin, retractable tentacles.

ABUNDANCE & DISTRIBUTION: Occasional Florida, Bahamas, Caribbean.

HABITAT & BEHAVIOR: Float on surface, propelled by wind. Large individuals are often accompanied by a school of small, banded Man-of-War Fish, *Nomeus gronovii*.

EFFECT ON DIVERS: Highly toxic; contact with tentacles will produce intense sting causing redness, welting and blistering. Numerous stings may require medical attention. Beware, tentacles often extend far behind or below float. If washed ashore, they remain toxic for some time.

VISUAL ID: Small, bubble-like float above stem bears numerous, highly contractile tentacles. When contracted [pictured], colony is only one or two inches in length. Relaxed tentacles may reach 30 feet. Transparent to translucent. Do not have swimming bells below float.

ABUNDANCE & DISTRIBUTION: Occasional Caribbean.

HABITAT & BEHAVIOR: Float in open water. Control depth by amount of carbon monoxide gas secreted into float.

EFFECT ON DIVERS: Toxic; contact with tentacles will produce an intense, but short-lived, sting. May cause minor redness and welts.

NOTE: There are two species, *R. filiformis* which is greenish, and *R. eysenhardti* which is pale pink. In young individuals [pictured], this coloration is not always obvious.

JELLY HYDROMEDUSA
Aequorea aequorea
ORDER:
Hydroids
Hydroida

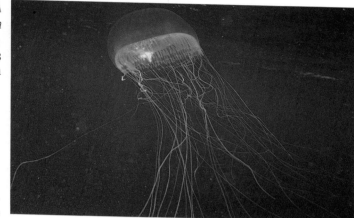

SIZE: 1.½ - 4 in.
DEPTH: 0 - 20 ft.

PORTUGUESE MAN-OF-WAR
Physalia physalis
ORDER:
Siphonophores
Siphonophora
SUBORDER:
Cystonectae

SIZE: Float 2 - 6 in.
Tentacles 10 - 30 ft.
DEPTH: Float on surface.

FLOATING SIPHONOPHORE
Rhizophysa spp.
ORDER:
Siphonophores
Siphonophora
SUBORDER:
Cystonectae

SIZE: See ID
DEPTH: 0 - 130 ft.

Siphonophores – Jellyfish

VISUAL ID: Below a tiny gas float is a series of paired swimming bells that range from less than one to several inches in length. Below the bells is a rigid structure (siphosome) that appears to be constructed of angular brackets. Numerous tentacles may extend below, often in a spiral pattern that can reach 12 inches in length. Transparent to translucent.

ABUNDANCE & DISTRIBUTION: Occasional South Florida, Bahamas, Caribbean.

HABITAT & BEHAVIOR: Float in open water. When feeding they extend (relax) their tentacles, spreading them in a wide spiral pattern by rotating in the water.

EFFECT ON DIVERS: Toxic; contact with tentacles will produce an intense, but short-lived, sting. May cause minor redness and welts.

NOTE: Species identification can be confirmed by noting the dot-like attachments to the tentacles, called tentilla. When relaxed, two long, lateral projecting parts are visible. In the pictured specimen, they are apparent only from the fourth tentilla down.

VISUAL ID: Beneath a tiny gas float, sticking out in all directions, are numerous swimming bells that may range from less than one to several inches in length. Beneath, attached to a stem, are numerous dot-like appendages, called palpons, that contain a red pigment. Also attached to the stem are numerous tentacles which, when relaxed, can reach several inches in length. Transparent to translucent.

ABUNDANCE & DISTRIBUTION: Occasional South Florida, Bahamas, Caribbean.

HABITAT & BEHAVIOR: Float in open water. Extend (relax) long tentacles to ensnare prey.

EFFECT ON DIVERS: Toxic; contact with tentacles will produce an intense, but short-lived, sting. May cause minor redness and welt.

NOTE: Species identification confirmed by being the only member of the family found within safe scuba diving depths.

VISUAL ID: Surface of dome has nematocyst-bearing warts. Eight highly contractile marginal tentacles and four long, frilly oral arms. Translucent, often pinkish with pink warts and tentacles, occasionally purple, yellow or brown. Luminescent at night.

ABUNDANCE & DISTRIBUTION: Occasional circumtropical.

HABITAT & BEHAVIOR: Inhabit surface oceanic waters, occasionally blown over reefs.

EFFECT ON DIVERS: Toxic; contact with bare skin can produce an intense sting. May cause redness and welts.

PAIRED-BELL SIPHONOPHORE

Agalma okeni

ORDER:
Siphonophores
Siphonophora
SUBORDER:
Physonectae
FAMILY:
Agalmidae

SIZE: See ID
DEPTH: 0 - 130 ft.

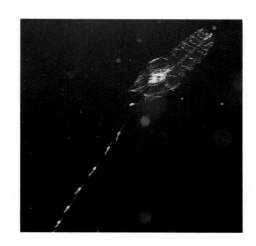

RED-SPOTTED SIPHONOPHORE

Forskalia edwardsi

ORDER:
Siphonophores
Siphonophora
SUBORDER:
Physonectae
FAMILY:
Forskaliidae

SIZE: See ID
DEPTH: 0 - 130 ft.

WARTY JELLYFISH

Pelagia noctiluca

CLASS:
Jellyfish
Scyphozoa

SIZE: ³/₄ - 1¹/₄ in.,
4 in. max.
DEPTH: 0 - 10 ft.

VISUAL ID: Blue to blue-green with white spots. Thick dome, finely grained surface. Oral arms have long, club-like appendages and filaments hanging from them. No marginal tentacles.

ABUNDANCE & DISTRIBUTION: Occasional Caribbean.

HABITAT & BEHAVIOR: Inhabit surface waters, often in harbors and bays, occasionally over reefs.

EFFECT ON DIVERS: Mildly toxic; contact with bare skin can produce sting. May cause redness and welts.

VISUAL ID: Saucer-shaped dome with numerous short, fringe-like tentacles around margin. Four-leaf-clover-shaped reproductive organs can be seen through translucent dome. Four frilly oral arms (not always obvious). Whitish, often shaded with pink or blue.

ABUNDANCE & DISTRIBUTION: Common Florida, Bahamas, Caribbean. Worldwide distribution. At times can be abundant.

HABITAT & BEHAVIOR: Inhabit surface waters, often over reefs.

EFFECT ON DIVERS: Mildly toxic; can sting bare sensitive skin and cause slight itchy rash.

VISUAL ID: Bulb-shaped dome with short, forked oral arms around stout protruding feeding tube. No marginal tentacles. Milky, often with tints of blue or yellow, markings around margin of dome usually brown or white, can be yellow or lavender.

ABUNDANCE & DISTRIBUTION: Occasional Florida, Caribbean. Not reported Bahamas. Can be abundant at times.

HABITAT & BEHAVIOR: Inhabit surface waters near shore, often in harbors and bays, occasionally over reefs.

EFFECT ON DIVERS: None.

BLUE-TINTED JELLYFISH
Phyllorhiza punctata
CLASS:
Jellyfish
Scyphozoa

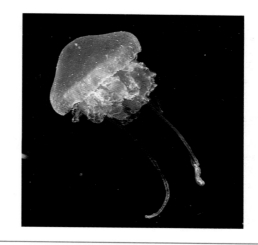

SIZE: 6 - 8 in.,
20 in. max.
DEPTH: 0 - 15 ft.

MOON JELLY
Aurelia aurita
CLASS:
Jellyfish
Scyphozoa

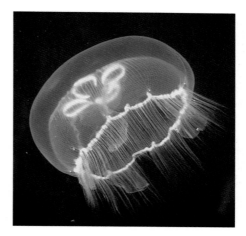

SIZE: 6 - 8 in.,
16 in. max.
DEPTH: 0 - 20 ft.

CANNONBALL JELLY
Stomolophus meleagris
CLASS:
Jellyfish
Scyphozoa

SIZE: 4 - 6 in.,
7 1/4 in. max.
DEPTH: 0 - 20 ft.

Jellyfish

VISUAL ID: Marbled markings on white dome, with lappets around margin. Grape-like clustered oral arms, may equal in length the diameter of bell. Numerous filaments extend from arms.

ABUNDANCE & DISTRIBUTION: Rare Caribbean.

HABITAT & BEHAVIOR: Inhabit surface waters, occasionally over reefs.

EFFECT ON DIVERS: Toxic; contact with bare skin can produce an intense sting. May cause redness and welts.

NOTE: The pictured specimen may be *L. lucerna* which is found in the waters off Brazil or it may be an undescribed species. Laboratory examination of specimen required for positive identification.

VISUAL ID: Smooth, saucer-shaped dome with lappets around margin. Numerous tentacles, and four large, cauliflower-like liplobes around feeding snout. Usually lavender to purple (color of pictured specimen uncommon). Caribbean's largest jellyfish.

ABUNDANCE & DISTRIBUTION: Uncommon South Florida, Bahamas, Caribbean. Its appearance is sporadic and at times can be locally abundant.

HABITAT & BEHAVIOR: Inhabit surface waters. Juvenile pelagic fish often live within the protection of the tentacles. Feed on Moon Jellies [pg. 83]

EFFECT ON DIVERS: Highly toxic; contact with bare skin can produce an intense sting, redness, welts and blistering. Pour vinegar on affected area. Severe stings may cause muscle cramps and breathing difficulty, treat for shock and seek medical attention.

VISUAL ID: Brown, thimble-shaped dome. A few short tentacles around margin of dome.

ABUNDANCE & DISTRIBUTION: Occasional circumtropical.

HABITAT & BEHAVIOR: Inhabit surface waters; usually appear in swarms in springtime.

EFFECT ON DIVERS: Mildly toxic; contact with sensitive skin may produce a mild sting and redness.

MARBLED JELLY
Lychnorhiza sp.
CLASS:
Jellyfish
Scyphozoa

SIZE: 4 - 6 in.
DEPTH: 0 - 15 ft.

STINGING CAULIFLOWER
Drymonema dalmatinum
CLASS:
Jellyfish
Scyphozoa

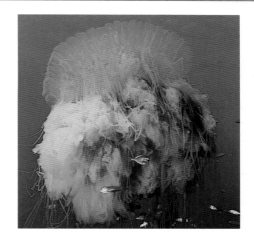

SIZE: 1 - 2$\frac{1}{2}$ ft.,
3 ft. max.
DEPTH: 0 - 20 ft.

SEA THIMBLE
Linuche unguiculata
CLASS:
Jellyfish
Scyphozoa

SIZE: $\frac{1}{2}$ - $\frac{3}{4}$ in.
DEPTH: 0 - 10 ft.

VISUAL ID: Flattened, disc-like bell with grape-like clustered, branched oral arms. Small leaf-shaped or paddle-like appendages on oral arms. Arms about three quarters the length of dome radius. Usually yellowish-brown with white markings. No marginal tentacles.

ABUNDANCE & DISTRIBUTION: Common Florida, Bahamas, Caribbean. May be locally abundant.

HABITAT & BEHAVIOR: Inhabit shallow sand flats in back reef areas and lagoons. Occasionally washed over nearby reefs. Rest on bottom with oral arms oriented upward to speed growth of symbiotic single-celled algae, called zoozanthellae, that grow in their tissues. Receive part of their nourishment from the zoozanthellae.

EFFECT ON DIVERS: Mildly toxic; contact with bare skin can produce sting. May cause redness and welt.

VISUAL ID: Flattened, disc-like dome with grape-like clustered, branched oral arms. Long leaf-shaped or ribbon-like appendages on oral arms. Arms about one half times length of dome radius. May be gray, purplish, greenish or yellow-brown with white markings. No marginal tentacles.

ABUNDANCE & DISTRIBUTION: Common Florida, Bahamas, Caribbean. May be abundant locally.

HABITAT & BEHAVIOR: Inhabit shallow mangrove bays and lagoons with mud and sand bottoms. Occasionally tidally washed over nearby reefs. Rest on bottom with oral arms oriented upward to speed growth of symbiotic single-celled algae, called zoozanthellae, that grow in their tissues. Receive part of their nourishment from the zoozanthellae.

EFFECT ON DIVERS: Mildly toxic; contact with bare skin can produce sting. May cause redness and welt.

VISUAL ID: Tall, translucent, rectangular-shaped dome with a tentacle hanging from each of the four corners of the dome at oral end. May have reddish or bluish tints.

ABUNDANCE & DISTRIBUTION: Occasional Florida, Bahamas, Caribbean.

HABITAT & BEHAVIOR: Inhabit shallow water at night, often over reefs. Attracted to light at night, often swarm.

EFFECT ON DIVERS: Highly toxic; contact with bare skin can produce an intense sting, redness and welts. Pour vinegar on affected area. Severe stings may cause muscle cramps and breathing difficulty, treat for shock and seek medical attention.

SIMILAR SPECIES: Warty Sea Wasp, *C. marsupialis*, smaller with shorter dome, covered with numerous nematocyst-bearing warts. Also attracted to light at night and highly toxic.

UPSIDEDOWN JELLY
Cassiopea frondosa
CLASS:
Jellyfish
Scyphozoa

SIZE: 4 - 5 in.,
10 ½ in. max.
DEPTH: 1 - 25 ft.

MANGROVE UPSIDEDOWN JELLY
Cassiopea xamachana
CLASS:
Jellyfish
Scyphozoa

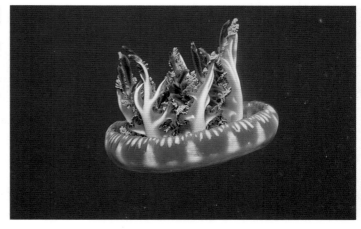

SIZE: 6 - 7 in.,
12 in. max.
DEPTH: 1 - 15 ft.

SEA WASP
Carybdea alata
CLASS:
Jellyfish
Scyphozoa
ORDER:
Box Jellyfish
Cubomedusae

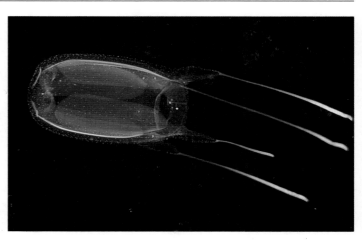

SIZE: 2 - 3 ¼ in.
dome height
DEPTH: 0 - 10 ft.

VISUAL ID: Largest of Caribbean anemones. Tentacles and body white, often with tints of gray, brown, yellow or green. Tentacles are long with slightly enlarged tips that may be pink, lavender, yellow, chartreuse or, occasionally, white.

ABUNDANCE & DISTRIBUTION: Common South Florida, Bahamas, Caribbean.

HABITAT & BEHAVIOR: Inhabit reef and lagoonal areas. Bodies are usually partially or completely hidden from view, in recesses. Tentacles are normally extended, but retract if disturbed. Diamond Blenny, *Malacoctenus boehlkei*, Pederson's Cleaner Shrimp [pg. 151], Spotted Cleaner Shrimp [pg. 151], Squat Anemone Shrimp [pg. 149], and Banded Clinging Crab [pg. 169] are known to associate with this anemone.

EFFECT ON DIVERS: Not considered toxic, but may produce mild irritation to sensitive skin.

VISUAL ID: Hundreds of short, thick tentacles with rounded tips cover flattened oral disc. Tentacles and oral disc are green to brown.

ABUNDANCE & DISTRIBUTION: Common to occasional Bahamas, eastern and southern Caribbean; rare northwestern Caribbean.

HABITAT & BEHAVIOR: Inhabit shallow back reefs. Dense clusters may carpet an area. The following are known to associate with this anemone: Squat Anemone Shrimp [pg. 149], and Banded Clinging Crab [pg. 169].

EFFECT ON DIVERS: Toxic; will sting bare skin and occasionally produce blistering.

VISUAL ID: Numerous knob-like tentacles cover flat oral disc. Tentacles and oral disc are light to dark gray and brown.

ABUNDANCE & DISTRIBUTION: Uncommon to rare from Jamaica to the Leeward and Windward Islands to Curacao.

HABITAT & BEHAVIOR: Inhabit areas of sand and coral rubble; occasionally reefs. The following are known to associate with this anemone: Spotted Cleaner Shrimp [pg. 151], Squat Anemone Shrimp [pg. 149], and Banded Clinging Crab [pg. 169].

EFFECT ON DIVERS: Not considered toxic.

GIANT ANEMONE
Condylactis gigantea
ORDER:
Anemones
Actiniaria

SIZE: 6 - 12 in. across
tentacles & body
DEPTH: 15 - 100 ft.

SUN ANEMONE
Stichodactyla helianthus
ORDER:
Anemones
Actiniaria

SIZE: Disc 4 - 6 in.
DEPTH: 3 - 30 ft.

ELEGANT ANEMONE
Actinoporus elegans
ORDER:
Anemones
Actiniaria

SIZE: Disc 7 - 9 in.
DEPTH: 10 - 60 ft.

VISUAL ID: About 200 short, tapering, often banded or striped tentacles around rim of oral disc. Rows of small, bead-like warts radiate from the central oral opening. Tentacles and oral disc gray to tan to olive, occasionally have reddish or lavender tints. Underside of disc often has reddish or lavender warts.

ABUNDANCE & DISTRIBUTION: Occasional Bahamas, Caribbean.

HABITAT & BEHAVIOR: Inhabit back reefs, sand and coral rubble. Bodies usually buried in sand or hidden in recesses.

EFFECT ON DIVERS: Not considered toxic.

VISUAL ID: Numerous long, thin, pointed tentacles are translucent and marked with whitish "corkscrew-like" markings. Tentacles and body shades of gray, brown or green.

ABUNDANCE & DISTRIBUTION: Common Florida, Bahamas, Caribbean.

HABITAT & BEHAVIOR: Inhabit reefs and areas of sand and coral rubble. Bodies usually hidden from view in small recesses, frequently in openings of dead conch shells. If disturbed, will rapidly retract tentacles, often completely from view. Red Snapping Shrimp [pg. 153] and Pederson's Cleaning Shrimp [pg. 151] are known to associate with this anemone.

EFFECT ON DIVERS: Mildly toxic; will sting sensitive skin.

VISUAL ID: Numerous nematocyst-bearing knobs on long, thin, pointed, translucent tentacles. Tentacles and body shades of gray to brown or green.

ABUNDANCE & DISTRIBUTION: Common Florida, Bahamas, Caribbean.

HABITAT & BEHAVIOR: Inhabit reefs and areas of sand and coral rubble, prefer clear water fore reefs. Bodies usually hidden in recesses. If disturbed, will rapidly retract tentacles, often completely from view.

EFFECT ON DIVERS: Toxic; will sting bare skin.

* NOTE: Formerly, inappropriately classified in the genus *Heteractis*. At printing, a proper genus has yet to be described.

BEADED ANEMONE
Epicystis crucifer
ORDER:
Anemones
Actiniaria

SIZE: Disc 3 - 5 in.
DEPTH: 5 - 30 ft.

CORKSCREW ANEMONE
Bartholomea annulata
ORDER:
Anemones
Actiniaria

SIZE: 4 - 7 in. across
exposed tentacles
DEPTH: 5 - 130 ft.

KNOBBY ANEMONE
* lucida
ORDER:
Anemones
Actiniaria

SIZE: Tentacles 3 - 4 in.
2 $^{1}/_{2}$ - 4 $^{1}/_{2}$ in. across
exposed tentacles
DEPTH: 5 - 100 ft.

VISUAL ID: Long, thin, pointed, transparent tentacles encircle brownish to bluish white oral disc. Often in groups, but may be solitary.

ABUNDANCE & DISTRIBUTION: Common to occasional Florida, Bahamas, Caribbean.

HABITAT & BEHAVIOR: Inhabit reefs, wrecks and rocky areas. Often attach to exposed surfaces, such as sides of wrecks.

EFFECT ON DIVERS: Not considered toxic.

NOTE: In Florida, has been reported by a junior name, *A. pallida*.

VISUAL ID: Tentacles with enlarged, "club-like" tips ring the protruding central oral opening. Tentacles and oral disc whitish, brown or lavender, often mottled and marked with flecks and splotches. Body column large and barrel-shaped, diameter about equal to that of oral disc.

ABUNDANCE & DISTRIBUTION: Common to occasional central, eastern and southern Caribbean; rare northwestern Caribbean, Bahamas. Not reported Florida.

HABITAT & BEHAVIOR: Inhabit caves and other dark recesses. Extend oral discs from under rocks and other protected areas. Bodies usually hidden, but occasionally exposed, especially in protected recesses.

EFFECT ON DIVERS: Not considered toxic.

VISUAL ID: Long pseudotentacles with slightly enlarged tips extend from fissure. Brown to dark gray to bluish-green with shaded line and ring markings. Pseudotentacles tips are slightly enlarged, often darker and occasionally double lobed.

ABUNDANCE & DISTRIBUTION: Occasional Bahamas, Caribbean.

HABITAT & BEHAVIOR: Inhabit narrow fissures in coral heads, with only the ends of pseudotentacles extended from openings. If disturbed, will retract pseudotentacles, often completely from view. Long, unbranched, true tentacles may be extended at night.

EFFECT ON DIVERS: Toxic; will sting bare skin.

PALE ANEMONE
Aiptasia tagetes
ORDER:
Anemones
Actiniaria

SIZE: Disc 1 - 2 in.
DEPTH: 5 - 60 ft.

CLUB-TIPPED ANEMONE
Telmatactis americana
ORDER:
Anemones
Actiniaria

SIZE: Disc 1 - 4 in.
DEPTH: 5 - 40 ft.

HIDDEN ANEMONE
Lebrunia coralligens
ORDER:
Anemones
Actiniaria

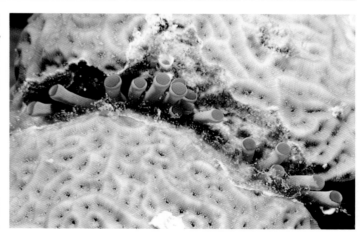

SIZE: 1$^1/_2$-2$^1/_2$ in.
tentacle spread
DEPTH: 3-40 ft.

VISUAL ID: Stubby, branching pseudotentacles have prominent, nematocyst-bearing knobs. Usually shades of brown to dark gray with lighter colored markings, occasionally in shades of blue-green.

ABUNDANCE & DISTRIBUTION: Common Florida, Bahamas, Caribbean.

HABITAT & BEHAVIOR: Inhabit reefs. Bodies hidden from view in recesses, and concealed by the branch-work bed of pseudotentacles. If disturbed, will rapidly retract pseudotentacles, often completely from view. Long, unbranched, true tentacles are only extended at night.

EFFECT ON DIVERS: Toxic; will sting bare skin.

VISUAL ID: Whitish, translucent to transparent tentacles and body.

ABUNDANCE & DISTRIBUTION: Common to occasional Florida, Bahamas, Caribbean.

HABITAT & BEHAVIOR: Attach to blades of turtle grass.

EFFECT ON DIVERS: Highly toxic; will sting bare skin and occasionally produce blistering.

NOTE: Scientific name may be junior to and synonymous with *Bunodeopsis antilliensis*.

VISUAL ID: Shape of tentacles is distinctive; ends are enlarged and bulbous, and tipped with a thin, elongated, curling point. Transparent to translucent tentacles and body. Marked, ringed and banded in shades of green, tan and white.

ABUNDANCE & DISTRIBUTION: Common northern Gulf Coast of Florida.

HABITAT & BEHAVIOR: Inhabit reefs, wrecks and rocky areas.

EFFECT ON DIVERS: Not toxic.

NOTE: Although this anemone is relatively common, its living appearance has not been matched with a scientific identification. Collection of a photographed specimen and microscopic examination is necessary to establish visual identification. Possibly an undescribed species.

BRANCHING ANEMONE
Lebrunia danae
ORDER:
Anemones
Actiniaria

SIZE: 3 - 10 in. across
exposed pseudotentacles
DEPTH: 5 - 130 ft.

TURTLE GRASS ANEMONE
Viatrix globulifera
ORDER:
Anemones
Actiniaria

SIZE: Disc ¹/₄ - ³/₄ in.
DEPTH: 1 - 20 ft.

LIGHT BULB ANEMONE

ORDER:
Anemones
Actiniaria

SIZE: Disc 2 - 3 in.
DEPTH: 30 - 130 ft.

VISUAL ID: Transparent to translucent brownish tentacles marked with white bands and speckles. Oral disc brownish translucent with white speckles; occasionally has white center around oral opening.

ABUNDANCE & DISTRIBUTION: Common Caribbean.

HABITAT & BEHAVIOR: Associate with sponges. Grow from folds and depressions in surface, and around bases.

NOTE: Although this anemone is relatively common, its living appearance has not been matched with a scientific identification. Collection of a photographed specimen and microscopic examination is necessary to establish visual identification. Possibly an undescribed species.

VISUAL ID: Large, tightly packed, knob-like outgrowths cover the body column. When contracted, usually during day, overall appearance resembles a head of cauliflower. When expanded, usually only at night, translucent tentacles protrude from upper part of body column and knob-like outgrowths appear as berry clusters on a tree trunk. Whitish-gray areas on outgrowths are concentrations of defensive stinging nematocysts.

ABUNDANCE & DISTRIBUTION: Rare Florida, Bahamas.

HABITAT & BEHAVIOR: Inhabit rocky outcroppings, shipwrecks and reefs.

EFFECT ON DIVERS: Toxic; will sting bare skin.

VISUAL ID: Colonies encrust Feather Bush Hydroids [pg. 73]. Body and tentacles are orange to pale yellow to brown or green.

ABUNDANCE & DISTRIBUTION: Occasional Florida, Bahamas, Caribbean.

HABITAT & BEHAVIOR: Inhabit reefs where Feather Tree Hydroids grow.

EFFECT ON DIVERS: None from zoanthid, but Feather Tree Hydroid will sting.

SPONGE ANEMONE

ORDER:
Anemones
Actinaria

SIZE: Disc $^3/_4$ - $1^1/_4$ in.
DEPTH: 25 - 130 ft.

BERRIED ANEMONE
Alicia mirabilis
ORDER:
Anemones
Actiniaria

SIZE: 2 - 4 in. across
outgrowths & body
DEPTH: 30 - 130 ft.

HYDROID ZOANTHID
Parazoanthus tunicans
ORDER:
Zoanthids
Zoanthidea

SIZE: $^1/_4$ in.
DEPTH: 30 - 130 ft.

VISUAL ID: Blunt tentacles numbering to 28 are brown, yellow-brown, light greenish-brown or greenish yellow; oral disk somewhat darker. Body white to grayish-white. Large communities inhabit surfaces of a wide variety of sponges.

ABUNDANCE & DISTRIBUTION: Common Florida, Bahamas, Caribbean.

HABITAT & BEHAVIOR: Inhabit sponges. Frequently grow on Branching Vase Sponge [pg. 25], Pink Vase Sponge [pg. 27], Lavender Rope Sponge [pg. 39], and Red Boring Sponge [pg. 57].

SIMILAR SPECIES: Brown Sponge Zoanthids, *P. catenularis*, are distinguished by 20 brown to yellow-brown, pointed tentacles; oral disk brown, darker toward center; body whitish, usually deeper than 60 ft. Yellow Sponge Zoanthids, *Epizoanthus cutressi*, are distinguished by their yellow color; known only from reefs and dropoffs.

VISUAL ID: Brilliant gold to yellow body and tentacles. Encrust surfaces of several species of sponges.

ABUNDANCE & DISTRIBUTION: Common Caribbean, Bahamas.

HABITAT & BEHAVIOR: Colonies grow in meandering, band-like rows. When polyps are closed, colonies appear as golden patches. Frequently grow on Thin Rope Sponge [pg. 41], Green Finger Sponge [pg. 43] and Brown Tube Sponge [pg. 23].

VISUAL ID: Body and tentacles dark maroon, burgundy or purple. Tentacles may be somewhat translucent. Large communities inhabit surfaces of several species of sponge.

ABUNDANCE & DISTRIBUTION: Common Caribbean.

HABITAT & BEHAVIOR: Inhabit sponges. Often grow on Brown Tube Sponges [pg. 23] and Dark Volcano Sponges [pg. 33]. Most common sponge zoanthid at depths below 65 ft.

SPONGE ZOANTHID
Parazoanthus parasiticus
ORDER:
Zoanthids
Zoanthidea

SIZE: ¹/₄ in.
DEPTH: 25 - 100 ft.

GOLDEN ZOANTHID
Parazoanthus swiftii
ORDER:
Zoanthids
Zoanthidea

SIZE: ¹/₄ in.
DEPTH: 40 - 130 ft.

MAROON SPONGE ZOANTHID
Parazoanthus puertoricense
ORDER:
Zoanthids
Zoanthidea

SIZE: ¹/₄ in.
DEPTH: 40 - 100 ft.

VISUAL ID: One of the largest zoanthids. Highly flattened oral disc is green to brown and often somewhat mottled. Short, light brown tentacles ring outer edge.
ABUNDANCE & DISTRIBUTION: Uncommon Caribbean.
HABITAT & BEHAVIOR: Inhabit mid-range to deep reefs. Attach to rocky, and usually somewhat sheltered, substrate. Several may grow in close proximity, but do not form mats. If disturbed, edges will curl inward revealing underside of oral disc.

VISUAL ID: Grow in dense mats. When circular oral discs are fully expanded, they often pack so tightly together that they become polygonal. Two rows of stubby tentacles around outer edge of oral disc. Colors and patterns vary, usually mottled in earthtones. On deeper reefs, occasionally fluoresce a dayglow-orange color which is not visible when lit by a hand light or strobe.
ABUNDANCE & DISTRIBUTION: Common Caribbean, Bahamas.
HABITAT & BEHAVIOR: Inhabit reef tops. Under stands of antler coral and in shallow cracks and crevices. If disturbed, tentacles curl inward and retract, forming a dome capped column [right].
SIMILAR SPECIES: Row Zoanthid, *Z. sociatus*, colonies tend to grow in rows from thin, band-like, occasionally branching bases. Oral disc small (about ¼ in.). Bodies usually hidden in sand or algae. Rarely deeper than 15 ft.

SUN ZOANTHID
Palythoa grandis
ORDER:
Zoanthids
Zoanthidea

SIZE: Disc ³/₄ - 1¹/₄ in.
DEPTH: 40 - 120 ft.

MAT ZOANTHID
Zoanthus pulchellus
ORDER:
Zoanthids
Zoanthidea

SIZE: Disc ¹/₄-¹/₂ in.
DEPTH: 20 - 60 ft.

Color Varieties

VISUAL ID: Grow in clusters. Flat oral disc is shades of brown, and often has blue and/or green overtones and white blotch in center. Two rings of thin, pointed tentacles around outer edge.

ABUNDANCE & DISTRIBUTION: Occasional Caribbean.

HABITAT & BEHAVIOR: Inhabit coral reefs. Small clusters grow in secluded, protected areas of reef.

NOTE: Although this distinctive zoanthid is relatively common, its living appearance has never been matched with a scientific identification. Collection of a photographed specimen and microscopic examination are necessary to establish visual identification. Possibly an undescribed species.

VISUAL ID: Brownish-white colonies form mats that encrust substrate. Oral discs push against one another when fully expanded. Two rings of short tentacles around outer edge.

ABUNDANCE & DISTRIBUTION: Occasional South Florida, Caribbean, Bahamas.

HABITAT & BEHAVIOR: Inhabit shallow reefs; prefer areas with some water movement. If disturbed, tentacles curl inward and retract forming dome-like lumps [below].

SIMILAR SPECIES: Knobby Zoanthid, *Palythoa mammillosa*, colonies form small mats, rarely exceeding 4 inches across. Oral discs do not touch when fully expanded and are separated by polygonal dividing lines.

NOTE: Has been reported by junior name *P. caribaea*.

BROWN ZOANTHID

ORDER:
Zoanthids
Zoanthidea

SIZE: Disc $^1/_4$ - $^1/_2$ in.
DEPTH: 20 - 60 ft.

WHITE ENCRUSTING ZOANTHID
Palythoa caribaeorum
ORDER:
Zoanthids
Zoanthidea

SIZE: Disc $^1/_4$ - $^1/_2$ in.
DEPTH: 10 - 40 ft.

Polyps Closed

Corallimorphs

VISUAL ID: Spherical, knob-like tentacles cover the oral disc, with elongated tentacles around edge. Completely extended and flattened disc reveals distinctive, radial, spoke-like arrangement of tentacles. Usually green overall, but may be, or have mixed in, shades of yellow, orange, brown and blue. Colors may fluoresce.

ABUNDANCE & DISTRIBUTION: Occasional Florida, Bahamas, Caribbean.

HABITAT & BEHAVIOR: Attach to solid reef structures. Often cover area in the form of mat-like communities, occasionally so compact that individual polyps are difficult to distinguish. Curl inward if disturbed.

VISUAL ID: Flattened oral disc with wart-like tentacles having forked extensions. These tentacles may be numerous and compacted together, or few and widely separated. Thin short tentacles around outer edge. Green overall, often has bluish overtones, and may be somewhat translucent.

ABUNDANCE & DISTRIBUTION: Occasional Florida, Bahamas, Caribbean.

HABITAT & BEHAVIOR: Attach to solid reef structures. Solitary, or grow in small groups, occasionally form mat-like communities so compacted that the individual polyps are difficult to distinguish. Curl inward if disturbed.

NOTE: This species was formerly classified in the genus *Rhodactis*.

VISUAL ID: Tiny, widely separated, forked tentacles cover oral disc. Green, brown and bluish-gray splotches cover oral disc. Often somewhat translucent.

ABUNDANCE & DISTRIBUTION: Uncommon Caribbean.

HABITAT & BEHAVIOR: Attach to solid reef structures. Prefer secluded areas. Grow as solitary polyp, or in small groups. Curl inward if disturbed.

NOTE: This species was formerly classified in the genus *Rhodactis*.

FLORIDA CORALLIMORPH
Ricordea florida
ORDER:
Corallimorphs
Corallimorpharian

SIZE: Disc 1½ - 2 in.
DEPTH: 15 - 100 ft.

WARTY CORALLIMORPH
Discosoma sanctithomae
ORDER:
Corallimorphs
Corallimorpharian

SIZE: Disc 2 - 3½ in.
DEPTH: 10 - 75 ft.

FORKED TENTACLE CORALLIMORPH
Discosoma carlgreni
ORDER:
Corallimorphs
Corallimorpharian

SIZE: Disc 1½ - 2½ in.
DEPTH: 10-60 ft.

Coralllimorphs – Tube-Dwelling Anemones

VISUAL ID: Extremely flattened oral disc with short, squarish, irregular tentacles around edge. Light green to olive to dark brown oral disc, occasionally streaked or splotched.

ABUNDANCE & DISTRIBUTION: Rare Florida, Bahamas, Caribbean.

HABITAT & BEHAVIOR: Attach to solid reef structures. Prefer shaded, secluded areas and caves. Grow as solitary polyps.

NOTE: This species was formerly classified in the genus *Paradiscosoma*.

VISUAL ID: Bright orange body column and ball-like tips on nearly transparent tentacles. On rare occasion may be pale yellow or white.

ABUNDANCE & DISTRIBUTION: Uncommon Caribbean.

HABITAT & BEHAVIOR: Inhabit reefs and sandy areas near reefs. Nocturnal, solitary polyps extend from recesses or sand. If disturbed or lighted, will retract.

NOTE: Because of their visual resemblance to anemones, this species is often called the "Orange Ball Anemone", which is a misnomer.

VISUAL ID: Translucent brown-and-white banded outer tentacles, whitish oral disc and central tentacles.

ABUNDANCE & DISTRIBUTION: Occasional South Florida, Bahamas, Caribbean.

HABITAT & BEHAVIOR: Inhabit areas of sand and coral rubble. Nocturnal, solitary polyps extend from parchment-like tube buried in sand. If disturbed or lit by a diver's light, retract into tube.

NOTE: Identification is tentative. Because there are several similar appearing species, positive identification requires microscopic examination.

UMBRELLA CORALLIMORPH
Discosoma neglecta
ORDER:
Corallimorphs
Corallimorpharian

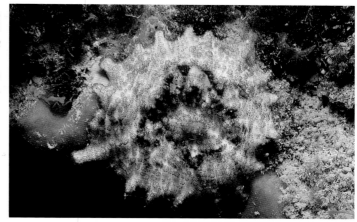

SIZE: Disc 1¹/₂ - 2¹/₂ in.
DEPTH: 30 - 90 ft.

ORANGE BALL CORALLIMORPH
Pseudocorynactis caribbeorum
ORDER:
Corallimorphs
Corallimorpharian

SIZE: Disc 1 - 2 in.
Tentacles 1 - 2 in.
DEPTH: 20 - 80 ft.

BANDED TUBE-DWELLING ANEMONE
Arachnanthus nocturnus
ORDER:
Tube-Dwelling Anemones
Ceriantharia

SIZE: Disc ³/₄ - 1¹/₄ in.
Tentacles 1 - 2 in.
DEPTH: 10 - 80 ft.

IDENTIFICATION GROUP 3
Phylum Ctenophora
(Tee-NOFF-for-uh / L. to bear combs)
Comb Jellies

Ctenophores comprise a small phylum of transparent, free-floating marine invertebrates that are often mistaken for jellyfish. However, there are a few distinct features that easily distinguish the group. Comb jellies are usually small, no more than one or two inches across, and have either two **tentacles** or lack them altogether. Their delicate body, which breaks apart easily when touched, often tends to be oval or pear-shaped, rather than having the open-dome shape of most jellyfish. Stinging nematocysts are absent in this phylum.

The phylum's most important visual distinction is the presence of eight rows or bands of hair-like cilia, called **combs.** Beating of the cilia in coordinated waves gives most of these animals their means of movement. This beating action appears as sets of iridescent lights moving along the comb rows.

Divers generally observe comb jellies just beneath the surface where the animals prey upon tiny planktonic animals. The best way to spot these animals is to look up toward the surface light, which makes them more visible as it passes through their transparent bodies. They occasionally appear in such large numbers that a haze is created across the surface. Ctenophores are noted for their bioluminescence. When disturbed at night, they produce a spectacular greenish-blue glow.

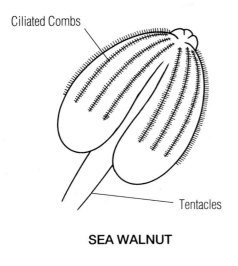

Ciliated Combs

Tentacles

SEA WALNUT

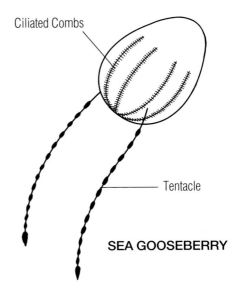

Ciliated Combs

Tentacle

SEA GOOSEBERRY

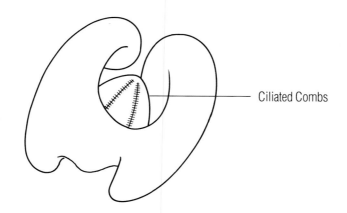

Ciliated Combs

WINGED COMB JELLY

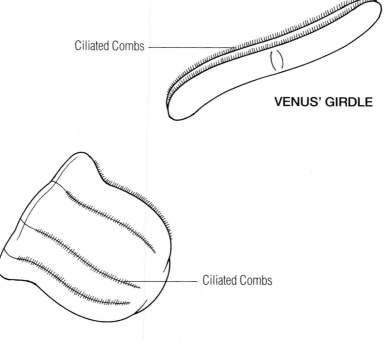

Ciliated Combs

VENUS' GIRDLE

Ciliated Combs

FLATTENED HELMET

VISUAL ID: Walnut or occasionally pear-shaped, with large oral lobes and some lateral compression. Often bespeckled with numerous small warts. Opalescent or translucent, frequently with a greenish-amber cast.

ABUNDANCE & DISTRIBUTION: Common Florida, Bahamas, Caribbean.

HABITAT & BEHAVIOR: Float near surface. Often appear in large aggregations over reefs, in bays and harbors, especially in summer months. Bioluminescent; when disturbed at night produce a greenish-blue light.

VISUAL ID: Largest comb jelly. Easily distinguished by numerous long, conical papillae. Transparent to translucent, occasionally with some yellowish markings, oral lobes tinted brown. Two short tentacles.

ABUNDANCE & DISTRIBUTION: Occasional Florida, Bahamas, Caribbean.

HABITAT & BEHAVIOR: During calm weather often float near surface of open water. May appear in large aggregations over reefs, especially in spring and summer. Bioluminescent; when disturbed at night produce a greenish-blue light.

VISUAL ID: Distinguished by two large, prominent oral lobes and compressed body. Transparent to translucent. May have some milky warts on outer surface of oral lobes.

ABUNDANCE & DISTRIBUTION: Occasional Florida, Bahamas, Caribbean.

HABITAT & BEHAVIOR: Float near surface of open water, found deeper when water is rough. May appear in large aggregations, especially on calm days of spring and early summer. Actively swim with flapping movements of oral lobes, usually with two or three pulsations followed by a brief rest period. Bioluminescent; when disturbed at night produce a greenish-blue light.

SEA WALNUT
Mnemiopsis Mccradyi
CLASS:
Comb Jellies
Tentaculata

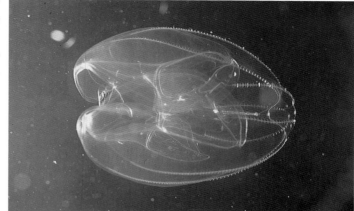

SIZE: 2 - 2¹/₂ in.,
4 in. max.
DEPTH: 0-15 ft.

WARTY COMB JELLY
Leucothea multicornis
CLASS:
Comb Jellies
Tentaculata

SIZE: 2 - 3 in.,
8 in. max.
DEPTH: 0 - 130 ft.

WINGED
COMB JELLY
Ocyropsis crystallina
CLASS:
Comb Jellies
Tentaculata

SIZE: 1 - 2 in.,
3¹/₂ in. max.
DEPTH: 1 - 15 ft.

VISUAL ID: Four conspicuous brown spots on large, prominent oral lobes, body compressed. Body and lobes whitish and translucent.

ABUNDANCE & DISTRIBUTION: Occasional Florida, Bahamas, Caribbean.

HABITAT & BEHAVIOR: Float near surface of open water, found deeper when water is rough. May appear in large aggregations after several days of calm. Actively swim with flapping movements of oral lobes, usually with two or three pulsations followed by a brief rest period. Bioluminescent; when disturbed at night produce a greenish-blue light.

VISUAL ID: Transparent, narrow, elongated body with small oral lobes (about one-quarter of body's length). Pores in the combs of cilia contain a red, oily, dye-like substance that make the combs appear as rows of brilliant red dots. Extremely fragile.

ABUNDANCE & DISTRIBUTION: Occasional Florida, Bahamas, Caribbean.

HABITAT & BEHAVIOR: Inhabit open oceanic waters, only occasionally over reefs. Near surface only on calm days. Swim solely by means of the ciliated combs. When disturbed red dye is ejected into the water as a fluorescing cloud. Bioluminescent; when disturbed at night produce a greenish-blue light.

VISUAL ID: Egg-shaped body, narrowing at the oral end. Comb rows extend from the aboral pole two-thirds to three-quarters the body's length. Two long tentacles with side branching filaments. When contracted, the filaments coil tightly into a tear-drop shape. Transparent to translucent with slight red pigmentation along edges of comb rows.

ABUNDANCE & DISTRIBUTION: Occasional Caribbean.

HABITAT & BEHAVIOR: Float near surface, found deeper when water is rough. Swim by means of the ciliated combs which they can reverse, causing a spinning action that spreads the tentacles in a corkscrew pattern. Filaments usually remain in coiled position, extending only when they contact food. Bioluminescent; when disturbed at night produce a greenish-blue light.

NOTE: Positive identification of this genus cannot be confirmed without light-microscopic examination of the tentacles. Pictured specimen may be an undescribed species.

SPOT-WINGED COMB JELLY

Ocyropsis maculata

CLASS:
Comb Jellies
Tentaculata

SIZE: 1¹/₂ - 2¹/₂ in.,
4 in. max.
DEPTH: 0 - 15 ft.

RED-SPOT COMB JELLY

Eurhamphaea vexilligera

CLASS:
Comb Jellies
Tentaculata

SIZE: 1 - 2 in.,
3¹/₂ in. max.
DEPTH: 1 - 130 ft.

SEA GOOSEBERRY

Euplokamis sp.

CLASS:
Comb Jellies
Tentaculata

SIZE: ¹/₂ - ³/₄ in.
DEPTH: 1 - 130 ft.

VISUAL ID: Long, ribbon-shaped body. Young are transparent; they become violet with age and often display a greenish-blue fluorescence. Edge of body curves out from central axis. Similar, smaller species, Small Venus' Girdle [next], has straight edge extending from central axis.

ABUNDANCE & DISTRIBUTION: Occasional Florida, Bahamas, Caribbean.

HABITAT & BEHAVIOR: Inhabit open oceanic waters, only occasionally over deeper reefs. Swim with undulating movements of body. Bioluminescent; when disturbed at night produce a greenish-blue light.

VISUAL ID: Transparent, ribbon-shaped body. Often display a blue to violet fluorescence. Edge of body straight from central axis. Similar, larger species, Venus' Girdle [previous], has curving edge extending from central axis.

ABUNDANCE & DISTRIBUTION: Occasional Florida, Bahamas, Caribbean.

HABITAT & BEHAVIOR: Inhabit open oceanic waters, occasionally over deeper reefs. Swim with undulating movements of body. Bioluminescent; when disturbed at night produce a greenish-blue light.

NOTE: Formally classified in the genus *Folia*.

VISUAL ID: Flat, helmet-shaped body. Transparent to translucent, often steely-blue, occasionally milky. Internal canals often pink to reddish-brown. Young are spotted.

ABUNDANCE & DISTRIBUTION: Occasional Florida, Bahamas, Caribbean.

HABITAT & BEHAVIOR: Habitat ranges from shallow-water mangrove bays to oceanic open water. Swim rapidly, solely by means of its ciliated combs. Bioluminescent; when disturbed at night produce a greenish-blue light.

VENUS' GIRDLE
Cestum veneris
CLASS:
Comb Jellies
Tentaculata

SIZE: 1 - 2 ft.,
5 ft. max.
DEPTH: 1 - 130 ft.

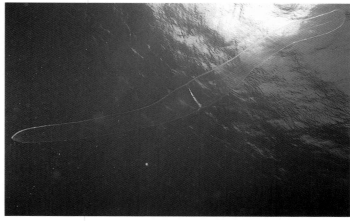

SMALL VENUS' GIRDLE
Velamen parallelum
CLASS:
Comb Jellies
Tentaculata

SIZE: 1 - 3 in.,
6 in. max.
DEPTH: 1 - 130 ft.

FLATTENED HELMET COMB JELLY
Beroe ovata
CLASS:
Comb Jellies
Nuda

SIZE: 2 - 3 in.,
6 in. .max.
DEPTH: 1 - 130 ft.

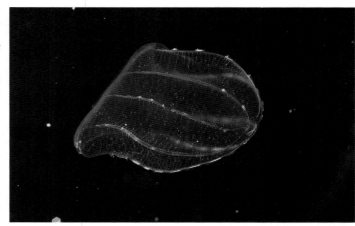

Phylum Platyhelminthes

(Plat-ee-hell-MIN-theez / Gr. broad flat worm)

Flatworms

Flatworms are flat, elongated ovals, that range in length from one to five inches. The only animal on the reef that they could be confused with are the thick-bodied nudibranchs (shell-less snails) which, like flatworms, are often brightly colored and oval-shaped. Remembering that flatworms are thin and leaf-like alleviates confusion.

Most marine flatworms observed by divers are in the Class Turbellaria, Order Polycladida. Although not particularly uncommon, flatworms are rarely sighted because they spend the majority of their time under rocks and in dark recesses, scavenging for small invertebrates and the remains of dead animals. Their slow, gliding movement over the bottom is accomplished primarily by the beating of cilia on the underside. In larger species, muscular waves, or ripples, running the length of the body, assist in movement. On rare occasions they may be observed swimming in open water using an undulating motion.

Flatworms are simple animals, but the phylum is biologically significant. They are the most primitive animals to have similar right and left sides, a definite front and rear end, and a dorsal and ventral surface. The primitive beginnings of specialized body organs, a complex nervous system, and three tissue layers are present. One body-opening, located centrally on the underside, serves as both **mouth** and **anus**. On the heads of most reef species are rudimentary sensory organs in the form of **antennae**. Eye spots, that function simply in the detection of light, are developed in many species. Flatworms have the capacity to regenerate parts severed from their body, and often can regenerate another complete animal from only the severed part.

Phylum Rhynchocoela

(Rin-co-SEE-luh / L. stout belly)

Ribbon Worms

Ribbon worms are long, slender and somewhat flattened. Those occurring on tropical reefs are often brightly colored and striped. In many respects they are similar to flatworms, but are more highly organized, and have both mouth and anus. They are not uncommon reef inhabitants, but are rarely observed in the open. Ribbon worms hide under rocks, or beneath algae and in deep recesses, where they prey on small invertebrates.

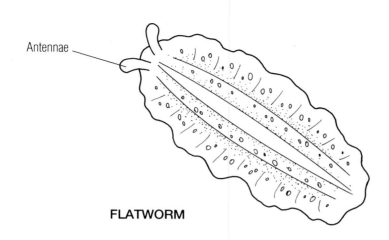

Antennae

FLATWORM

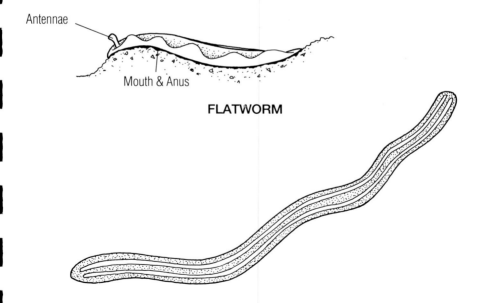

Antennae

Mouth & Anus

FLATWORM

RIBBONWORM

Flatworms

VISUAL ID: Dark reddish-brown with orange spots ringed in black, margin trimmed in black with white spots. Two short sensory antennae at head.

ABUNDANCE & DISTRIBUTION: Occasional South Florida, Bahamas, Caribbean.

HABITAT & BEHAVIOR: Inhabit coral reefs. Often hide under rocks and rubble. Occasionally swim in open water with an undulating motion of entire body.

VISUAL ID: White to light grayish brown or green with numerous, thin, dark brown lines crisscrossing body. Two short sensory antennae at head.

ABUNDANCE & DISTRIBUTION: Occasional Florida, Bahamas, Caribbean.

HABITAT & BEHAVIOR: Inhabit shallow areas of rocks and coral rubble, patch reefs, and around mangroves. Occasionally swim in open water with an undulating motion of entire body.

NOTE: Also commonly known as "Crozier's Flatworm."

VISUAL ID: White, light gray or tan with brown, net-like pattern over body. Two short sensory antennae at head.

ABUNDANCE & DISTRIBUTION: Occasional Florida, Bahamas.

HABITAT & BEHAVIOR: Inhabit coral reefs. Often hide under rocks and rubble. Occasionally swim in open water with an undulating motion of entire body.

LEOPARD FLATWORM
Pseudoceros pardalis
CLASS:
Flatworms
Turbellaria
ORDER:
Polycladida

SIZE: 1 - 2 in.
DEPTH: 15 - 75 ft.

LINED FLATWORM
Pseudoceros crozieri
CLASS:
Flatworms
Turbellaria
ORDER:
Polycladida

SIZE: 1 - 2 in.
DEPTH: 1 - 35 ft.

NETTED FLATWORM
Pseudoceros texarus
CLASS:
Flatworms
Turbellaria
ORDER:
Polycladida

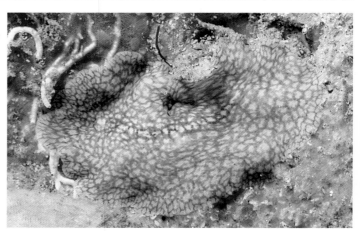

SIZE: 1 - 2 in.
DEPTH: 1 - 35 ft.

VISUAL ID: Dark brown central area, with scattered white spots and scalloped border. Margin of body is white with pale green to yellow edge. Two short sensory antennae at head.

ABUNDANCE & DISTRIBUTION: Uncommon to rare Florida, Bahamas, Caribbean.

HABITAT & BEHAVIOR: Inhabit shallow patch reefs, areas of sand, rubble and sea grass beds.

VISUAL ID: Navy blue to dark purple body, with narrow, orange to gold margin and dark purple edge. Two short sensory antennae at head.

ABUNDANCE & DISTRIBUTION: Rare Florida, Bahamas, Caribbean. Circumtropical. Common in some Indo-Pacific regions.

HABITAT & BEHAVIOR: Inhabit coral reefs and areas of rubble. Often hide under rocks and rubble. Occasionally swim in open water with an undulating motion of entire body.

VISUAL ID: Two red stripes running down back are bordered by three narrow white stripes. Belly is pale grayish-white.

ABUNDANCE & DISTRIBUTION: Uncommon Florida, Bahamas, Caribbean.

HABITAT & BEHAVIOR: Inhabit reefs and areas of coral rubble. Hide under rocks, debris and recesses in reef.

NOTE: Many species of ribbon worms vary greatly in color and markings. Microscopic examination of tissue is required to determine genus and species.

BICOLORED FLATWORM
Pseudoceros bicolor

CLASS:
Flatworms
Turbellaria
ORDER:
Polycladida

SIZE: ½ - 1¾ in.
DEPTH: 1 - 35 ft.

SPLENDID FLATWORM
Pseudoceros splendidus

CLASS:
Flatworms
Turbellaria
ORDER:
Polycladida

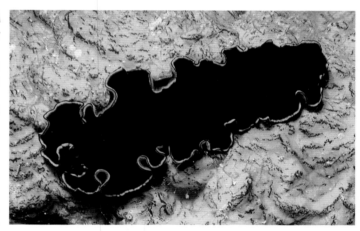

SIZE: 1 - 2 in.
DEPTH: 10 - 75 ft.

RED & WHITE STRIPED RIBBON WORM

Phylum:
Ribbon worms
Rhynchocoela

SIZE: 3 - 10 in.
DEPTH: 1 - 130 ft.

IDENTIFICATION GROUP 5
Phylum Annelida
(Aah-NELL-id-uh / L. little rings)
Segmented Worms

Common earthworms, as well as many marine worms, are members of this phylum. Their distinguishing characteristic is repetitive segments which divide the worm's body. Marine worms that inhabit reefs belong to the class Polychaeta, and are commonly referred to as polychaetes.

FIRE WORMS

Class Polychaeta (Polly-KEY-tuh / Gr. many hairs)
Subclass Errantia (Air-RAN-tee-uh / L. free-moving)
Family Amphinomidae (Am-fin-NOME-ih-dee / L. moving round about)

For defense, free-living fire worms have developed the sensory hairs on each segment into bundles of tiny, white, sharp, detachable bristles. Also, extending from the segments are clusters of reddish, irregular-branching **gill filaments**, part of their circulatory system. Located on the head is a fleshy plate, called a **caruncle**; its size and shape is often a clue for species identification. These somewhat flattened worms can grow to 12 inches in length. They prefer the cover of rocks during the day, but occasionally can be found crawling about the reef, where they feed on branched corals and gorgonians. When disturbed, fire worms flare their sharp, detachable bristles. These bristles can easily penetrate the skin and break off, causing a painful, long-lasting irritation.

FEATHER DUSTER WORMS

Class Polychaeta
Subclass Sedentaria (Said-den-TAIR-ee-uh / L. to remain stationary)
Family Sabellidae (Suh-BELL-ih-dee / L. sand)

Feather dusters, also known as fan worms, do not appear to be worms at all, because their bodies are hidden inside **parchment-like tubes** attached to the reef. The flexible tube is constructed of fine sand held together with glue that is secreted by collar glands just below the head. Feather dusters have a highly modified head with a crown of feather-like appendages called **radioles** that are normally extended from the tube. These work as both gills, and for capturing plankton, which is moved to its mouth at the center of the feathery crown. The dramatic colors and patterns of the radioles are often the keys to visual identification. Feather duster worms are very sensitive to nearby movement and changes in light intensity and, if disturbed, instantly retract the crown.

CALCAREOUS TUBE WORMS

Class Polychaeta, Subclass Sedentaria
Family Serpulidae (Sir-PYULE-ih-dee / L. to creep)

Serpulids build hard, calcareous tubes which are often hidden in or on rock, coral, or, occasionally, sponge. Their extended crown of colorful **radioles** form spirals and whorls. Like fan worms, the radioles are used to catch food, and will instantly retract when disturbed. A hardened structure, called an **operculum**, covers the tube opening when the worm withdraws. **Horn-like growths** that often extend from the operculum are useful in species identification.

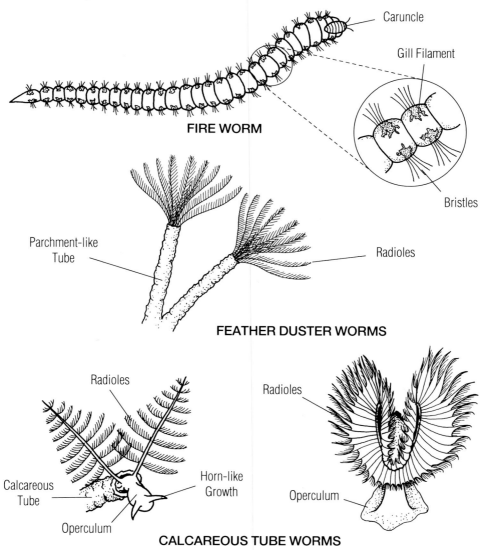

Caruncle

FIRE WORM

Gill Filament

Bristles

Parchment-like Tube

Radioles

FEATHER DUSTER WORMS

Radioles

Radioles

Calcareous Tube

Horn-like Growth

Operculum

Operculum

Operculum

CALCAREOUS TUBE WORMS

Fireworms

VISUAL ID: Large, pleated and branched (beard-like) appendage of flesh on head, called a caruncle, distinguishes this species. Segments have short tufts of white bristles and stalks of red, branched-gill filaments. Color varies from shades of red to green to brown.

ABUNDANCE & DISTRIBUTION: Common Florida, Bahamas, Caribbean.

HABITAT & BEHAVIOR: Inhabit reefs, areas of reef rubble and sea grass beds. Often hide under rocks, slabs of coral and in recesses. Occasionally forage in open. Feed on a variety of attached marine invertebrates, including gorgonians, anemones and hard corals.

EFFECT ON DIVERS: When disturbed display bristles, which can easily penetrate and break off in skin, causing a painful burning sensation and irritating wound.

NOTE: Color pattern of juveniles [below] was confirmed by collection of pictured specimen and microscopic examination.

Juvenile

VISUAL ID: Long, numerous bristles along sides are tipped or banded with red and/or orange. Caruncle is small, ribbed and divided longitudinally. Tufts of gill-filaments on each side of segments. Body color varies from pale green to shades of brown, often in patterned designs.

ABUNDANCE & DISTRIBUTION: Occasional Florida, Bahamas, Caribbean. Also along Pacific coast of Central America.

HABITAT & BEHAVIOR: In all marine habitats, especially in the areas of debris or reef rubble, occasionally on reefs. These voracious predators often forage in the open, can swim and will even take a fisherman's bait!

EFFECT ON DIVERS: When disturbed display bristles, which can easily penetrate and break off in skin, causing a very painful burning sensation and irritating wound.

BEARDED FIREWORM
Hermodice carunculata
SUBCLASS:
Errantia
FAMILY:
Fireworms
Amphinomidae

SIZE:4 - 6 in.,
12 in. max.
DEPTH:1 - 130 ft.

Greenish Variety

RED-TIPPED FIREWORM
Chloeia viridis
SUBCLASS:
Errantia
FAMILY:
Fireworms
Amphinomidae

SIZE:3 - 5 in.,
6 in. max.
DEPTH:1 - 130 ft.

Scale Worms – Sponge Worms – Lug Worms

VISUAL ID: This family of segmented worms is characterized by two paired rows of overlapping, plate-like scales, called elytra, that run down the back. Frequently in shades of brown to gray to black. Most species require microscopic examination to determine genus and species.

ABUNDANCE & DISTRIBUTION: Occasional Florida, Bahamas, Caribbean.

HABITAT & BEHAVIOR: Found in most marine habitats. Hide under rock slabs, coral and shell rubble, and in recesses.

REACTION TO DIVERS: Many species will roll into a tight ball when threatened.

VISUAL ID: Thousands of tiny white worms on inner walls of sponges.

ABUNDANCE & DISTRIBUTION: Common Florida, Bahamas, Caribbean.

HABITAT & BEHAVIOR: Inhabit sponges on which they feed by inserting their proboscis into individual cells. They are most commonly observed in Touch-Me-Not Sponges [pg. 37].

NOTE: Until recently, sponge worms of this type were all thought to be *Syllis spongicola*, a species first described from the Mediterranean. Many scientists, however, now believe that there are several species instead, all in the genus *Haplosyllis*.

VISUAL ID: Volcanic-cone-shaped mound in sand. The worms, which are never above the surface, reside in U-shaped burrows beneath sand. They are colored in shades of green to brown, with brownish-red tufts of gill filaments.

ABUNDANCE & DISTRIBUTION: Common Florida, Bahamas, Caribbean.

HABITAT & BEHAVIOR: Inhabit sand flats, where hundreds of the conical mounds may be observed. Worms ingest sandy bottom material, digest organic debris, then blow excreted sand from burrows by water pressure, forming the conical mounds (see photograph).

SCALE WORMS

SUBCLASS:
Errantia
FAMILY:
Scale Worms
Polynoidae

SIZE: 1 - 4 in.
DEPTH: 0 - 130 ft.

SPONGE WORMS

Haplosyllis sp.
SUBCLASS:
Errantia
FAMILY:
Sponge Worms
Syllidae

SIZE: $^1/_{16}$ - $^1/_8$ in.
DEPTH: 10 - 130 ft.

SOUTHERN LUGWORM

Arenicola cristata
SUBCLASS:
Sedentaria
FAMILY:
Lugworms
Arenicolidae

SIZE: 4 - 6 in.
DEPTH: 3 - 60 ft.

Feather Duster Worms

VISUAL ID: Large crown of radioles arranged in a double circular pattern. Banded pattern comes in a variety of colors, including shades of brown, brownish-red, reddish-purple, gold, tan and white. Parchment-like tubes are often hidden in recesses or encased in coral. Largest of Caribbean feather dusters.

ABUNDANCE & DISTRIBUTION: Common to uncommon Florida, Bahamas, Caribbean

HABITAT & BEHAVIOR: Inhabit reefs, sand and gravel bottoms, pilings and wrecks. Often grow from coral heads.

REACTION TO DIVERS: Shy; instantly retract crowns into tubes when approached. If diver waits motionless, for several minutes, crowns may slowly extend and reopen.

VISUAL ID: Grow in clusters. Crowns of radioles arranged in circular patterns, extend from parchment-like tubes that are usually exposed. Crowns' color variable, although generally consistent within a geographical area; for example, tend to be violet in Cayman Islands, white in Cozumel, and light brown in Belize. Color usually more intense near mouth, shading to white around outer part of crown; occasionally display some banding.

ABUNDANCE & DISTRIBUTION: Common Caribbean, Bahamas.

HABITAT & BEHAVIOR: Inhabit reefs. Prefer areas with some water movement. Reproduce asexually and are, consequently, usually found in clusters.

REACTION TO DIVERS: Shy; instantly retract crowns into tubes when approached. If diver waits motionless, for several minutes, crowns may slowly extend and reopen.

NOTE: Specimens in all three photographs were collected and visual identification confirmed by microscopic examination.

Brown-Banded Variety

MAGNIFICENT FEATHER DUSTER
Sabellastarte magnifica
SUBCLASS:
Sedentaria
FAMILY:
Feather Duster Worms
Sabellidae

SIZE: Crown 3 - 6 in.
DEPTH: 10 - 60 ft.

SOCIAL FEATHER DUSTER
Bispira brunnea
SUBCLASS:
Sedentaria
FAMILY:
Feather Duster Worms
Sabellidae

SIZE: Crown ³/₄ - 1¹/₄ in.
DEPTH: 15 - 60 ft.

Violet Variety

Feather Duster Worms

VISUAL ID: Circular crown of radioles often variegated [below right] or banded [below] in shades of brown, maroon and violet, although color is occasionally uniform [opposite]. Parchment-like tubes usually hidden. Dark eyespots are often visible on stems of radioles.

ABUNDANCE & DISTRIBUTION: Occasional Florida, Bahamas, Caribbean.

HABITAT & BEHAVIOR: Inhabit reefs and surrounding areas of rubble and sand. Often congregate in small groups. Tubes are usually hidden in sand, under rocks or in recesses.

REACTION TO DIVERS: Shy; instantly retract crowns into tubes when approached. If diver waits motionless, for several minutes, crowns may slowly extend and reopen.

NOTE: Specimens in all three photographs were collected and visual identifications confirmed by microscopic examination. Often reported by junior names *Sabella melanostigma* and *S. bipunctuta*.

Banded Variety

VISUAL ID: Circular crown of radioles is nearly colorless to white, with three very faint maroon bands and darker ring just above mouth. Usually cluster in large groups, with parchment-like tubes protruding from the sand.

ABUNDANCE & DISTRIBUTION: Common Florida, Bahamas, Caribbean.

HABITAT & BEHAVIOR: Inhabit sandy areas around reefs where solid substrate or coral rock is at or near sand's surface. Tube bases often encased in coral rock.

REACTION TO DIVERS: Extremely sensitive to any movement. Even when approached from several feet away, instantly retract crowns into tubes. If diver waits motionless, for several minutes, crowns may slowly extend and reopen.

NOTE: Photographed specimens were collected and visual identification of genus determined by microscopic examination. Probably an undescribed species.

VARIEGATED FEATHER DUSTER
Bispira variegata
SUBCLASS:
Sedentaria
FAMILY:
Feather Duster Worms
Sabellidae

SIZE: Crown ³/₄ - 1¹/₄ in.
DEPTH: 20 - 75 ft.

Variegated Variety

GHOST FEATHER DUSTERS
Anamobaea sp.
SUBCLASS:
Sedentaria
FAMILY:
Feather Duster Worms
Sabellidae

SIZE: Crown ¹/₂ - ³/₄ in.
DEPTH: 15 - 60 ft.

Feather Duster Worms

VISUAL ID: Circular crown of radioles is yellow, and occasionally spotted or thinly banded with dark purple. Also reported white, red and/or purple on occasion. Parchment-like tubes usually hidden.

ABUNDANCE & DISTRIBUTION: Common to occasional Florida, Bahamas, Caribbean.

HABITAT & BEHAVIOR: Inhabit older areas of reefs without much living coral. Prefer shaded areas, often under ledges, rocks or in recesses. Tubes usually encased in coral rock.

REACTION TO DIVERS: Shy; instantly retract crowns into tubes when approached. If diver waits motionless, for several minutes, crowns may slowly extend and reopen.

NOTE: Photographed specimen was collected and visual identification confirmed by microscopic examination. Has previously been incorrectly reported as *Hypsicomus elegans*.

VISUAL ID: Circular crown of radioles is spotted and banded, in shades of white, brown and purple. Parchment-like tubes usually hidden.

ABUNDANCE & DISTRIBUTION: Common to occasional Florida, Bahamas, Caribbean.

HABITAT & BEHAVIOR: Inhabit older areas of reefs with little living coral. Prefer shaded areas, often under ledges, rocks and in recesses. Tubes usually encased in coral rock.

REACTION TO DIVERS: Shy; instantly retract crowns into tubes when approached. If diver waits motionless, for several minutes, crowns may slowly extend and reopen.

NOTE: Photographed specimen was collected and visual identification confirmed by microscopic examination. Has previously been reported by junior name *Protulides elegans*.

VISUAL ID: Circular crown of radioles form a pleated design. Yellowish with a white ring around outer edge and white band near mouth. About one inch of parchment-like tube is usually visible.

ABUNDANCE & DISTRIBUTION: Occasional Caribbean.

HABITAT & BEHAVIOR: Inhabit coral reefs, especially along walls. Prefer somewhat protected areas, often under ledges and in depressions along walls. Tubes usually encased in coral rock.

REACTION TO DIVERS: Shy; instantly retract crowns into tubes. If diver waits motionless, for several minuets, crowns may slowly extend and reopen.

NOTE: Photographed specimen was collected and identification made by microscopic examination. This was a previously unreported genus in the Caribbean and is probably an undescribed species.

132

YELLOW FANWORM

Notaulax occidentalis
SUBCLASS:
Sedentaria
FAMILY:
**Feather Duster
Worms**
Sabellidae

SIZE: Crown ³/₄ - 1¹/₄ in.
DEPTH: 10 - 70 ft.

BROWN FANWORM

Notaulax nudicollis
SUBCLASS:
Sedentaria
FAMILY:
**Feather Duster
Worms**
Sabellidae

SIZE: Crown ³/₄ - 1¹/₄ in.
DEPTH: 10 - 70 ft.

RUFFLED
FEATHER DUSTER

Hypsicomus sp.
SUBCLASS:
Sedentaria
FAMILY:
**Feather Duster
Worms**
Sabellidae

SIZE: Crown ¹/₄ - ³/₄ in.
DEPTH: 25 - 75 ft.

133

VISUAL ID: Radioles arranged in an oval pattern, with a longitudinal split of the crown into mirrored halves. Color variable in shades of brown, orangish-brown, maroon and violet, often with white spots and bands. Parchment-like tubes usually hidden.

ABUNDANCE & DISTRIBUTION: Common Florida, Bahamas, Caribbean.

HABITAT & BEHAVIOR: Inhabit reefs and adjacent areas. May be solitary or in small groups of three or four. Tubes often deeply encased in coral rock.

REACTION TO DIVERS: Shy; instantly retract crowns into tubes when approached. If diver waits motionless, for several minutes, crowns may slowly extend and reopen.

NOTE: Photographed specimens were collected and visual identification confirmed by microscopic examination.

VISUAL ID: Radioles form distinctive horseshoe-shaped crown. Banded in shades of brown and white. Rows of black eyespots are visible on the radioles' stems. Parchment-like tube usually hidden.

ABUNDANCE & DISTRIBUTION: Common South Florida, Bahamas; occasional Caribbean.

HABITAT & BEHAVIOR: Inhabit reefs. Tubes usually in crevices or encased in sponges.

REACTION TO DIVERS: Shy; instantly retract crowns into tubes when approached. If diver waits motionless, for several minutes, crowns may slowly extend and reopen.

NOTE: Photographed specimen was collected and visual identification confirmed by microscopic examination.

VISUAL ID: Radioles of crown form circular pattern with a distinctive V-shaped fold into one side. Banded and spotted in shades of brown and white. Parchment-like tube usually hidden.

ABUNDANCE & DISTRIBUTION: Occasional South Florida, Bahamas, Caribbean.

HABITAT & BEHAVIOR: Inhabit reefs. Tubes usually in narrow, tight crevices or recesses. Multi-faceted eyespots on tips of radioles allow this worm to be unusually sensitive to movement.

REACTION TO DIVERS: Extremely sensitive to any movement. Even when approached from several feet away, instantly retract crowns into tubes. Do not extend crowns for several minutes after retraction. An extremely slow approach is required to view these worms closely.

NOTE: Photographed specimen was collected and identification of genus determined by microscopic examination. Probably an undescribed species.

SPLIT-CROWN FEATHER DUSTER

Anamobaea orstedii

SUBCLASS:
Sedentaria
FAMILY:
Feather Duster Worms
Sabellidae

SIZE: Crown 1¹/₂ - 2 in.
DEPTH: 15 - 75 ft.

BLACK-SPOTTED FEATHER DUSTER

Branchiomma nigromaculata

SUBCLASS:
Sedentaria
FAMILY:
Feather Duster Worms
Sabellidae

SIZE: Crown ¹/₂ - 1 in.
DEPTH: 6 - 75 ft.

SHY FEATHER DUSTER

Megalomma sp.

SUBCLASS:
Sedentaria
FAMILY:
Feather Duster Worms
Sabellidae

SIZE: Crown ¹/₂ - 1 in.
DEPTH: 6 - 75 ft.

Calcareous Tube Worms

VISUAL ID: Two spiraled crowns of radioles, with double-horned operculum between. Tubes usually hidden; a single sharp spike protrudes from edge of opening. Color and patterns of radioles variable, though most frequently shades of brown, orange, maroon and white.

ABUNDANCE & DISTRIBUTION: Abundant Florida, Bahamas, Caribbean.

HABITAT & BEHAVIOR: Inhabit all areas of reef. Tubes usually encased in living coral.

REACTION TO DIVERS: Shy; when approached instantly retract crowns into tube and close openings with operculum. If diver waits motionless, for several minutes, crown may slowly extend and reopen.

VISUAL ID: Double fold of radioles form U-shaped crown. Long, heavy-stalked operculum has circular tip with no horns or heavy spikes; at the center is a star-shaped pattern of fine spines, that is often overgrown with algae. Colors and patterns of radioles variable, though most commonly in shades of red, orange, yellow and white. Tubes usually hidden.

ABUNDANCE & DISTRIBUTION: Abundant Florida, Bahamas, Caribbean.

HABITAT & BEHAVIOR: Inhabit all areas of reef. Tubes usually encased in living coral.

REACTION TO DIVERS: Shy; when approached instantly retract crowns into tube and close openings with operculum. If diver waits motionless, for several minutes, crowns may slowly extend and reopen.

NOTE: Specimens in all four photographs were collected and visual identifications confirmed by laboratory examination.

CHRISTMAS TREE WORM
Spirobranchus giganteus
SUBCLASS:
Sedentaria
FAMILY:
**Calcareous
Tube Worms**
Serpulidae

SIZE: Crown 1 - 1½ in.
DEPTH: 10 - 100 ft.

STAR HORSESHOE WORM
Pomatostegus stellatus
SUBCLASS:
Sedentaria
FAMILY:
**Calcareous
Tube Worms**
Serpulidae

SIZE: Crown 1 - 1½ in.
DEPTH: 10 - 100 ft.

Color and Pattern Varieties

Calcareous Tube Worms

VISUAL ID: Double fold of white radioles with red spots form a deep, rounded, U-shaped crown. Tube hidden; opening has a trumpet-like flair. No operculum.

ABUNDANCE & DISTRIBUTION: Common Caribbean.

HABITAT & BEHAVIOR: Inhabit reefs. Prefer secluded, shaded areas, often in small recesses under lower edges of corals.

REACTION TO DIVERS: Shy; retract crowns into tubes instantly when approached. If diver waits motionless, for several minutes, crowns may slowly extend and reopen.

NOTE: Photographed specimen was collected and visual identification of genus confirmed by microscopic examination. Possibly an undescribed species.

VISUAL ID: Small fan-shaped crown of radioles is translucent with white markings. Circular operculum on long stalk. Tubes hidden.

ABUNDANCE & DISTRIBUTION: Common to occasional Florida, Bahamas, Caribbean.

HABITAT & BEHAVIOR: Live in association with Touch-Me-Not Sponges [pg. 37]. Tubes become encased as their rate of extension matches that of host sponge's growth. Not found on all Touch-Me-Not Sponges, but when present they are usually numerous.

REACTION TO DIVERS: Shy; instantly retract crowns into tubes when approached. If diver waits motionless, for several minutes, crowns may slowly extend and reopen.

VISUAL ID: Tangles and twinings of tiny white tubes. Often encrust, but may grow in disordered masses. Tiny crowns of radioles at tubes' heads are barely visible.

ABUNDANCE & DISTRIBUTION: Common Florida, Bahamas, Caribbean.

HABITAT & BEHAVIOR: Primarily inhabit reefs. Prefer shaded, protected areas. Often encrust areas around base of rope and tube sponges and under ledge overhangs. The branches of black coral trees occasionally support disordered masses.

REACTION TO DIVERS: Shy; instantly retract crowns into tubes when approached. If diver waits motionless, for several minutes, crowns may slowly extend and reopen.

RED-SPOTTED HORSESHOE WORM

Protula sp.

SUBCLASS
Sedentaria
FAMILY:
**Calcareous
Tube Worms**
Serpulidae

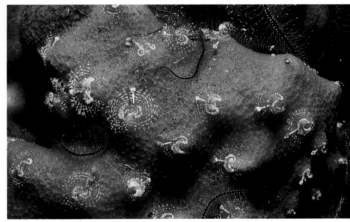

SIZE: Crown 1 - 1¹/₄ in.
DEPTH: 15 - 60 ft.

TOUCH-ME-NOT FANWORM

Hydroides spongicola

SUBCLASS:
Sedentaria
FAMILY:
**Calcareous
Tube Worms**
Serpulidae

SIZE: Crown ¹/₂ - 1 in.
DEPTH: 10 - 100 ft.

SEA FROST

Filograna huxleyi

SUBCLASS:
Sedentaria
FAMILY:
**Calcareous
Tube Worms**
Serpulidae

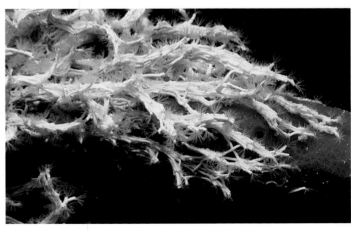

SIZE: Crown ¹/₁₆ in.
Tubes to 6 in.
DEPTH: 20 - 130 ft.

Calcareous Tube Worms – Spaghetti Worms

VISUAL ID: Tiny reddish fans on surface of Blushing Star Coral, *Stephanocenia michelini*. Tubes encased in coral.

ABUNDANCE & DISTRIBUTION: Occasional South Florida, Bahamas, Caribbean.

HABITAT & BEHAVIOR: Apparently always live in association with Blushing Star Coral (see note), which form medium-sized, rounded mounds.

REACTION TO DIVERS: Shy; instantly retract crowns into tubes when approached; the coral's tiny polyps also retract simultaneously. The overall effect is that the coral head appears to "blush" white. If diver waits motionless, for several minutes, crowns and coral polyps may slowly extend and reopen.

NOTE: Pictured specimens were collected and visual identification of genus determined by microscopic examination. Little is known about this worm, and it is probably an undescribed species.

VISUAL ID: Long, smooth, transparent to translucent whitish tentacles extend from hiding place and spread over sand.

ABUNDANCE & DISTRIBUTION: Common Florida, Bahamas, Caribbean.

HABITAT & BEHAVIOR: Inhabit reefs and adjacent areas of sand and rubble. Hide under rocks, debris, coral heads and in cracks along the bases of reefs. Live in tubes constructed of fine sand and mucus.

REACTION TO DIVERS: Retract tentacles when disturbed.

NOTE: Photographed specimen was collected and identified by laboratory examination. There are several species of similar worms and identification beyond family often requires the disturbance of worm's habitat to see its body, a practice not encouraged.

VISUAL ID: Long, smooth, bluish or greenish translucent tentacles with whitish spots and rings. Tentacles extend from hiding place and spread over sand. Body grayish with whitish or pinkish bands.

ABUNDANCE & DISTRIBUTION: Common Florida, Bahamas, Caribbean.

HABITAT & BEHAVIOR: Inhabit reefs and adjacent areas of sand and rubble. Hide under rocks, debris, coral heads and in cracks along bases of reefs. Live in tubes constructed of fine sand and mucus.

REACTION TO DIVERS: Retract tentacles when disturbed.

NOTE: There are several species of similar worms and identification beyond family often requires the disturbance of worm's habitat to see its body, a practice not encouraged.

BLUSHING STAR CORAL FANWORM
Vermiliopsis n. sp.
SUBCLASS:
Sedentaria
FAMILY:
**Calcareous
Tube Worms**
Serpulidae

SIZE: Crown to ¼ in.
DEPTH: 10 - 130 ft.

SPAGHETTI WORM
Eupolymnia crassicornis
SUBCLASS:
Sedentaria
FAMILY:
Spaghetti Worms
Terebellidae

SIZE: Tentacles to 18 in.
DEPTH: 10 - 130 ft.

MEDUSA WORM
Loimia medusa
SUBCLASS:
Sedentaria
FAMILY:
Spaghetti Worms
Terebellidae

SIZE: Tentacles to 18 in.
DEPTH: 10 - 130 ft.

Phylum Arthropoda

(Are-THROP-uh-duh / Gr. jointed leg))

Class Crustacea

Shrimps, Lobsters, Crabs, Barnacles

Arthropods make up the largest phylum in the Animal Kingdom, with nearly two million described species. They include the insects and spiders, as well as many marine creatures. At this writing, many zooligists believe arthropods should be re-classified into several phyla and additional subdivisions. This text, however, uses the traditional classifications. The group's most distinguishing feature is jointed legs, coupled with an often elaborate exoskeleton. A cuticular material is secreted to form an array of plates and tubes which are connected by flexible membranes to allow movement. While the exoskeleton provides excellent protection, it has the drawback of restricting growth. To remedy this problem, all arthropods periodically molt — shedding their old covering and replacing it with a new, enlarged version. Because the animal is vulnerable to predators during this process, molting usually takes place in protected recesses of the reef.

The most frequently observed arthropods on the reef are in the Class Crustacea, and are distinguished among other things by two pairs of antennae, and three distinct body parts — head, thorax and abdomen. The largest order of crustaceans is the decapods. They have **five pairs of legs**, and include shrimp, lobsters, crabs and their relatives. The head and thorax of these animals are fused and covered by a dorsal shell called a **carapace**.

SHRIMPS

Class Crustacea (Krus-STAY-shuh / L. covered by a hard shell)
Order Decapoda (Deck-ah-POE-duh / Gr. ten legs)
Suborder Natantia (Nuh-TAN-tee-uh / L. swimming)

The most distinguishing characteristic of shrimp is their **long, hair-like antennae** which help divers locate them in their daytime hiding places, just inside dark recesses and near the openings of sponges. They are often beautifully colored and patterned. Their bodies tend to be laterally compressed, with a well-developed **abdomen**, making them highly adapted for swimming. A number of species, called cleaning shrimp, feed by removing parasites and bacterial debris from fish. A few species find protection by living in association with anemones. Although normally secretive, most come out into the open to feed on the reef at night.

LOBSTERS

Class Crustacea, Order Decapoda
Suborder Palinura (Pal-uh-NUR-uh / Gr. backwards by tail)

Lobsters are bottom-dwellers that use well-developed legs to crawl about. If

strokes of a heavy, muscular abdomen and wide, flattened tail. Spiny lobsters have a pair of **long, conical antennae** that often give away their hiding places on reefs during the day. They do not have claws for protection; instead, they rely on sharp spikes that cover their carapace and antennae. Slipper lobsters are also clawless, but have **flattened, rounded plate-like antennae**, and a second pair of **thin, short antennae**. They rely on their shell and camouflage for protection.

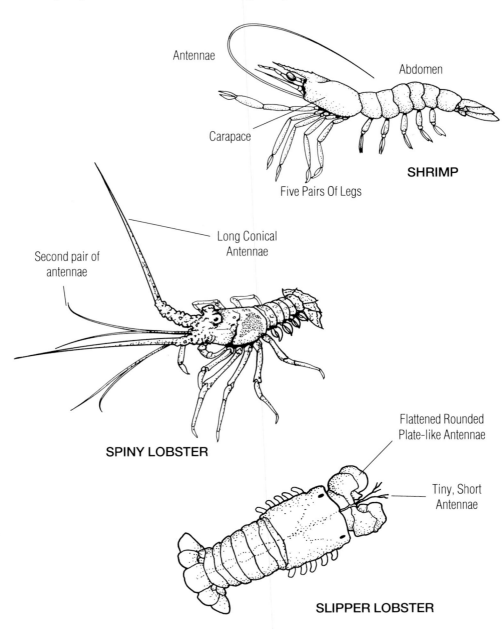

Antennae

Abdomen

Carapace

SHRIMP

Five Pairs Of Legs

Long Conical
Antennae

Second pair of
antennae

SPINY LOBSTER

Flattened Rounded
Plate-like Antennae

Tiny, Short
Antennae

SLIPPER LOBSTER

HERMIT CRABS & PORCELAIN CRABS

Class Crustacea, Order Decapoda
Section Anomura (An-oh-MURE-uh / Gr. irregular tail)

Hermit crabs use discarded **sea shells** as mobile homes. They occupy the shell by wrapping their long abdomen around the internal spirals of the shell and extend only head, antennae and legs from the opening. If threatened, they withdraw completely into the shell for protection. When they outgrow their homes, they simply move into a larger shell. This section also includes the porcelain crabs that look much like true crabs, but are distinguished by the presence of **long antennae** and **three pairs of walking legs**.

TRUE CRABS

Class Crustacea, Order Decapoda
Section Brachyura (Brack-ee-YOUR-uh / Gr. short tail)

Crabs have greatly reduced abdomens and tails, which are kept curled under their large, rounded, and often flattened carapace. Their first pair of legs have developed claws that are used for protection and for the manipulation of objects. If disturbed, these claws are raised toward the danger in a threatening manner. Using the remaining **four pairs of legs**, crabs can move rapidly in a sideways direction. Many species are quite small and secretive, and therefore difficult to find.

MANTIS SHRIMP

Class Crustacea
Order Stomatapoda (Stow-ma-tuh-POE-duh / Gr. mouth-like leg)

Mantis shrimp inhabit both reefs and burrows in sandy areas. They resemble the praying mantis insect with their large, **stalked eyes** and long, **spiked foreclaws** which, when not in use, fold back into a claw slot in the leg. These powerful claws can slice a finger as well as capture prey. Species vary in length from a few inches to nearly a foot. These crustaceans are not decapods, and have only **three pairs of walking legs**. They are usually observed peering from the burrow entrance, but are occasionally spotted out in the open. They have an elongated body and **feather-like gills** attached to the lower abdomen.

BARNACLES

Class Crustacea
Subclass Cirripedia (Seer-uh-PED-ee-uh / L. curled or ringed legs)

Barnacles are gregarious crustaceans that permanently attach to a variety of substrate, including animals like whales and turtles. They have been described as shrimp-like animals that stand on their head and kick food into their mouths. Barnacles secrete a protective exoskeleton, composed of **shell plates**. Because they have shells they are often mistaken for mollusks. They can be distinguished by fan-like legs, called **cirri**, that extend from the shell and sweep the water for food. There are two basic types: **sessile barnacles** attach their shells directly to the substrate; the shells of **gooseneck barnacles**, are attached by an intervening **stalk**.

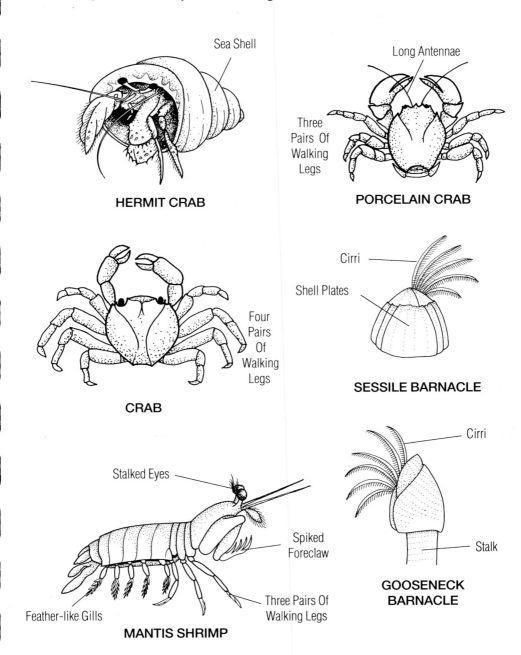

Sea Shell

HERMIT CRAB

Long Antennae

Three Pairs Of Walking Legs

PORCELAIN CRAB

Four Pairs Of Walking Legs

CRAB

Cirri

Shell Plates

SESSILE BARNACLE

Cirri

Stalk

GOOSENECK BARNACLE

Stalked Eyes

Spiked Foreclaw

Feather-like Gills

Three Pairs Of Walking Legs

MANTIS SHRIMP

Shrimp

VISUAL ID: Red to reddish-brown with white bandings on legs, body and claws. Second pair of legs bear long, cylindrical, large claws with short somewhat slender pincers.

ABUNDANCE & DISTRIBUTION: Common Florida, Bahamas, Caribbean.

HABITAT & BEHAVIOR: Inhabit coral reefs.

REACTION TO DIVERS: When approached, retreat into protective recesses.

VISUAL ID: Red and white banded body and claws, with bands occasionally bordered in purple. Two pairs of long, white, hair-like antennae. Walking legs and some parts of the body are often translucent. Third (middle) pair of legs are enlarged and bear large claws. Although the large claws break off easily, they can be regenerated and, as a consequence, are sometimes of unequal size.

ABUNDANCE & DISTRIBUTION: Common Florida, Bahamas, Caribbean.

HABITAT & BEHAVIOR: Inhabit reefs. Cleaning shrimp that perch near the openings of recesses or sponges and slowly wave their antennae to attract fish.

REACTION TO DIVERS: When approached, retreat into protective recesses. If a bare hand is slowly extended toward the shrimp, it may leave its retreat and even attempt to clean fingers.

NOTE: Also commonly known as "Barber Pole Shrimp."

VISUAL ID: Yellow body and legs, with red and occasionally white bands on abdomen and claws. Two pairs of long white, hair-like antennae. Walking legs and some parts of the body are often translucent. Third (middle) pair of legs which are enlarged and bear large claws. Although the large claws break off easily, they can be regenerated and, as a consequence, are sometimes of unequal size.

ABUNDANCE & DISTRIBUTION: Occasional to uncommon Florida, Bahamas, Caribbean.

HABITAT & BEHAVIOR: Inhabit reefs. Cleaning shrimp that perch near the openings of recesses or sponges, and slowly wave their antennae to attract fish.

REACTION TO DIVERS: When approached, retreat into protective recesses. If a bare hand is slowly extended toward the shrimp, it may leave its retreat and even attempt to clean fingers.

TWO CLAW SHRIMP

Brachycarpus biunguiculatus

ORDER:
Decapoda
SUBORDER:
Shrimp
Natantia
FAMILY:
Palaemonidae

SIZE: 1 - 2¹/₂ in.
DEPTH: 1 - 130 ft.

BANDED CORAL SHRIMP

Stenopus hispidus

ORDER:
Decapoda
SUBORDER:
Shrimp
Natantia
FAMILY:
Stenopodidae

SIZE: 1¹/₂ - 2 in.
DEPTH: 3 - 130 ft.

GOLDEN CORAL SHRIMP

Stenopus scutellatus

ORDER:
Decapoda
SUBORDER:
Shrimp
Natantia
FAMILY:
Stenopodidae

SIZE: ³/₄ - 1¹/₄ in.
DEPTH: 10 - 130 ft.

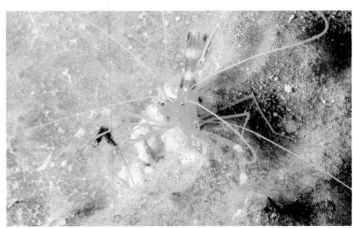

Shrimp

VISUAL ID: Pale, pinkish-white body and appendages marked with fine, bright red to reddish-orange lines.

ABUNDANCE & DISTRIBUTION: Occasional Florida, Bahamas, Caribbean.

HABITAT & BEHAVIOR: Inhabit reefs; often inside tube sponges. Cleaning shrimp.

REACTION TO DIVERS: Quite shy; retreat into sponge when approached.

VISUAL ID: Two broad red stripes, with a narrow white stripe between, extend down back to tail. Pale cream to yellow body and legs. Two pairs of long, white, hair-like antennae.

ABUNDANCE & DISTRIBUTION: Occasional to uncommon Florida, Bahamas, Caribbean.

HABITAT & BEHAVIOR: Inhabit reefs. Cleaning shrimp that perch near the openings of recesses or sponges and slowly wave their antennae to attract fish. Pictured specimens are cleaning a Nassau Grouper, *Epinephalus striatus.*

REACTION TO DIVERS: When approached, retreat into protective recesses. If a bare hand is slowly extended toward the shrimp, it may leave its retreat and even attempt to clean fingers.

VISUAL ID: Brown to gray body with three white saddles across back, and several spots on sides and tail. Saddles and spots are often outlined in dark brown and violet. Two pairs of short banded antennae. Large protruding eyes and upward pointing tail.

ABUNDANCE & DISTRIBUTION: Common South Florida, Bahamas, Caribbean.

HABITAT & BEHAVIOR: Live in association with a variety of anemones, especially the Giant, Sun and Elegant Anemones [pg. 89].

REACTION TO DIVERS: When closely approached or molested, they retreat into the tentacles or under the anemone's body.

NOTE: Identification is probable. This genus was recently split into three groups, due to minute anatomical differences, positive identification requires microscopic examination.

PEPPERMINT SHRIMP

Lysmata wurdemanni

ORDER:
Decapoda
SUBORDER:
Shrimp
Natantia
FAMILY:
Hippolytidae

SIZE: 1 - 1 ³/₄ in.
DEPTH: 3 - 90 ft.

SCARLET-STRIPED CLEANING SHRIMP

Lysmata grabhami

ORDER:
Decapoda
SUBORDER:
Shrimp
Natantia
FAMILY:
Hippolytidae

SIZE: 1¹/₄ - 2 in.
DEPTH: 3 - 90 ft.

SQUAT ANEMONE SHRIMP

Thor amboinensis

ORDER:
Decapoda
SUBORDER:
Shrimp
Natantia
FAMILY:
Hippolytidae

SIZE: ¹/₄ - ³/₄ in.
DEPTH: 10 - 60 ft.

Shrimp

VISUAL ID: Slender, elongated body with long, pointed snout and prominent abdominal hump. Color varies from translucent to gray, purple or green

ABUNDANCE & DISTRIBUTION: Occasional Florida, Bahamas, Caribbean.

HABITAT & BEHAVIOR: Found in all shallow habitats. Color usually matches background, such as green on turtle grass, purple on sea plumes, etc.

VISUAL ID: Transparent body and legs covered with purple to lavender spots. Two pairs of long, white, hair-like antennae. Rows of pinkish eggs are occasionally attached to belly [see photograph].

ABUNDANCE & DISTRIBUTION: Common South Florida, Bahamas, Caribbean.

HABITAT & BEHAVIOR: Live in association with a variety of anemones, especially Corkscrew [pg. 91], Branching [pg. 95], Giant [pg. 89], and Knobby [pg. 91]. Cleaning shrimp that perch on the tentacles of anemones, and sway their bodies and wave their antennae to attract fish.

REACTION TO DIVERS: Unafraid; if a bare hand is slowly extended, shrimp may swim out and attempt to clean fingers.

VISUAL ID: Body is transparent, with three or four tan and white saddle markings across back, and several white spots along sides. Legs and claws banded with white and purple, lavender or red. Two pairs of long, white, hair-like antennae with dark bands. Rows of pinkish eggs are occasionally attached to belly.

ABUNDANCE & DISTRIBUTION: Common South Florida, Bahamas, Caribbean.

HABITAT & BEHAVIOR: Live in association with a variety of anemones, especially Corkscrew [pg. 91], Branching [pg. 95], and Giant Anemones [pg. 89]. Cleaning shrimp that perch on the tentacles of anemones, and sway their bodies and wave their antennae to attract fish.

REACTION TO DIVERS: Unafraid.

NOTE: Identification is probable. Because there are several similar appearing species, positive identification requires microscopic examination.

ARROW SHRIMP
Tozeuma carolinense
ORDER:
Decapoda
SUBORDER:
Shrimp
Natantia
FAMILY:
Hippolytidae

SIZE: 1 - 1¹/₂ in.
DEPTH: 1 - 50 ft.

PEDERSON CLEANER SHRIMP
Periclimenes pedersoni
ORDER:
Decapoda
SUBORDER:
Shrimp
Natantia
FAMILY:
Palaemonidae

SIZE: ³/₄ - 1 in.
DEPTH: 10 - 60 ft.

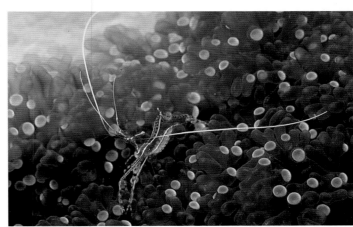

SPOTTED CLEANER SHRIMP
Periclimenes yucatanicus
ORDER:
Decapoda
SUBORDER:
Shrimp
Natantia
FAMILY:
Palaemonidae

SIZE: ³/₄ - 1 in.
DEPTH: 10 - 60 ft.

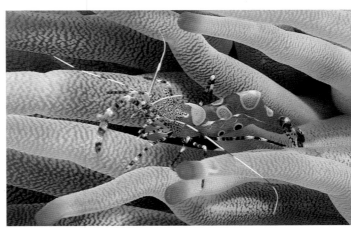

Shrimp

VISUAL ID: Red and white banded antennae. Body ranges from bright red to orange to light brown, with white spots and markings. Blue markings often appear on tail. Each of their first legs bears a claw; one is a greatly enlarged snapping claw, the other is much smaller.

ABUNDANCE & DISTRIBUTION: Common South Florida, Bahamas, Caribbean

HABITAT & BEHAVIOR: Live with Corkscrew Anemone [pg. 91]. Often only their antennae can be seen protruding from anemone. They use their powerful snapping claw to produce loud popping sounds which ward off intruders and helps them capture food.

REACTION TO DIVERS: When threatened, often dart forward and snap large claw.

NOTE: Also commonly known as "Pistol Shrimp."

VISUAL ID: Members of this genus can be identified by their first legs; one bears a smooth, cylindrical, highly enlarged snapping claw; the other a much smaller claw. There are over 30 species in this genus and most require microscopic examination for identification.

ABUNDANCE & DISTRIBUTION: Common Florida, Bahamas, Caribbean.

HABITAT & BEHAVIOR: Found in all habitats. Hide in dark recesses. Several species live inside the canals of sponges. They use their powerful snapping claw to produce a loud popping sound which wards off intruders and helps them capture food.

VISUAL ID: Body is red and may have white to tan bands and spots. Large black eyes.

ABUNDANCE & DISTRIBUTION: Abundant Florida Keys, Bahamas, Caribbean.

HABITAT & BEHAVIOR: Inhabit coral reefs. Nocturnal; hide deep in reefs by day, and appear in large numbers at night. Eyes glow red when illuminated by a diver's light.

REACTION TO DIVERS: Shy; when approached retreat into protective recesses.

RED SNAPPING SHRIMP
Alpheus armatus
ORDER:
Decapoda
SUBORDER:
Shrimp
Natantia
FAMILY:
Alpheidae

SIZE: 1 - 2 in.
DEPTH:3 - 40 ft.

LARGE-CLAW SNAPPING SHRIMP
Synalpheus sp.
ORDER:
Decapoda
SUBORDER:
Shrimp
Natantia
FAMILY:
Alpheidae

SIZE: $^1/_2$ - $^3/_4$ in.
DEPTH:1 - 130 feet.

RED NIGHT SHRIMP
Rhynchocinetes rigens
ORDER:
Decapoda
SUBORDER:
Shrimp
Natantia
FAMILY:
Rhynchocinetidae

SIZE: $1^1/_4$ - 2 in.
DEPTH: 20 - 90 ft.

Spiny Lobsters

VISUAL ID: Carapace has shaded areas of brown and tan with a few dark spots, while abdomen is brown and tan banded with a few light spots. They have sharp "horns" above their eyes and pair of long, conical antennae.

ABUNDANCE & DISTRIBUTION: Common Florida, Bahamas, Caribbean. May be abundant in areas where they are not harvested.

HABITAT & BEHAVIOR: Inhabit reefs. Hide in protective recesses during day, and forage in the open at night. When disturbed, can swim backwards rapidly using powerful strokes of their tails. Females, during reproduction, carry clusters of tiny orange eggs under their abdomens and should be left undisturbed.

REACTION TO DIVERS: Wary; when approached retreat into protective recesses.

VISUAL ID: Dark brown body with lavender markings, brown and white banded legs, and a whitish band on tail.

VISUAL ID: Body is brown to dark purple, and covered with numerous white spots. Last segment of legs has brown stripes.

ABUNDANCE & DISTRIBUTION: Occasional Florida, Bahamas, Caribbean.

HABITAT & BEHAVIOR: Inhabit reefs. Hide in protective recesses during the day, and forage in the open at night. When disturbed, can swim backwards rapidly using powerful strokes of their tails.

REACTION TO DIVERS: Wary; retreat into protective recesses when approached.

SIMILAR SPECIES: Smoothtail Spiny Lobster, *P. laevicauda*, distinguished by bluish-green to purplish cast and large white spots along sides of abdomen. Rare.

NOTE: Also commonly known as the "Spanish Lobster."

CARIBBEAN SPINY LOBSTER

Panulirus argus

ORDER:
Decapoda
SUBORDER:
Palinura
FAMILY:
Spiny Lobsters
Palinuridae

SIZE: 6 - 10 in.,
2 ft. max.
DEPTH: 3 - 130 ft.

Juvenile

SIZE: Photographed
specimen about 1 in.

SPOTTED SPINY LOBSTER

Panulirus guttatus

ORDER:
Decapoda
SUBORDER:
Palinura
FAMILY:
Spiny Lobsters
Palinuridae

SIZE: 5 - 8 in.,
18 in. max.
DEPTH: 6 - 75 ft.

VISUAL ID: Legs have wide red bands and a few narrow white bands and spots. Antennae are banded in red and gold. Body is marked in shades of red and gold. First legs of males modified into large claws.

ABUNDANCE & DISTRIBUTION: Uncommon South Florida, Bahamas, Caribbean

HABITAT & BEHAVIOR: Inhabit deep reefs. Hide in deep recesses and caves during the day, and forage near openings at night.

REACTION TO DIVERS: Wary; when approached retreat into protective recesses.

VISUAL ID: Reddish-orange to reddish-brown body and appendages, with no dramatic markings. Lacks large, numerous spines, but is somewhat hairy. Body is flatter than other spiny lobsters.

ABUNDANCE & DISTRIBUTION: Uncommon South Florida, Bahamas, Caribbean.

HABITAT & BEHAVIOR: Inhabit caves in deep coral reefs. Rarely venture far from cave, even at night.

REACTION TO DIVERS: Shy; when approached rapidly retreat deep inside cave.

VISUAL ID: Four or five purple spots on first segment of abdomen. Abdomen segments are relatively smooth compared with Ridged Slipper Lobster [next]. Body reddish-brown to orangish-brown. Legs yellow with tiny brown spots. Flattened, plate-like antennae are smooth, and the forward portion of the second plate is squared-off (compare with Sculptured Slipper Lobster [pg. 161]).

ABUNDANCE & DISTRIBUTION: Occasional South Florida, Bahamas, Caribbean.

HABITAT & BEHAVIOR: Inhabit coral reefs. Hide in protective recesses during day, and forage in the open at night. When disturbed, can swim backwards rapidly using powerful strokes of their tails.

REACTION TO DIVERS: Wary; when approached retreat into protective recesses.

NOTE: Also commonly known as the "Shovel-nosed Lobster."

RED BANDED LOBSTER
Justitia longimanus
ORDER:
Decapoda
SUBORDER:
Palinura
FAMILY:
Spiny Lobsters
Palinuridae

SIZE: 5 - 8 in.
DEPTH: 40 - 130 ft.

COPPER LOBSTER
Palinurellus gundlachi
ORDER:
Decapoda
SUBORDER:
Palinura
FAMILY:
Spiny Lobsters
Palinuridae

SIZE: 5 - 8 in.
DEPTH: 60 - 130 ft.

SPANISH LOBSTER
Scyllarides aequinoctialis
ORDER:
Decapoda
SUBORDER:
Palinura
FAMILY:
Slipper Lobsters
Scyllaridae

SIZE: 6 - 12 in.
DEPTH: 30 - 130 ft.

VISUAL IDENTIFICATION: Numerous spines and stiff, bristol-like hairs project from edges of flattened antenna and carapace. Antenna and carapace have rough, cobblestone-like texture. Carapace low, wide and rounded. Mottled tan to yellow-brown and brown.

ABUNDANCE & DISTRIBUTION: Occasional Bahamas, Caribbean; uncommon South Florida. Circumtropical.

HABITAT & BEHAVIOR: Inhabit rocky areas and coral reefs. Hide in protective recesses during day, and forage in open at night. When disturbed, can swim backwards rapidly using powerful strokes of their tails.

REACTION TO DIVERS: Wary; when approached retreat into protective recesses.

VISUAL ID: Numerous spikes project from edges of plate-like antennae. Carapace is relatively smooth, but with deep sculpturing on the abdomen. Numerous bristle-like hairs on body, especially along sides. Body tan to yellowish with red and blue shading [pictured].

ABUNDANCE & DISTRIBUTION: Occasional to uncommon Bahamas, Caribbean. Not known Florida.

HABITAT & BEHAVIOR: Inhabit coral reefs and areas of sand and sea grass. Hide in protective recesses during day, and forage in the open at night. When disturbed, can swim backwards rapidly using powerful strokes of their tails.

REACTION TO DIVERS: Wary; when approached retreat into protective recesses.

VISUAL ID: Large lavender-gray to reddish-gray to reddish-brown claws of nearly equal size (right slightly larger), with a surface texture resembling irregular, overlapping scales. Red and white banded antennae. Green or blue-green eyes. Largest Caribbean hermit crab.

ABUNDANCE & DISTRIBUTION: Occasional Florida, Bahamas, Caribbean.

HABITAT & BEHAVIOR: Inhabit sand and areas of sea grass, often near reefs. Occupy large shells, most commonly those of the Queen Conch [pg. 201].

REACTION TO DIVERS: Wary; pull back into shell when approached. After quiet, motionless wait crab often reappears.

SCULPTURED SLIPPER LOBSTER
Parribacus antarcticus
ORDER:
Decapoda
SUBORDER:
Palinura
FAMILY:
Slipper Lobsters
Scyllaridae

SIZE: 4-7 in.
DEPTH: 20-75 ft.

REGAL SLIPPER LOBSTER
Arctides guineensis
ORDER:
Decapoda
SUBORDER:
Palinura
FAMILY:
Slipper Lobsters
Scyllaridae

SIZE: 4 - 7 in.
DEPTH: 25 - 60 ft.

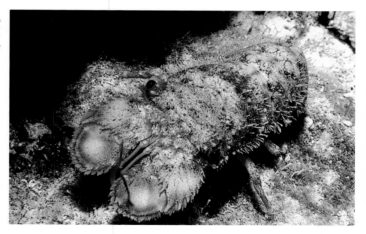

GIANT HERMIT
Petrochirus diogenes
ORDER
Decapoda
SECTION
Anomura
FAMILY
Hermit Crabs
Diogenidae

SIZE: 5 - 8 in.,
12 in. max.
DEPTH: 3 - 100 ft.

Hermit Crabs

VISUAL ID: Blue to blue-green eyes, with dark pupils and distinctive star-like design. Legs are banded in a variety of colors that may include white, cream, red, lavender, orange and reddish-brown. Claws often shaded in lavender. Numerous bristle-like hairs.

ABUNDANCE & DISTRIBUTION: Occasional Florida, Bahamas, Caribbean.

HABITAT & BEHAVIOR: In a wide variety of habitats, including reefs.

REACTION TO DIVERS: Wary; pull back into shell when approached. After quiet, motionless wait crab often reappears.

SIMILAR SPECIES: Bareye Hermit, *D. fucosus*, has a dark horizontal bar across the eye when viewed from the front. These two species are so similar in appearance that laboratory examination is often required for positive identification.

VISUAL ID: Carapace, legs, claws and eyestalks shades of red-brown to brown and covered with raised, scattered, white speckles. Equal sized claws.

ABUNDANCE & DISTRIBUTION: Occasional Caribbean.

HABITAT & BEHAVIOR: In a wide variety of habitats, including reefs.

REACTION TO DIVERS: Wary; pull back into shell when approached. After quiet, motionless wait crab often reappears.

NOTE: There are two other species with similar coloration and appearance, *P. grayi* and *P. wassi*.

VISUAL ID: Cream to tan legs and claws with red bands and large spots. Tentacles and eyestalks gold; eyes blue. Equal sized claws.

ABUNDANCE & DISTRIBUTION: Occasional Caribbean.

HABITAT & BEHAVIOR: In a wide variety of habitats, including reefs.

REACTION TO DIVERS: Wary; pull back into shell when approached. After quiet, motionless wait crab often reappears.

NOTE: There are several similar appearing species and varieties of color patterns within this species, positive identification may require laboratory examination.

STAREYE HERMIT
Dardanus venosus
ORDER:
Decapoda
SECTION:
Anomura
FAMILY:
Hermit Crabs
Diogenidae

SIZE: 3 - 5 in.
DEPTH: 2 - 130 ft.

WHITE SPECKLED HERMIT
Paguristes punticeps
ORDER:
Decapoda
SECTION:
Anomura
FAMILY:
Hermit Crabs
Diogenidae

SIZE: 3 - 5 in.
DEPTH: 2 - 130 ft.

RED BANDED HERMIT
Paguristes erythrops
ORDER:
Decapoda
SECTION:
Anomura
FAMILY:
Hermit Crabs
Diogenidae

SIZE: 2 - 3 in.,
4 in. max.
DEPTH: 2 - 130 ft.

Hermit Crabs

VISUAL ID: Bright red legs and carapace, may have some white spots. Greenish eyes on pale eyestalks.

ABUNDANCE & DISTRIBUTION: Common South Florida, Bahamas, Caribbean.

HABITAT & BEHAVIOR: Inhabit coral reefs. Often form small aggregations during the day.

REACTION TO DIVERS: Wary; pull back into shell when approached. After quiet, motionless wait crab often reappears in opening.

VISUAL ID: Legs and claws, which may be shades of orange, red, maroon or dark reddish-brown, are covered with fine white spots and tipped with white or yellow. Orange antennae and eyestalks. Tip of eyestalks white, eyes black. One claw enlarged.

ABUNDANCE & DISTRIBUTION: Occasional South Florida, Bahamas, Caribbean.

HABITAT & BEHAVIOR: Inhabit coral reefs and rocky substrates. Often in small aggregations during day.

REACTION TO DIVERS: Wary; pull back into shell when approached. After quiet, motionless wait crab often reappears in opening.

VISUAL ID: Legs white to cream and boldly striped in shades of red or brown. One claw greatly enlarged; base mottled gray, movable pincer is white.

ABUNDANCE & DISTRIBUTION: Occasional South Florida, Bahamas, Caribbean.

HABITAT & BEHAVIOR: Inhabit coral reefs.

REACTION TO DIVERS: Wary; pull back into shell when approached. After quiet, motionless wait crab often reappears in opening.

RED REEF HERMIT
Paguristes cadenati
ORDER:
Decapoda
SECTION:
Anomura
FAMILY:
Hermit Crabs
Diogenidae

SIZE: $^1/_2$ -1 in.
DEPTH: 25-95 ft.

ORANGECLAW HERMIT
Calcinus tibicen
ORDER:
Decapoda
SECTION:
Anomura
FAMILY:
Hermit Crabs
Diogenidae

SIZE: $^1/_2$ -1 in.
DEPTH: 1-100 ft.

RED-STRIPE HERMIT
Phimochirus holthuisi
ORDER:
Decapoda
SECTION:
Anomura
FAMILY:
Hermit Crabs
Paguridae

SIZE: $^1/_2$ -1 in.
DEPTH: 20-65 ft.

VISUAL ID: Right claw is greatly enlarged, base is maroon with large white dots; movable pincer is white. Legs and left claw red to reddish-brown. Eyestalks are white with maroon band, eyes are blue.

ABUNDANCE & DISTRIBUTION: Occasional South Florida, Bahamas, Caribbean.

HABITAT & BEHAVIOR: Inhabit coral reefs.

REACTION TO DIVERS: Wary; pull back into shell when approached. After quiet, motionless wait crab often reappears in opening.

VISUAL ID: Red to orange and covered with large white and violet spots ringed in red.

ABUNDANCE & DISTRIBUTION: Occasional Florida, Bahamas, Caribbean.

HABITAT & BEHAVIOR: Found in a variety of habitats. May be free-living, but commonly associate with Giant Hermits [pg. 159], Stareye Hermits [pg. 161], and Queen Conchs [pg. 201].

REACTION TO DIVERS: Shy; retreat to protective cover when approached.

VISUAL ID: Body and appendages are mottled shades of green. Antennae long and translucent.

ABUNDANCE & DISTRIBUTION: Occasional Florida, Bahamas, Caribbean.

HABITAT & BEHAVIOR: Found in a variety of habitats, including reefs.

REACTION TO DIVERS: Shy; retreat to protective cover when approached.

NOTE: A small isopod is attached to the left side of photographed specimen's carapace.

POLKADOTTED HERMIT
Phimochirus operculatus
ORDER:
Decapoda
SECTION:
Anomura
FAMILY:
Hermit Crabs
Paguridae

SIZE: $^1/_2$ - 1 in.
DEPTH: 20 - 65 ft.

SPOTTED PORCELAIN CRAB
Porcellana sayana
ORDER:
Decapoda
SECTION:
Anomura
FAMILY:
Porcelain Crabs
Porcellanidae

SIZE: $^1/_2$ - 1 in.
DEPTH: 10 - 100 ft.

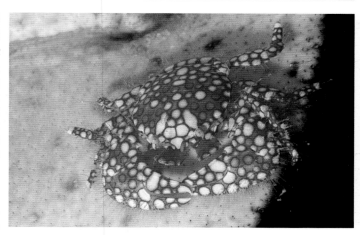

GREEN PORCELAIN CRAB
Petrolisthes armatus
ORDER:
Decapoda
SECTION:
Anomura
FAMILY:
Porcelain Crabs
Porcellanidae

SIZE: $^1/_2$ - 1 in.
DEPTH: 20 - 75 ft.

True Crabs

VISUAL ID: Smooth carapace in shades of orange, red or brown with white and yellow spots and markings. Legs are red with purple shading.
ABUNDANCE & DISTRIBUTION: Common Bahamas, Caribbean. Uncommon to rare in many locations due to over-harvesting.
HABITAT & BEHAVIOR: Inhabit shallow coral reefs. Hide during day in protective recesses; forage in open at night.
REACTION TO DIVERS: Shy; when approached retreat into protective recesses.
NOTE: Also commonly known as "Coral Crab", "Red Coral Crab", and "Queen Crab".

VISUAL ID: Smooth carapace and claws are dark red (underwater may appear dark without artificial light).
ABUNDANCE & DISTRIBUTION: Occasional South Florida, Bahamas, Caribbean.
HABITAT & BEHAVIOR: Inhabit small recesses in reef and areas of rubble.
REACTION TO DIVERS: Shy; when approached retreat into protection of recesses.

VISUAL ID: Carapace appears to be eroded into numerous uneven ridges and bumps. Cream colored with red, maroon, orange and tan blotches and spots. Walking legs have yellowish tips.
ABUNDANCE & DISTRIBUTION: Occasional Florida, Bahamas, Caribbean.
HABITAT & BEHAVIOR: Inhabit small holes and recesses in shallow reefs, and algae-covered, rocky bottoms. Hide during day by wedging into holes, forage in open at night.
REACTION TO DIVERS: Generally remain motionless, relying on their camouflage for concealment.

BATWING CORAL CRAB
Carpilius corallinus
ORDER:
Decapoda
SECTION:
True Crabs
Brachyura
FAMILY:
Xanthidae

SIZE: 3$^1/_2$ - 4$^1/_2$ in.,
6 in. max.
DEPTH: 3 - 45 ft.

BLACK CORAL CRAB
Paraliomera dispar
ORDER:
Decapoda
SECTION:
True Crabs
Brachyura
FAMILY:
Xanthidae

SIZE: $^1/_2$ - $^3/_4$ in.
DEPTH: 10 - 45 ft.

ERODED MUD CRAB
Glyptoxanthus erosus
ORDER:
Decapoda
SECTION:
True Crabs
Brachyura
FAMILY:
Xanthidae

SIZE: 1$^1/_4$ - 2 in.
DEPTH: 3 - 45 ft.

True Crabs

VISUAL ID: Carapace is smooth and heavy. Claws are enlarged and stout. Juveniles are dark blue to purple and often spotted, claw tips are dark. Adults are reddish-brown and spotted with gray or white, claw tips are dark brown to black.

ABUNDANCE & DISTRIBUTION: Common Florida, Bahamas, South Caribbean.

HABITAT & BEHAVIOR: Juveniles often inhabit reefs and rocky areas of moderate depth. Adults inhabit burrows in mud-bottom bays and harbors and are rarely observed by divers.

REACTION TO DIVERS: Retreat to protective recesses or burrows when approached.

NOTE: In Florida, Stone Crab claws are highly prized as food. Legally, only the claws may be taken, which the crabs regenerate. However, only one claw should be taken because it greatly improves the crab's chances of survival.

VISUAL ID: Green carapace is covered with smooth, rounded nodules. Claws are smooth with blunt tips. Legs hairy.

ABUNDANCE & DISTRIBUTION: Common South Florida, Bahamas, Caribbean. Can be locally abundant.

HABITAT & BEHAVIOR: Inhabit shallow reefs and adjacent areas of coral rubble, sand and sea grass. Hide in small recesses and under coral debris.

REACTION TO DIVERS: Unafraid; normally allow close non-threatening approach, retreating only when molested.

VISUAL ID: Smooth, blunt-tipped claws are cream colored and banded in dark reddish-brown. Smooth carapace is cream colored with dark reddish-brown markings and covered with rounded nodules. Legs hairy.

ABUNDANCE & DISTRIBUTION: Common South Florida, Bahamas, Caribbean.

HABITAT & BEHAVIOR: Inhabit coral reefs and adjacent areas. Usually live in association with anemones, especially Giant and Sun Anemones [pg. 89].

REACTION TO DIVERS: Shy; retreat into protection of tentacles or under anemone when approached.

NOTE: Also commonly known as the "Anemone Crab."

FLORIDA STONE CRAB

Menippe mercenaria
Juvenile
ORDER:
Decapoda
SECTION:
True Crabs
Brachyura
FAMILY:
Xanthidae

SIZE: Adults 2¹/₂ - 4 in.
Juveniles ³/₄ - 1 in.
DEPTH: 0 - 60 ft.

GREEN CLINGING CRAB

Mithrax sculptus
ORDER:
Decapoda
SECTION:
True Crabs
Brachyura
FAMILY:
Majidae

SIZE: ¹/₂ - ³/₄ in.
DEPTH: 1 - 40 ft.

BANDED CLINGING CRAB

Mithrax cinctimanus
ORDER:
Decapoda
SECTION:
True Crabs
Brachyura
FAMILY:
Majidae

SIZE: ¹/₂ - ³/₄ in.
DEPTH: 10 - 45 ft.

VISUAL ID: Red carapace is covered with smooth rounded nodules. Pointed cone-shaped projections are prominent around sides of carapace. Smooth claws have blunt tips.

ABUNDANCE & DISTRIBUTION: Occasional South Florida, Bahamas, Caribbean.

HABITAT & BEHAVIOR: Inhabit reefs and adjacent areas of coral rubble and algae-covered, rocky bottoms. During the day hide in small holes and recesses.

REACTION TO DIVERS: Unafraid; normally allow close non-threatening approach, retreating only when molested.

VISUAL ID: Reddish-brown carapace and walking legs. Smooth claws purplish-gray, with a single row of nodules running along the outer edge. Blunt claw tips. Numerous short spines and nodules cover legs. Largest species of Caribbean reef crab.

ABUNDANCE & DISTRIBUTION: Common to occasional Florida, Bahamas, Caribbean.

HABITAT & BEHAVIOR: Inhabit rocky areas and coral reefs. Often in caves or under ledge overhangs during the day; forage in the open at night. Frequently covered with encrusting organisms, algal growth and debris.

REACTION TO DIVERS: Relatively unafraid, but retreat when closely approached.

NOTE: Also commonly known as "Reef Spider Crab," "Spiny Spider Crab," "Coral Crab" and "King Crab."

VISUAL ID: Hairy carapace and appendages are reddish-brown. Numerous spines on walking legs and claw arms. Claws are relatively narrow with blunt tips.

ABUNDANCE & DISTRIBUTION: Rare Florida, Bahamas, Caribbean.

HABITAT & BEHAVIOR: Inhabit rocky areas and reefs. Reclusive, hide in deep caves and recesses.

REACTION TO DIVERS: Shy; retreat deep into protective recesses when approached.

RED-RIDGED CLINGING CRAB

Mithrax forceps
ORDER:
Decapoda
SECTION:
True Crabs
Brachyura
FAMILY:
Majidae

SIZE: $^1/_2$ - $^3/_4$ in.
DEPTH: 10 - 45 ft.

CHANNEL CLINGING CRAB

Mithrax spinosissimus
ORDER:
Decapoda
SECTION:
True Crabs
Brachyura
FAMILY:
Majidae

SIZE: Carapace 5 - 7 in.
DEPTH: 10 - 130 ft.

HAIRY CLINGING CRAB

Mithrax pilosus
ORDER:
Decapoda
SECTION:
True Crabs
Brachyura
FAMILY:
Majidae

SIZE: 2 - 4 in.
DEPTH: 15 - 45 ft.

171

True Crabs

VISUAL ID: Yellowish to orangish-white, with spots and irregular areas of varying sizes; the larger areas are red to orange with dark outlines. Carapace is smooth, rounded and hemispherical. Claws are flattened and have several longitudinal ridges.

ABUNDANCE & DISTRIBUTION: Occasional Florida, Bahamas, Caribbean.

HABITAT & BEHAVIOR: Inhabit shallow areas of sand, coral rubble, patch and fringing reefs.

REACTION TO DIVERS: Relatively unafraid, retreat if molested.

VISUAL ID: Rough carapace covered with ridges and nodules. A "pinched-in" area located just behind front of carapace distinguishes this species. Color varies from pale yellow to orange to brown, with a scattering of dark spots on front of carapace and upper claws. Encrustations on shell often hide true color.

ABUNDANCE & DISTRIBUTION: Occasional Florida, Bahamas, Caribbean.

HABITAT & BEHAVIOR: Inhabit sandy bottoms. Often hide by burying up to their eyes in sand.

REACTION TO DIVERS: Generally remain motionless, relying on their camouflage for concealment.

SIMILAR SPECIES: Flame Box Crab, *C. flammea*, distinguished by relatively smooth, grayish carapace with purplish-brown flame markings and banding on legs.

VISUAL ID: Carapace is flattened, discus-shaped and dark brown to olive with an iridescent green line around front. Brown legs are marked with yellow-gold bands.

ABUNDANCE & DISTRIBUTION: Common Florida, Bahamas, Caribbean. Also Pacific coast of Central America.

HABITAT & BEHAVIOR: Inhabit reefs and rocky areas. Often hide under Long-spined Urchins [pg. 287] for protection.

REACTION TO DIVERS: When approached, retreat under protective spines of urchins.

NOTE: This species is also commonly known as the "Urchin Crab."

172

GAUDY CLOWN CRAB
Platypodiella spectabilis
ORDER:
Decapoda
SECTION:
True Crabs
Brachyura
FAMILY:
Xanthidae

SIZE: $^1/_4$ - $^3/_4$ in.
DEPTH: 1 - 35 ft.

ROUGH BOX CRAB
Calappa gallus
ORDER:
Decapoda
SECTION:
True Crabs
Brachyura
FAMILY:
Calappidae

SIZE: $1^1/_2$ - 3 in.
DEPTH: 3 - 45 ft.

NIMBLE SPRAY CRAB
Percnon gibbesi
ORDER:
Decapoda
SECTION:
True Crabs
Brachyura
FAMILY:
Grapsidae

SIZE: $^3/_4$ - $1^1/_4$ in.
DEPTH: 3 - 75 ft.

VISUAL ID: Pure white. Carapace is rounded and hemispherical. Legs hairy.
ABUNDANCE & DISTRIBUTION: Occasional Florida, Bahamas, Caribbean.
HABITAT & BEHAVIOR: Live among spines of Red Heart Urchin [pg. 293] for protection.

VISUAL ID: Brown to tan with two large, dark reddish-brown spots ringed in white on rear of carapace. Rear pair of legs have developed into paddle-like appendages which are used for swimming.
ABUNDANCE & DISTRIBUTION: Occasional South Florida, Bahamas, Caribbean.
HABITAT & BEHAVIOR: Inhabit reefs and sea grass beds.
REACTION TO DIVERS: Wary; retreat to protective recesses when approached.
SIMILAR SPECIES: Redhair Swimming Crab, *P. ordwayi*, carapace reddish on top, yellowish underside, pincers distinctively light and dark banded.

VISUAL ID: Carapace and appendages are shades of golden brown, and occasionally marked with white blotches. Rear pair of legs have developed into paddle-like appendages which are used for swimming.
ABUNDANCE & DISTRIBUTION: Occasional South Florida, Bahamas, Caribbean.
HABITAT & BEHAVIOR: Inhabit large floats of sargassum. May occasionally drop onto reefs.
REACTION TO DIVERS: Wary; retreat to protective recesses when approached.

HEART URCHIN PEA CRAB

Dissodactylus primitivus

ORDER:
Decapoda
SECTION:
True Crabs
Brachyura
FAMILY:
Pinnotheridae

SIZE: $^1/_4$ - $^1/_2$ in.
DEPTH: 3 - 130 ft.

OCELLATE SWIMMING CRAB

Portunus sebae

ORDER:
Decapoda
SECTION:
True Crabs
Brachyura
FAMILY:
Portunidae

SIZE: $2^1/_2$ - $3^1/_2$ in.
DEPTH: 15 - 90 ft.

SARGASSUM SWIMMING CRAB

Portunus sayi

ORDER:
Decapoda
SECTION:
True Crabs
Brachyura
FAMILY:
Portunidae

SIZE: $2^1/_2$ - $3^1/_2$ in.
DEPTH: 20 - 60 ft.

True Crabs

VISUAL ID: Members of this genus have a wide carapace with a long, sharp spine protruding from the widest point on each side; between this spine and eye is a row of pointed "teeth." Gray to brown with variable tints from blue to green. Positive identification usually requires microscopic examination.

ABUNDANCE & DISTRIBUTION: Common Florida, Bahamas, Caribbean.

HABITAT & BEHAVIOR: Generally inhabit shallow sand and mud bottoms. May be in sandy areas around patch reefs.

REACTION TO DIVERS: Aggressively rear back on hind legs with claws raised for attack when approached.

NOTE: Pictured species probably *C. ornatus*, distinguished by its greenish tint, white-tips on teeth and bluish legs with reddish tips. The Common Blue Crab, *C. sapidus*, known for its edibility, is the largest (6-8 in.), blue-gray with bright blue claws. There are several additional species and sub-species.

VISUAL ID: Golden-brown, triangular body with long pointed snout (rostrum). Carapace decorated with fine dark lines. Long, slender, spider-like legs. Claws often have violet tips.

ABUNDANCE & DISTRIBUTION: Abundant Florida, Bahamas, Caribbean.

HABITAT & BEHAVIOR: Found in a wide variety of habitats, including reefs.

REACTION TO DIVERS: Unafraid; retreat only if molested.

VISUAL ID: A decorator crab; the attachment of living sponge to its carapace and legs is distinctive of this species. Legs flattened. Light blue to purple claws with scattering of dark speckles.

ABUNDANCE & DISTRIBUTION: Common South Florida, Bahamas, Caribbean.

HABITAT & BEHAVIOR: Inhabit reefs.

REACTION TO DIVERS: Unafraid; remain motionless, relying on their camouflage for concealment.

BLUE CRABS

Callinectes sp.

ORDER:
Decapoda
SECTION:
True Crabs
Brachyura
FAMILY:
Portunidae

SIZE: 4 - 6 in.
DEPTH: 5 - 50 ft.

YELLOWLINE ARROW CRAB

Stenorhynchus seticornis

ORDER:
Decapoda
SECTION:
True Crabs
Brachyura
FAMILY:
Majidae

SIZE: $1^1/_2$ - $2^1/_2$ in.
DEPTH: 10 - 130 ft.

CRYPTIC TEARDROP CRAB

Pelia mutica

ORDER:
Decapoda
SECTION:
True Crabs
Brachyura
FAMILY:
Majidae

SIZE: $^1/_2$ - $^3/_4$ in.
DEPTH: 20 - 130 ft.

VISUAL ID: A decorator crab; the attachment of hydroids and other organisms to the legs at right angles is distinctive of this genus. At head a long rostrum extends from triangular carapace. Eye protrudes at right angles from sides of rostrum. Long, thin, spider-like legs.

ABUNDANCE & DISTRIBUTION: Common Florida, Bahamas, Caribbean.

HABITAT & BEHAVIOR: Inhabit reefs. Often on seafans and other gorgonians.

REACTION TO DIVERS: Unafraid; remain motionless, relying on their camouflage for concealment.

NOTE: Pictured species is probably the Shortfinger Neck Crab, *P. sidneyi*, which is distinguished by a blunt, scooped-out frontal spine. Similar Curvedspine Neck Crab, *P. curvirostris*, is distinguished by a curved frontal spine, while the Unicorn Neck Crab, *P. gracilipes*, has a triangular frontal spine.

VISUAL ID: A decorator crab; the attachment of massive amounts of sponge, other organisms and debris distinguishes this species. Red claws speckled and white banded. Two horn-like projections extend from front of head.

ABUNDANCE & DISTRIBUTION: Common South Florida, Bahamas, Caribbean.

HABITAT & BEHAVIOR: Inhabit reefs.

REACTION TO DIVERS: Unafraid; remain motionless, relying on their camouflage for concealment.

NOTE: This species is also commonly known as the "Two-Horned Spider Crab".

VISUAL ID: Large, double-lobed eyes on stalks. Cream colored, with darkish bands crossing body. Tail is distinctively covered with spinules and nodules, giving the surface a scaly appearance. Claws have eight to eleven sharp spines. The largest mantis shrimp in Florida and the Caribbean.

ABUNDANCE & DISTRIBUTION: Occasional Florida, Bahamas, Caribbean.

HABITAT & BEHAVIOR: Inhabit burrows on flat sand bottoms.

REACTION TO DIVERS: Aggressive if molested; claws can inflict deep, painful gashes. Known as "thumb-splitters" by Caribbean fishermen.

NOTE: Identification is tentative and based on eye shape, coloration, size and habitat. Specimen must be fully visible for positive identification.

NECK CRABS

Podochela sp.

ORDER:
Decapoda
SECTION:
True Crabs
Brachyura
FAMILY:
Majidae

SIZE: 1 ^{1}/$_2$ - 2 ^{1}/$_2$ in.
DEPTH: 15 - 100 ft.

SPECK-CLAW DECORATOR CRAB

Microphrys bicornuta

ORDER:
Decapoda
SECTION:
True Crabs
Brachyura
FAMILY:
Majidae

SIZE: ^{1}/$_2$ - ^{3}/$_4$ in.
DEPTH: 20 - 130 ft.

SCALY-TAILED MANTIS

Lysiosquilla scabricauda

ORDER:
Mantis Shrimp
Stomatopoda
FAMILY:
Squillidae

SIZE: 4 - 6 in.,
1 ft. max.
DEPTH: 10 - 100 ft.

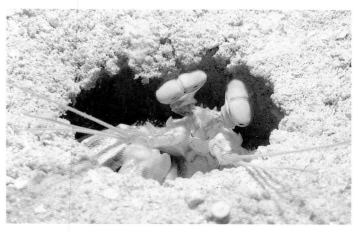

Mantis Shrimp

VISUAL ID: Large double-lobed eyes on stalks. Mottled in shades of dark brown to reddish-brown to tan.
ABUNDANCE & DISTRIBUTION: Occasional South Florida, Bahamas, Caribbean.
HABITAT & BEHAVIOR: Inhabit burrows in sandy areas on coral reefs.
REACTION TO DIVERS: Aggressive if molested; claws can inflict deep, painful gashes. Known as "thumb-splitters" by Caribbean fishermen.
NOTE: Identification is tentative and based on eye shape, coloration and habitat. Specimen must be fully visible for positive identification.

VISUAL ID: Four sharp spikes protrude from outer edges of last two plates. Final or tail plate has a medial ridge. Claw has no spines and its base is enlarged. Stalked eyes have a single lobe. Color varies, though commonly cream with brown or green shading and mottling.
ABUNDANCE & DISTRIBUTION: Occasional South Florida, Bahamas, Caribbean.
HABITAT & BEHAVIOR: Inhabit reefs and adjacent areas. Often burrow under rocks in sand. Forage in cracks and recesses, under ledges and in other protected areas.
REACTION TO DIVERS: Shy; retreat to protective recesses when approached.

VISUAL ID: Uniformly dark olive to brown coloration is distinctive. Eyes have a single lobe.
ABUNDANCE & DISTRIBUTION: Occasional South Florida, Bahamas, Caribbean.
HABITAT & BEHAVIOR: Inhabit reefs. Forage in cracks and recesses, under ledges and in other protected areas.
REACTION TO DIVERS: Shy; retreat to protective recesses when approached.

REEF MANTIS
Lysiosquilla glabriuscula
ORDER:
Mantis Shrimp
Stomatopoda
FAMILY:
Squillidae

SIZE: 4 - 7 in.
DEPTH: 15 - 75 ft.

SWOLLEN-CLAW MANTIS
Gonodactylus oerstedii
ORDER:
Mantis Shrimp
Stomatopoda
FAMILY:
Squillidae

SIZE: 1 - 2 in.
DEPTH: 1 - 75 ft.

DARK MANTIS
Gonodactylus curacaoensis
ORDER:
Mantis Shrimp
Stomatopoda
FAMILY:
Squillidae

SIZE: 1¹/₄ - 2 in.
DEPTH: 25 - 75 ft.

VISUAL ID: Dark gray to brown, oval-shaped and segmented. These bug-like animals attach to fishes' heads or gill plate covers.

ABUNDANCE & DISTRIBUTION: Occasional Florida, Bahamas, Caribbean.

HABITAT & BEHAVIOR: Parasites that attach to a wide variety of reef fishes, most commonly butterflyfishes and Blackbar Soldierfish, *Myripristis jacobus.*

NOTE: Species identification is tentative; based on the host, Blackbar Soldierfish, which is commonly known to carry this species. There are several similar parasitic isopods, necessitating laboratory examination for positive identification.

VISUAL ID: The tiny shrimp of this genus appear as small clouds of white to transparent specks hovering over reef. Often mistaken for fish larva. Close observation may reveal their typical shrimp shape.

ABUNDANCE & DISTRIBUTION: Common South Florida, Bahamas, Caribbean.

HABITAT & BEHAVIOR: Inhabit reefs. Frequently hover near urchins and anemones where they hide when threatened. Occasionally over sea grass beds. Often swim in open, near surface at night.

NOTE: There are three primary Atlantic reef species, *M. columbiae, M. gracile,* and *M. integrum.* Microscopic examination of specimen is required for species identification.

VISUAL ID: Sessile barnacles permanently affix at the base of their shells to the substrate. The outer shell is composed of one to eight plates, depending upon genus; most genera observed by divers have six. The opening is protected by two paired movable plates. When feeding, six cirri are repeatedly flicked in and out from opening. Identification of species is generally based on structures not observable underwater.

ABUNDANCE & DISTRIBUTION: Common worldwide.

HABITAT & BEHAVIOR: Attach to wide range of surfaces. Commonly on dock pilings, buoys, ship bottoms and shipwrecks. Often well camouflaged by other organisms, such as sponges, fire corals, hydroids and algae that attach and overgrow their shells.

NOTE: Photographed specimens were collected and by laboratory examination determined to include two species, *Megabalanus tintinnabulum* and *Balanus trigonus.*

SOLDIERFISH ISOPOD
Anilocra laticaudata
ORDER:
Isopods
Isopoda

SIZE: $^{1}/_{2}$ - $^{3}/_{4}$ in.
DEPTH: 15 - 75 ft.

MYSID SHRIMP
Mysidium spp.
ORDER:
Mysid Shrimp
Mysidacea

SIZE: $^{1}/_{16}$ - $^{1}/_{8}$ in.
DEPTH: 15 - 65 ft.

SESSILE BARNACLES

SUBCLASS:
Barnacles
Cirripedia
ORDER:
Thoracica

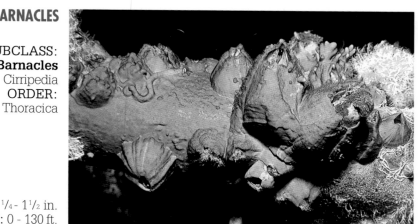

SIZE: $^{1}/_{4}$ - 1$^{1}/_{2}$ in.
DEPTH: 0 - 130 ft.

VISUAL ID: Body encased in flattened formation of five smooth, translucent, white to bluish-white shell plates. Attached to substrate by stalk that may reach nearly one inch in length when fully extended.

ABUNDANCE & DISTRIBUTION: Common worldwide.

HABITAT & BEHAVIOR: Normally attach to floating objects such as driftwood, buoys and ship bottoms.

SIMILAR SPECIES: Grooved Goose-Neck Barnacle, *L. anserifera*, shell plates have fine radiating grooves, short stalk. Scaled Goose-Neck Barnacle, *L. pectinata*, shell plates are ridged with scales and occasionally spines.

NOTE: Visual identification was confirmed by collection of pictured specimens and laboratory examination.

VISUAL ID: Shell and stalk grayish black to reddish brown. Shells have pronounced hump where they join on back and dual knob-like tips at top.

ABUNDANCE & DISTRIBUTION: Occasional Caribbean.

HABITAT & BEHAVIOR: Attach to branches of Feather Black Coral, *Antipathes pennacea* and Bushy Black Coral, *A. salix*. Grow in small clusters.

NOTE: There are several similar appearing species of barnacles that associate with black corals. The pictured specimens were collected and identification made by laboratory examination.

VISUAL ID: Gray to brown. Carapace is smooth and horseshoe-shaped. Tail is long and spike-like.

ABUNDANCE & DISTRIBUTION: Common Florida.

HABITAT & BEHAVIOR: Inhabit shallow areas with soft or sandy bottoms, often in areas of sea grass and other algal growth.

SMOOTH GOOSE-NECK BARNACLE

Lepas anatifera

SUBCLASS:
Barnacles
Cirripedia
ORDER:
Thoracica
FAMILY:
Lepadidae

SIZE: ¹/₄ - 1¹/₂ in.
DEPTH: 0 - 130 ft.

BLACK CORAL BARNACLE

Oxynaspis gracilis

SUBCLASS:
Barnacles
Cirripedia
ORDER:
Thoracica
FAMILY:
Heteralepidae

SIZE: ¹/₄ - ¹/₂ in.
DEPTH: 45 - 130 ft.

HORSESHOE CRAB

Limulus polyphemus

CLASS:
Merostomata
SUBCLASS
Horseshoe Crab
Xiphosura

SIZE: 10 - 20 in.
DEPTH: 1 - 15 ft.

Phylum Ectoprocta

(Eck-toe-PROCK-tuh / Gr. outside anus)

Bryozoans

Bryozoans are tiny, colonial animals called **zooids**. Zooids have polyp-like **tentacles** encircling the mouth; but, unlike polyps, they have a complete digestive system, including an anus that lies outside the ring of tentacles. These animals form a colonial skeleton with chambers that partition and separate one zooid from the next. These skeletal **chambers** may be **oval, tubular, vase** or **rectangular-shaped** and are usually less than 1/16 inch across. The colonies of different species vary greatly in appearance. Some look like a clump of **seaweed** or moss, while others grow as **lacy fans**; some species simply form **encrustations**. Colonies are generally white, although shades of brown, yellow, red and purple occur. Because the composition of building materials varies among species, colonies can be flexible or rigid. Rigid colonies, though calcareous, are often extremely fragile.

Because of the many variables, members of the phylum are not easily recognized as a group. Observing zooids joined together to form a colonial structure is often the best clue in recognizing a formation as bryozoan. Some species can be identified by the colony's pattern of growth, while others can be distinguished only by the shape of the individual zooids, which often requires microscopic examination.

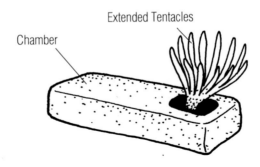

Chamber

Extended Tentacles

TYPICAL ZOOID

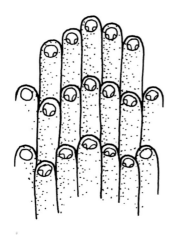

**OVAL SHAPED
ZOOID CHAMBERS**

**TUBULAR SHAPED
ZOOID CHAMBERS**

**VASE SHAPED
ZOOID CHAMBERS**

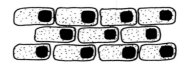

**RECTANGULAR SHAPED
ENCRUSTING ZOOID CHAMBERS**

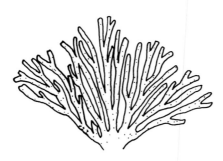

LACY FAN COLONY

**SEAWEED-LIKE
COLONY**

VISUAL ID: White, fan-shaped colonies. Structures are rigid and quite fragile.

ABUNDANCE & DISTRIBUTION: Common Caribbean. Not reported Florida.

HABITAT & BEHAVIOR: Inhabit coral reefs. Grow in protected areas, such as around the bases of coral heads, in crevices and recesses, under ledge overhangs and in depressions on walls.

VISUAL ID: Brown, fan-shaped colonies. Structures are flexible, have red tips, and occasional cross bars.

ABUNDANCE & DISTRIBUTION: Common Florida Keys, Bahamas, Caribbean.

HABITAT & BEHAVIOR: Inhabit coral reefs. Grow in protected areas, such as around the bases of coral heads, in crevices and recesses, under ledge overhangs and in depressions on walls.

VISUAL ID: Tan, fan-shaped colonies. Structures are flexible and somewhat crunchy to the touch.

ABUNDANCE & DISTRIBUTION: Common Gulf Coast of Florida. Genus is worldwide. (See note)

HABITAT & BEHAVIOR: Attach to hard substrate. Numerous colonies often grow in patches.

NOTE: This is the only genus to form tan, fan-like structures along the Gulf Coast of Florida. Species identification, however, requires laboratory examination of specimen.

WHITE FAN BRYOZOAN
Reteporellina evelinae
CLASS:
Bryozoans
Gymnolaemata

SIZE: Colony 1 - 2 in.
DEPTH: 25 - 100 ft.

BROWN FAN BRYOZOAN
Canda simplex
CLASS:
Bryozoans
Gymnolaemata

SIZE: Colony ³/₄ - 1¹/₄ in.
DEPTH: 25 - 130 ft.

TAN FAN BRYOZOAN
Scrupocellaria sp.
CLASS:
Bryozoans
Gymnolaemata

SIZE: Colony ³/₄ - 1¹/₄ in.
DEPTH: 15 - 100 ft.

VISUAL ID: Purple, fan-shaped colonies. Structures are flexible with somewhat widely spaced branches.

ABUNDANCE & DISTRIBUTION: Occasional Caribbean; uncommon Florida.

HABITAT & BEHAVIOR: Inhabit reefs. Grow in protected areas, such as around the bases of coral heads, in crevices and recesses, under ledge overhangs and in depressions on walls.

SIMILAR SPECIES: Purple Fan Bryozoan, *B. neritina*, is impossible to visually distinguish from the Purple Reef Fan, but can generally be differentiated by habitat and location. Tend to grow in bays and harbors rather than reefs; occasional Florida, rare Caribbean.

VISUAL ID: Tangled masses of white, thin, cylindrical branches. Calcareous structures are rigid and quite fragile.

ABUNDANCE & DISTRIBUTION: Occasional Florida, Bahamas, Caribbean.

HABITAT & BEHAVIOR: Inhabit deep walls. Grow under ledge overhangs, attach to rope sponges and branches of black coral trees.

NOTE: Visual identification confirmed by microscopic examination of small sample collected from pictured specimen.

VISUAL ID: White, branching, ribbon-shaped colonies. These calcareous structures are rigid and quite fragile. The tiny, rectangular zooid chambers are distinctive of this genus.

ABUNDANCE & DISTRIBUTION: Uncommon Caribbean.

HABITAT & BEHAVIOR: Inhabit deep walls. Grow under ledge overhangs, attach to rope sponges and branches of black coral trees.

NOTE: Because there are several similar appearing species in this genus, species identification requires microscopic examination.

PURPLE REEF FAN
Bugula minima
CLASS:
Bryozoans
Gymnolaemata
ORDER:
Cheilostomata

SIZE: Colony 1 - 2 in.
DEPTH: 25 - 100 ft.

WHITE TANGLED BRYOZOAN
Bracebridgia subsulcata
CLASS:
Bryozoans
Gymnolaemata
ORDER:
Cyclostomata

SIZE: Colony 1 - 5 in.
DEPTH: 50 - 130 ft.

TANGLED RIBBON BRYOZOAN
Membranipora sp.
CLASS:
Bryozoans
Gymnolaemata
ORDER:
Cheilostomata

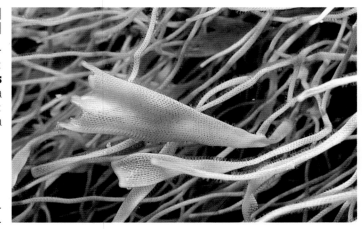

SIZE: Colony 1 - 5 in.
DEPTH: 50 - 130 ft.

VISUAL ID: Bushy, flexible, seaweed-like colonies are light orangish-brown to tan. Primary branches of the colony are the long axis for secondary branches that form a spiral pattern.

ABUNDANCE & DISTRIBUTION: Common North Florida; occasional South Florida. Not reported Caribbean.

HABITAT & BEHAVIOR: Attach to substrate in wide range of habitats, including dock pilings, sea grass beds, shipwrecks and rocky reefs.

VISUAL ID: Bushy, flexible, seaweed-like colonies are white to light gray or tan. Circular, fan-like structures tip the secondary branches.

ABUNDANCE & DISTRIBUTION: Common Florida; occasional Bahamas, Caribbean. Circumtropical.

HABITAT & BEHAVIOR: Attach to substrate in wide range of habitats, including dock pilings, sea grass beds, shipwrecks and rocky reefs.

NOTE: Visual identification confirmed by examination of small sample collected from pictured specimen.

VISUAL ID: Purplish-brown, calcified encrusting colonies that often form tubular, branching, horn-like structures.

ABUNDANCE & DISTRIBUTION: Occasional Florida, Bahamas, Caribbean.

HABITAT & BEHAVIOR: Generally inhabit harbors, bays and mangrove environments in the Caribbean, but may be found on reefs. In North Florida waters they inhabit deep rocky reefs.

NOTE: Visual identification confirmed by examination of small sample collected from pictured specimen.

SPIRAL-TUFTED BRYOZOAN
Bugula turrita
CLASS:
Bryozoans
Gymnolaemata
ORDER:
Cheilostomata

SIZE: Colonies to 1 ft.
DEPTH: 1 - 90 ft.

SEAWEED BRYOZOAN
Caulibugula dendrograpta
CLASS:
Bryozoans
Gymnolaemata
ORDER:
Cheilostomata

SIZE: Colonies to 1¹/₂ ft.
DEPTH: 10-130 ft.

TUBULAR-HORN BRYOZOAN
Schizoporella violacea
CLASS:
Bryozoans
Gymnolaemata
ORDER:
Cheilostomata
SUBORDER:
Ascophora

SIZE: Colony 1 - 4 in.
DEPTH: 1 - 100 ft.

VISUAL ID: Thin, encrusting colonies are red to pink and occasionally gold. In natural light usually fluoresce pale green. Calcified, relatively large, tooth-shaped zooid chambers give the surface of the colony a beaded texture.

ABUNDANCE & DISTRIBUTION: Common Caribbean. Possibly in Florida Keys and Bahamas.

HABITAT & BEHAVIOR: Inhabit reefs. Encrust in protected areas, such as around the bases of coral heads, in crevices and recesses, under ledge overhangs and in depressions on walls.

VISUAL ID: Pearly Orange Encrusting Bryozoan: Pearly orange color is distinctive. The thin, calcified encrusting colonies are composed of tiny zooids. Purple Encrusting Bryozoan: Purple color is distinctive. The thin, calcified encrusting colonies are composed of tiny zooids. Green coloration in picture comes from algae growth.

ABUNDANCE & DISTRIBUTION: Common Florida, Bahamas, Caribbean. Circumtropical.

HABITAT & BEHAVIOR: Encrust boat bottoms, dock pilings, and mangrove roots, but are also occasionally common on mid-range reefs.

NOTE: Pictured specimens were collected and visual identifications confirmed by laboratory examination. Purple Encrusting Bryozoan cannot be identified to species because of incomplete classification data for this and several similar appearing species. It is possibly *S. serialis* or *S. violacea*, but could also be an undescribed species.

VISUAL ID: Pearly red color is distinctive. Encrusting colonies are calcified and composed of large, rectangular zooids with rounded ends that lay in an overlapping, shingle-like pattern.

ABUNDANCE & DISTRIBUTION: Occasional Florida, Bahamas, Caribbean. Circumtropical.

HABITAT & BEHAVIOR: Encrust in dead areas of reefs, especially around the bases of coral heads, under ledge overhangs and in shallow recesses.

BLEEDING TEETH BRYOZOAN
Trematooecia aviculifera
CLASS:
Bryozoans
Gymnolaemata
ORDER:
Cheilostomata

SIZE: Colony ½ - 3 in.
DEPTH: 25 - 100 ft.

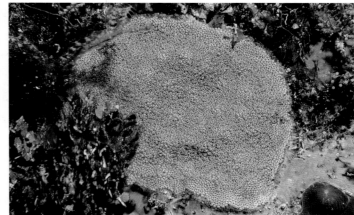

PEARLY ORANGE ENCRUSTING BRYOZOAN
Hippopodina feegeensis

PURPLE ENCRUSTING BRYOZOAN
Schizoporella sp.
CLASS:
Bryozoans
Gymnolaemata
ORDER:
Cheilostomata
SUBORDER:
Ascophora
SIZE: Colonies 1 - 3 in.
DEPTH: 2 - 75 ft.

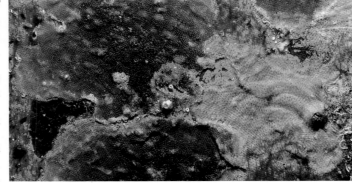

PEARLY RED ENCRUSTING BRYOZOAN
Steginoporella magnilabris
CLASS:
Bryozoans
Gymnolaemata

SIZE: Colonies 1 - 3 in.
DEPTH: 15 - 130 ft.

Phylum Mollusca

(Moe-LUS-kuh / L. soft body)

Snails, Shell-less Snails, Chitons, Bivalves, Octopuses, Squid

The Latin name Mollusca means soft body, which appropriately describes these animals because they lack a true skeleton. A majority of phylum members have an external shell for protection. Shells are made of calcium carbonate secreted from a specialized layer of the animals' outer tissues, called the **mantle**.

SNAILS

Class Gastropoda (Gas-tro-POE-duh / L. stomach foot)
Subclass Prosobranchia (Pro-so-BRAHNK-key-uh / Gr. forward gills)

Snails are, by far, the largest class of mollusks, containing more than 35,000 species. Typically, each animal secretes a tubular whorl that forms an ever-enlarging cone-shaped shell as the snail grows. Species are identified by their shells' shape, sculpturing, color pattern, or a combination of these features.

Normally, the snail's soft body is completely hidden within the shell. Occasionally, however, a tube-like mouth called the **proboscis**, and **two tentacles**, are seen extending from the shell's opening. **Eyes** are usually located at the base of these tentacles. A short leathery pad or **foot** is extended to slowly drag the snail about. Many species have a hard, cuticular disc, called an **operculum**, attached to the foot. This covers the opening of the shell when the animal withdraws. A few species, such as Flamingo Tongues and Cowries, extend their mantle over the entire shell as camouflage.

SHELL-LESS SNAILS

Class Gastropoda
Subclass Opisthobranchia (Oh-PISS-toe-BRAHNK-key-uh / Gr. back or rear gills)

Most members of this subclass lack an external shell, although several orders have reduced-external, or poorly-developed internal, shells. The body is typically a thick, elongated oval only a few inches in length. The mantle, which often has colorful, ornate designs, covers the animal's back. At the head are one or two pairs of tentacles; some have foot corner extensions that appear as an additional pairs of tentacles. Many opisthobranchs have specialized diets, feeding on only a single species of marine invertebrate or plant. Finding their food source is often the secret to locating many species. Several orders may be encountered on the reef; their similarity in appearance, however, makes them difficult to distinguish.

Headshield slugs, Order Cephalaspidea, have a distinctive **shield-shaped head**. They all have an internal or external shell.

Sea hares, Order Anaspidea, are large opisthobranchs having **two pairs of tentacles** and **mantle skin flaps** on their backs. Most are colored in shades of green and brown, a few are black. They have a small internal shell and internal gills. Sea hares feed on algae. When disturbed, many species are able to discharge a purple ink in defense.

Sidegill slugs, Order Notaspidea, have a **mantle skirt** that covers the gill on the body's right side. They usually have an internal shell and **one pair of tentacles** that resemble a rounded tip dowel. Members of this order feed primarily on tunicates.

Sea slugs, Order Sacoglossa, is a diverse order united by a sac in the alimentary canal that collects discarded teeth. Visually they vary greatly, although most are shades of green. Sea slugs respire by absorbing oxygen through their skin. Some can be identified by **skin ruffles** on their backs that increase the absorption area. They have **one pair of obvious tentacles** that resemble a rolled sheet of paper. All sea slugs have a shell, which may be external or internal and is usually reduced in size. Members of this order feed on algae.

Nudibranchs, Order Nudibranchia (L. naked gill), can be recognized by their external gills. Many species have developed true secondary gills, as in the Family Chromodoridae (Gr. colorful sea goddess). Their structure takes the form of a crown of feather-like appendages surrounding the anus, called **anal gills**. Others have developed appendages to increase skin area for the absorption of oxygen. These may take the form of skin ruffles, or fringe-like projections on the back, called cerata. Nudibranchs have a pair of sensory tentacles, called **rhinophores**, on their head; a second pair of **oral tentacles** is also present, although not obvious in some species. A few have foot corner extensions that resemble a third pair of tentacles. Members of this order have no shell and are carnivores.

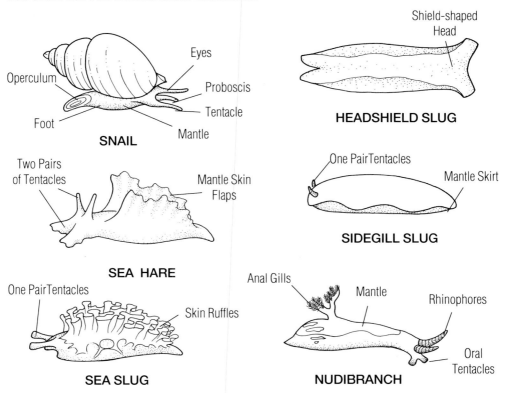

SNAIL

Operculum, Eyes, Proboscis, Tentacle, Mantle, Foot

HEADSHIELD SLUG

Shield-shaped Head

SEA HARE

Two Pairs of Tentacles, Mantle Skin Flaps

SIDEGILL SLUG

One Pair Tentacles, Mantle Skirt

SEA SLUG

One Pair Tentacles, Skin Ruffles

NUDIBRANCH

Anal Gills, Mantle, Rhinophores, Oral Tentacles

CHITONS

Class Amphineura (Am-fee-NUR-uh / L. nerves all around)

Chitons are easily recognized by their oval shape, formed by eight transverse, overlapping, **calcareous plates**. Around the edge is a fleshy border, called a **girdle**. The girdle's color, markings and texture are often important keys to species identification. Only an inch or two in length, they attach firmly to rocks with a large, muscular foot. Movement is imperceptibly slow as they graze on algae. Chitons generally inhabit shallow intertidal or subtidal water, but are occasionally found on reefs.

BIVALVES

Class Bivalvia (Buy-VALVE-ee-uh / L. two doors)

The soft-bodied animals of this class are protected by two shells, called **valves**, that are hinged together by a ligament. Special muscles, called abductors, contract to close the valves and relax to open. Species are identified by their valves' sculpturing, color pattern, or a combination of these features. When open, some species extend a curtain-like **mantle** that can be brightly colored. The mantle of a few species have **tentacles**, and **eye spots** for the detection of movement. Bivalves are filter-feeders. Water is drawn into a siphon, passed through a complex gill-filter to extract food and oxygen, and expelled out a second siphon.

SQUID, OCTOPUSES

Class Cephalopoda (Sef-uh-low-POE-duh / Gr. head and foot)

Cephalopods have long arms with powerful suction cups that are used to catch prey and bring it to the mouth. All are carnivores that have a pair of powerful, beak-like jaws to crush or tear prey. Of all the invertebrate animals, they have the most highly evolved nervous system, including eyes similar in structure to those of vertebrates. Octopuses and squid have no external shell, unlike their close relative, the chambered nautilus. Cephalopods can propel themselves rapidly by expelling water from a mantle cavity with a water-jet action. They can change body colors swiftly and dramatically, often to blend with their surroundings. This is accomplished by the expansion or contraction of specialized pigment cells called chromatophores.

Squid, Suborder Teuthoidea, can be recognized by the **eight arms** and **two longer tentacles** that stream behind their elongated body as they swim. Running along the sides are stabilizing **swim fins**. Squid are often seen in groups, moving over the reef in close formation. They prey primarily on fish.

Octopuses, Order Octopoda, have **eight arms** of about equal length, and a globular or bag-like body. They are primarily bottom-dwellers that use their arms and suction cups to move about; however, they have the ability to jet themselves backwards by rapidly expelling water from their mantle cavity. A cloud of dark ink is sometimes discharged to cover their escape. Crustaceans and shelled mollusks make up their basic diet.

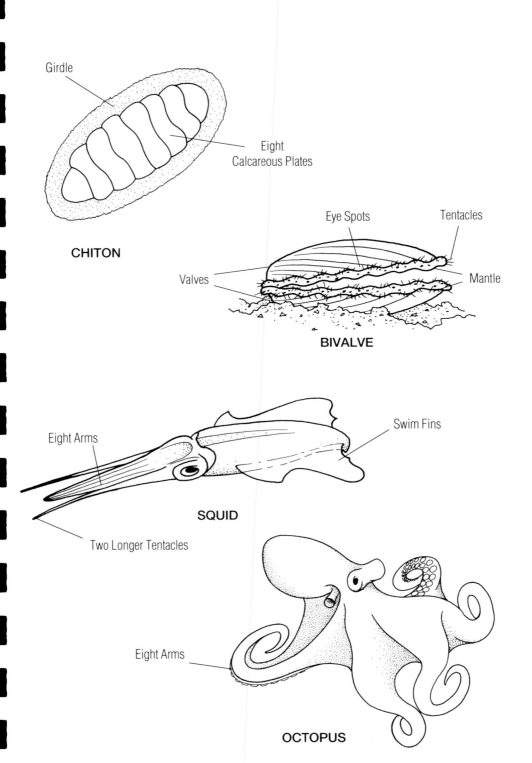

Girdle

Eight
Calcareous Plates

CHITON

Eye Spots

Tentacles

Valves

Mantle

BIVALVE

Swim Fins

Eight Arms

SQUID

Two Longer Tentacles

Eight Arms

OCTOPUS

VISUAL ID: Large shell has short conical spire with blunt spikes. Shell's exterior is orangish (not always apparent because of algal growth and debris); aperture rosy-pink. Mottled gray head with large proboscis and long eye stalks. Eye at tip of stalk, tentacles below. Long, claw-like operculum.

ABUNDANCE & DISTRIBUTION: Abundant to uncommon South Florida, Bahamas, Caribbean. Has become uncommon in many areas because of over-harvesting.

HABITAT & BEHAVIOR: Inhabit sea grass beds and sand flats, often around patch reefs. Pictured species relatively young, shell becomes thicker with age. Often more abundant between 40-100 feet because of difficulty in harvesting.

REACTION TO DIVERS: When approached, retract proboscis and eye stalks into shell. If diver waits, motionlessly, animal often reappears after a short time.

VISUAL ID: Thick, whitish exterior shell, cream colored lip and aperture. Short conical spire with large rounded spikes. Green head with large proboscis. Long, greenish-cream colored eye stalks with eye at tip and tentacle below. Long, claw-like operculum.

ABUNDANCE & DISTRIBUTION: Common to uncommon South Florida, Bahamas, Caribbean.

HABITAT & BEHAVIOR: Inhabit sea grass beds and sand flats, often around patch reefs.

REACTION TO DIVERS: When approached, retract proboscis and eye stalks into shell. If diver waits, motionlessly, animal often reappears after a short time.

VISUAL ID: Shell has short conical spire with two spikes on last whorl, aperture's upper lip is expanded and extends upward. Exterior mottled browns and purples (not always apparent because of algal growth and debris); aperture reddish. Long eye stalks with tentacles attached below eyes at tips. Long, claw-like operculum.

ABUNDANCE & DISTRIBUTION: Common South Florida, occasional Bahamas, Caribbean.

HABITAT & BEHAVIOR: Inhabit sea grass beds and sand flats, often around patch reefs.

REACTION TO DIVERS: When approached, retract proboscis and eye stalks into shell. If diver waits, motionlessly, animal often reappears after a short time.

QUEEN CONCH
Strombus gigas
CLASS:
Snails
Gastropoda
SUBCLASS:
Prosobranchia

SIZE: 6 - 9 in.,
12 in. max.
DEPTH: 3 - 100 ft.

MILK CONCH
Strombus costatus
CLASS:
Snails
Gastropoda
SUBCLASS:
Prosobranchia

SIZE: 4 - 6 in.
DEPTH: 3 - 40 ft.

HAWKWING CONCH
Strombus raninus
CLASS:
Snails
Gastropoda
SUBCLASS:
Prosobranchia

SIZE: 2¹/₂ - 3¹/₂ in.,
4¹/₂ in. max.
DEPTH: 3 - 80 ft.

VISUAL ID: Shell has knob-like spikes on next-to-last whorl of spire, and short, pointed spikes on final whorl. Aperture's upper lip slants downward. Exterior orangish-brown and may be mottled and/or banded; aperture reddish-cream. Mottled brown head with large white-tipped proboscis and long, whitish eye stalks. Long, claw-like operculum.

ABUNDANCE & DISTRIBUTION: Abundant West Florida; common East Florida. Not reported Caribbean.

HABITAT & BEHAVIOR: Inhabit sea grass beds and sand flats, often around shallow patch and fringing reefs.

REACTION TO DIVERS: When approached, retract proboscis and eye stalks into shell. If diver waits, motionlessly, animal often reappears after a short time.

SIMILAR SPECIES: West Indian Fighting Conch, *S. pugilis*, is distinguished by longer, more pointed spikes on last two whorls of spire, upper aperture lip "U"-shaped. Common Caribbean, occasional South Florida.

VISUAL ID: Shell has long, narrow extension of aperture's upper lip. Exterior is orangish, often blotched with white; aperture reddish-cream. Mottled brown head with large proboscis and long eye stalks. Eye at tip of stalk, tentacle below. Long, claw-like operculum.

ABUNDANCE & DISTRIBUTION: Rare South Florida, Bahamas, Caribbean.

HABITAT & BEHAVIOR: Inhabit sea grass beds and sand flats, often around shallow patch and fringing reefs.

REACTION TO DIVERS: When approached, retract proboscis and eye stalks into shell. If diver waits, motionlessly, animal often reappears after a short time.

VISUAL ID: Shell has long conical spire with small knobs. Exterior grayish-white to salmon or tan; orangish aperture. Body cream to reddish-orange. Shell often flaky. Long, claw-like operculum.

ABUNDANCE & DISTRIBUTION: Abundant to common Florida and Gulf of Mexico.

HABITAT & BEHAVIOR: Inhabit areas of sand, sea grass and patch reefs. Large adults tend to inhabit deeper waters.

REACTION TO DIVERS: When approached, retract into shell. If diver waits, motionlessly, animal often reappears after a short time.

NOTE ABOUT JUVENILES: Orange shell and red body to 3 ½ inches, usually in depths less than 30 feet.

FLORIDA FIGHTING CONCH

Strombus alatus

CLASS:
Snails
Gastropoda
SUBCLASS:
Prosobranchia

SIZE: 2¹/₂ - 3¹/₂ in.,
5 in. max.
DEPTH: 3 - 20 ft.

ROOSTERTAIL CONCH

Strombus gallus

CLASS:
Snails
Gastropoda
SUBCLASS:
Prosobranchia

SIZE: 3¹/₂ - 5 in.
DEPTH: 3 - 20 ft.

FLORIDA HORSE CONCH

Pleuroploca gigantea

CLASS:
Snails
Gastropoda
SUBCLASS:
Prosobranchia

SIZE: 10 - 14 in.,
30 in. max.
DEPTH: 3 - 100 ft.

VISUAL ID: Spindle-shaped shell with many broken, dark spiral stripes. Variable blotched color pattern, often in shades of gray, green or brown; in Florida, occasionally reddish-orange. Body black to reddish-brown with white speckles. Tear-shaped operculum is brown.

ABUNDANCE & DISTRIBUTION: Occasional Florida, Bahamas, Caribbean.

HABITAT & BEHAVIOR: Inhabit shallow sand and grass bottoms, prefer quiet water of bays. Occasionally found in deeper water.

VISUAL ID: Long, pointed spiral shell is variegated in shades ranging from cream to dark brown. Yellow and black banded tentacles. Body mottled reddish-brown.

ABUNDANCE & DISTRIBUTION: Occasional Southeast Florida, Bahamas, Caribbean. Has become rare in many areas because of over-collecting.

HABITAT & BEHAVIOR: Inhabit sandy bottoms and reefs. Hide in reef recesses during day. Feed on sea cucumbers at night, in the open.

VISUAL ID: Exterior shell of living specimen is covered with hair-like projections. Dark brown between white "teeth" on aperture lip. Body whitish, covered with dark, outlined gray spots.

ABUNDANCE & DISTRIBUTION: Occasional Florida, Bahamas, Caribbean.

HABITAT & BEHAVIOR: Inhabit coral reefs.

TRUE TULIP
Fasciolaria tulipa
CLASS:
Snails
Gastropoda
SUBCLASS:
Prosobranchia

SIZE: 3 - 6 in.,
10 in. max.
DEPTH: 0 - 35 ft.

ATLANTIC TRITON'S TRUMPET
Charonia variegata
CLASS:
Snails
Gastropoda
SUBCLASS:
Prosobranchia

SIZE: 10 - 14 in.,
18 in. max.
DEPTH: 20 - 60 ft.

ATLANTIC HAIRY TRITON
Cymatium pileare
CLASS:
Snails
Gastropoda
SUBCLASS:
Prosobranchia

SIZE: 1^1/$_2$ - 3^1/$_2$ in.,
4 in. max.
DEPTH: 20 - 80 ft.

VISUAL ID: Exterior shell in shades of reddish-brown in a wavy, netted pattern, with seven or eight dark stripes over outer lip. Five axial growth lines on shell. Flattened lip around aperture forms distinct triangle.

ABUNDANCE & DISTRIBUTION: Common to occasional Florida, Bahamas, Caribbean. Has become rare in many areas because of over-collecting.

HABITAT & BEHAVIOR: Inhabit shallow sand flats, often around patch and fringing reefs. During day usually burrow in sand with only small part of upper shell exposed. Hunt in open at night for sea urchins, which they attack with surprising speed, unimpeded by spines.

SIMILAR SPECIES: King Helmet, *C. tuberosa*, flattened lip around aperture is triangular, fine netted growth lines on shell, smaller shell, four inches maximum. Emperor or Queen Helmet, *C. madagascariensis*, flattened lip forms a rounded triangle, large shell to 12 inches.

VISUAL ID: Light brown netted pattern over creamy to white exterior. May occasionally have two or three dark bands; rarely all white with no markings.

ABUNDANCE & DISTRIBUTION: Common Florida, Bahamas, Caribbean.

HABITAT & BEHAVIOR: Inhabit sandy areas near shallow patch and back reefs. Crawl about, partially buried in sand, while searching for prey.

SIMILAR SPECIES: Lettered Olive *O. Sayana,* netted pattern over grayish-tan exterior, generally slimmer and larger (2 - 2¹/₂ inches), common Florida.

VISUAL ID: White shell with white spots and blotches, three faint, diffuse, yellowish bands. Translucent body blotched with white.

ABUNDANCE & DISTRIBUTION: Common Caribbean.

HABITAT & BEHAVIOR: Inhabit sand and sea grass bottoms, often near fringing reefs.

SIMILAR SPECIES: White-Spotted Marginella, *Marginella guttata,* distinguished by smaller spots and faint pinkish-brown bands.

FLAME HELMET
Cassis flammea
CLASS:
Snails
Gastropoda
SUBCLASS:
Prosobranchia

SIZE: 4 - 5 in.,
7 in. max.
DEPTH: 10 - 35 ft.

NETTED OLIVE
Oliva reticularis
CLASS:
Snails
Gastropoda
SUBCLASS:
Prosobranchia

SIZE: 1 - 1½ in.,
2 in. max.
DEPTH: 5 - 25 ft.

GLOWING MARGINELLA
Marginella pruniosum
CLASS:
Snails
Gastropoda
SUBCLASS:
Prosobranchia

SIZE: ¼ - ½ in.
DEPTH: 5 - 20 ft.

VISUAL ID: High, conical spire. Exterior usually covered with various growths including Red Coralline Algae.

ABUNDANCE & DISTRIBUTION: Common Caribbean.

HABITAT & BEHAVIOR: Inhabit grass beds and shallow reefs, often hide under rocks.

SIMILAR SPECIES: American Starsnail, *L. americanum*, is virtually indistinguishable, common Southeast Florida.

VISUAL ID: Width of lower whorl is half that of shell's overall length. Shallow-water specimens tend to have whitish spire with numerous small, dark, spiraled markings and prominent short spikes on spire. Deep-water specimens tend to have orange-brown to rust-brown mottling on spire, with less pronounced short spikes.

ABUNDANCE & DISTRIBUTION: Abundant South Florida, Bahamas, Caribbean.

HABITAT & BEHAVIOR: Inhabit wide range of marine environments including intertidal pools, sea grass beds and reefs. More common in shallow water.

SIMILAR SPECIES: There are numerous similar and easily confused species, all of which are somewhat more elongated.

VISUAL ID: Numerous whorls of chocolate-brown lines on sharp spire. Exterior in varying shades of light brown.

ABUNDANCE & DISTRIBUTION: Rare Florida Keys, Bahamas, Caribbean.

HABITAT & BEHAVIOR: Inhabit sandy areas and shallow coral reefs.

WEST INDIAN STARSNAIL

Lithopoma tectum

CLASS:
Snails
Gastropoda
SUBCLASS:
Prosobranchia

SIZE: 1 - 1¹/₂ in.,
2 in. max.
DEPTH: 5 - 25 ft.

STOCKY CERITH

Cerithium litteratum

CLASS:
Snails
Gastropoda
SUBCLASS:
Prosobranchia

SIZE: ³/₄ - 1¹/₄ in.,
1³/₄ in. max.
DEPTH: Intertidal - 100

CHOCOLATE-LINED TOPSNAIL

Calliostoma javanicum

CLASS:
Snails
Gastropoda
SUBCLASS:
Prosobranchia

SIZE: ³/₄ - 1 in.,
1¹/₄ in. max.
DEPTH: 2 - 35 ft.

VISUAL ID: Ribs run around shell from slit-like groove on back . White to tan to brownish-pink with three pairs of large, irregular, brownish spots on back. Highly decorated red to yellow camouflaging mantle may extend over outside of shell.

ABUNDANCE & DISTRIBUTION: Common Florida. Occasional Bahamas, Caribbean.

HABITAT & BEHAVIOR: Inhabit intertidal zones to deep reefs.

VISUAL ID: Bulbous-shaped shell (compare with more elongated shell of similar Measled Cowrie [next]). Covered with white spots, the larger of which often have brown centers. Lustrous shell in shades of brown, often has indistinct lighter and darker bands. Shell of young is banded and has no spots. Black, gray and brown mottled mantle with occasional white blotches and numerous fleshy, spike-like projections.

ABUNDANCE & DISTRIBUTION: Occasional to rare Florida, Bahamas, Caribbean.

HABITAT & BEHAVIOR: Inhabit reefs, often on underside of ledge overhangs and in recesses. Camouflage by extending mantle over shell. (Note the partial extension of mantle in photograph.)

VISUAL ID: Shell somewhat elongated (compare with more bulbous shell of similar Atlantic Deer Cowrie [previous]). Covered with whitish spots, the larger of which often have brown centers, especially around sides. Lustrous shell, in shades of brown, often has indistinct lighter and darker bands. Shell of young is banded and has no spots. Grayish mottled mantle and numerous fleshy, spike-like projections.

ABUNDANCE & DISTRIBUTION: Occasional to rare Southeast Florida, Bahamas, Caribbean.

HABITAT & BEHAVIOR: Inhabit reefs, often on underside of ledge overhangs and in recesses. Also found near protective rocks in shallow water. Camouflage by extending mantle over shell.

COFFEE BEAN TRIVIA
Trivia pediculus
CLASS:
Snails
Gastropoda
SUBCLASS:
Prosobranchia

SIZE: ³/₄ - 1 in.,
1¹/₄ in. max.
DEPTH: 2 - 80 ft.

ATLANTIC DEER COWRIE
Cypraea cervus
CLASS:
Cowries
Gastropoda
SUBCLASS:
Prosobranchia
FAMILY:
Cypraeidae

SIZE: 2 - 3 in.,
5 in. max.
DEPTH: 1 - 40 ft.

MEASLED COWRIE
Cypraea zebra
CLASS:
Cowries
Gastropoda
SUBCLASS:
Prosobranchia
FAMILY:
Cypraeidae

SIZE: 2 - 3¹/₂ in.,
4 in. max.
DEPTH: 6 - 35 ft.

VISUAL ID: Lustrous, medium-brown to mauve shell with dark-brown to black flecks. Mantle mottled in shades of brown and mauve, and covered with numerous fleshy warts with forked extensions.

ABUNDANCE & DISTRIBUTION: Common to uncommon Southeast Florida, Caribbean.

HABITAT & BEHAVIOR: Inhabit coral reefs, often on undersides of ledge overhangs and in recesses. Camouflage by extending mantle over shell.

VISUAL ID: Lustrous, yellow-brown shell with lighter spots. Mantle medium to dark-brown with numerous, lighter colored, fleshy warts with forked projections.

ABUNDANCE & DISTRIBUTION: Uncommon to rare Florida, Bahamas, Caribbean.

HABITAT & BEHAVIOR: Inhabit areas of reef rubble, often under rocks and in other sheltered locations. Camouflage by extending mantle over shell. (Note the partial extension of mantle in photograph.)

VISUAL ID: White mantle covered with gray to black, usually rounded spots, with darker outlines. Shell is porcelain white.

ABUNDANCE & DISTRIBUTION: Occasional to rare Florida, Bahamas.

HABITAT & BEHAVIOR: Attach to and feed on gorgonians in all types of habitats. Mantle normally extended over shell.

NOTE: Also commonly known as McGinty's Cyphoma.

ATLANTIC GRAY COWRIE
Cypraea cinerea
CLASS:
Cowries
Gastropoda
SUBCLASS:
Prosobranchia
FAMILY:
Cypraeidae

SIZE: ½ - 1 in.,
1½ in. max.
DEPTH: 20 - 50 ft.

ATLANTIC YELLOW COWRIE
Cypraea spurca acicularis
CLASS:
Cowries
Gastropoda
SUBCLASS:
Prosobranchia
FAMILY:
Cypraeidae

SIZE: ½ - 1 in.,
1½ in. max.
DEPTH: 15 - 50 ft.

SPOTTED CYPHOMA
Cyphoma macgintyi
CLASS:
Snails
Gastropoda
SUBCLASS:
Prosobranchia

SIZE: ¾ - 1 in.
DEPTH: 20 - 80 ft.

VISUAL ID: Cream-white mantle covered with orangish, often somewhat rectangular spots with black outlines. Shell is reddish-cream to white.

ABUNDANCE & DISTRIBUTION: Common Florida, Bahamas, Caribbean.

HABITAT & BEHAVIOR: Attach to and feed on gorgonians in all types of habitats. Mantle normally extended over shell.

VISUAL ID: White mantle with numerous finger print-like designs of black and gold. Shell white to cream, often with a few yellowish markings.

ABUNDANCE & DISTRIBUTION: Uncommon to rare Florida Keys, Bahamas, Caribbean.

HABITAT & BEHAVIOR: Attach to and feed on gorgonians in all types of habitats. Mantle normally extended over shell.

VISUAL ID: Mantle has fine network of lines and white spots; colored in various shades of purple, yellow or green. Shell is narrow and glossy, in various colors including lavender, yellow, green or white, with white border around aperture.

ABUNDANCE & DISTRIBUTION: Common Florida, Bahamas, Caribbean.

HABITAT & BEHAVIOR: Attach to and feed upon purple or yellow sea fans, and occasionally other gorgonians, including sea rods and sea whips. Change mantle color to match gorgonian.

NOTE: Although common, rarely observed because of its small size and excellent camouflage.

FLAMINGO TONGUE
Cyphoma gibbosum
CLASS:
Snails
Gastropoda
SUBCLASS:
Prosobranchia

SIZE: ³/₄ - 1 in.
DEPTH: 6 - 45 ft.

FINGERPRINT CYPHOMA
Cyphoma signatum
CLASS:
Snails
Gastropoda
SUBCLASS:
Prosobranchia

SIZE: ³/₄ - 1 in.
DEPTH: 6 - 45 ft.

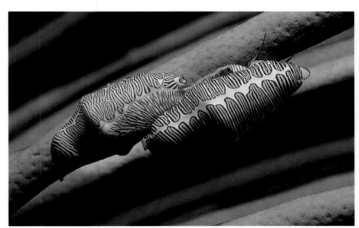

WEST INDIAN SIMNIA
Cymbovula acicularis
CLASS:
Snails
Gastropoda
SUBCLASS:
Prosobranchia

SIZE: ¹/₂ in.
DEPTH: 5 - 50 ft.

Tube-Worm Snails – Headshield Slugs

VISUAL ID: Circular shell opening (about 3/16 in.) protrudes slightly from sponge or dead coral surface. The animal's head, with two small tentacles, can be seen in the opening. Color varies, often yellow, orange or black. Shell (rarely visible) is a long tube with several curves, the tip is spiraled. Tube is marked with rings of reddish-brown to gray and muddy-white, the last quarter inch and spiraled tip are white.

ABUNDANCE & DISTRIBUTION: Common Florida, Bahamas, Caribbean.

HABITAT & BEHAVIOR: Grow in sponges and dead coral heads. Often grow in intertwining clumps in shallow water. On deeper reefs, more commonly solitary, although several individuals may inhabit a single sponge. Commonly found growing in Touch-Me-Not Sponges [pg.37]. Feed by sending out mucus thread [note photograph].

NOTE : Identification was made by collection of pictured specimen. This and several similar species can often be identified only by collection.

VISUAL ID: Thin black line design on polished, cream shell. Body translucent white with opaque white patches.

ABUNDANCE & DISTRIBUTION: Uncommon Florida, Bahamas, Caribbean. However, can be common in localized areas.

HABITAT & BEHAVIOR: Inhabit sandy areas, hide under rocks during day. Forage at night for polychaete worms.

VISUAL ID: Body and shell mottled brown with whitish flecks. Shell sculptured with widely spaced parallel grooves.

ABUNDANCE & DISTRIBUTION: Occasional Florida, Bahamas, Caribbean.

HABITAT & BEHAVIOR: Inhabit areas of sand, gravel and mud. Bury themselves during day, forage at night for algae.

FLORIDA WORMSNAIL
Vermicularia knorrii
CLASS:
Tube-Worm Snails
Gastropoda
SUBCLASS:
Prosobranchia

SIZE: Tube 3 - 5 in.
DEPTH: 5 - 60 ft.

MINIATURE MELO
Micromela undata
SUBCLASS:
Opisthobranchia
ORDER:
Headshield Slugs
Cephalaspidea
FAMILY:
Hydatinidae

SIZE: 1$^{1}/_{4}$ - 1$^{3}/_{4}$ in.,
2$^{1}/_{2}$ in. max.
DEPTH: 0 - 14 ft.

STRIATE BUBBLE
Bulla striata
SUBCLASS:
Opisthobranchia
ORDER:
Headshield Slugs
Cephalaspidea
FAMILY:
Bullidae

SIZE: 1 - 1$^{1}/_{2}$ in.,
2$^{1}/_{2}$ in. max.
DEPTH: 0 - 100 ft.

VISUAL ID: Rows of brilliant blue spots on mantle. Body finely lined in shades of olive and brown.

ABUNDANCE & DISTRIBUTION: Occasional Florida, Bahamas, Caribbean.

HABITAT & BEHAVIOR: Inhabit rocky areas. Feed on other opisthobranchs, especially Lettuce Slugs [pg. 227].

VISUAL ID: Orange, blue and black stripes, white patch mid-back.

ABUNDANCE & DISTRIBUTION: Occasional Florida, Bahamas, Caribbean.

HABITAT & BEHAVIOR: Inhabit sandy areas. Feed on other headshield slugs.

VISUAL ID: Olive-brown to tan with numerous very thin brown lines and small iridescent blue rings or spots. Long tapered tail.

ABUNDANCE & DISTRIBUTION: Uncommon Florida, Bahamas, Caribbean.

HABITAT & BEHAVIOR: Inhabit areas of rocky rubble and open sand. Feed on algae. When disturbed will discharge a scarlet fluid.

MYSTERIOUS HEADSHIELD SLUG

Navanax aenigmaticus

SUBCLASS:
Opisthobranchia
ORDER:
Headshield Slugs
Cephalaspidea
FAMILY:
Aglajidae

SIZE: 1¼ - 1¾ in.,
2½ in. max.
DEPTH: 3 - 30 ft.

LEECH HEADSHIELD SLUG

Chelidonura hirundinina

SUBCLASS:
Opisthobranchia
ORDER:
Headshield Slugs
Cephalaspidea
FAMILY:
Aglajidae

SIZE: ½ - ¾ in.,
1 in. max.
DEPTH: 3 - 60 ft.

BLUE-RING SEA HARE

Stylocheilus longicauda

SUBCLASS:
Opisthobranchia
ORDER:
Sea Hares
Anaspidea
FAMILY:
Notarchidae

SIZE: ¾ - 1¼ in.,
3 in. max.
DEPTH: 0 - 100 ft.

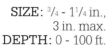

Sea Hares

VISUAL ID: Irregular skin flaps on back, interior edge lined with black or blue. Pale brown overall, with numerous white blotches and spots. Tips of rhinophores and oral tentacles darkened.

ABUNDANCE & DISTRIBUTION: Uncommon Caribbean. Circumtropical.

HABITAT & BEHAVIOR: Inhabit areas of rocky rubble and open sand. Feed on algae.

VISUAL ID: Light brown to green with irregular light spots outlined in black.

ABUNDANCE & DISTRIBUTION: Occasional to common Florida, Bahamas, Caribbean. Circumtropical and subtropical.

HABITAT & BEHAVIOR: Prefer grassy flats with scattered rocks. Feed on algae. When disturbed will discharge a harmless, thick, purple fluid.

VISUAL ID: Numerous hair-like skin papillae extend from body which is brown to tan.

ABUNDANCE & DISTRIBUTION: Uncommon Caribbean. Can be common in localized areas. Circumtropical.

HABITAT & BEHAVIOR: Inhabit sea grass beds. Feed on algae. During breeding season individuals form long lines while copulating.

WHITE-SPOTTED SEA HARE

Aplysia parvula

SUBCLASS:
Opisthobranchia
ORDER:
Sea Hares
Anaspidea
FAMILY:
Aplysiidae

SIZE: ³/₄ - 1 in.,
1¹/₂ in. max.
DEPTH: 0 - 20 ft.

SPOTTED SEA HARE

Aplysia dactylomela

SUBCLASS:
Opisthobranchia
ORDER:
Sea Hares
Anaspidea
FAMILY:
Aplysiidae

SIZE: 3 - 6 in.,
12 in. max.
DEPTH: 0 - 120 ft.

RAGGED SEA HARE

Bursatella leachii

SUBCLASS:
Opisthobranchia
ORDER:
Sea Hares
Anaspidea
FAMILY:
Aplysiidae

SIZE: 5 - 7 in.,
10 in. max.
DEPTH: 1 - 50 ft.

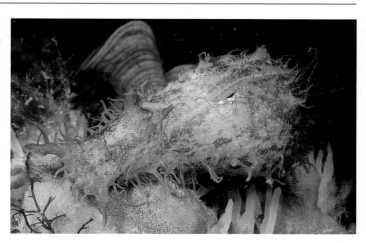

VISUAL ID: Numerous warts on back. Varies from dark reddish-brown to light golden-brown, occasionally pale yellow to white.

ABUNDANCE & DISTRIBUTION: Uncommon Caribbean; rare Bahamas. Also in eastern tropical Pacific.

HABITAT & BEHAVIOR: Inhabit rocky shallows and areas of reef rubble. Hide in recesses.

VISUAL ID: Orange, smooth, somewhat translucent body.

ABUNDANCE & DISTRIBUTION: Occasional Caribbean. Circumtropical.

HABITAT & BEHAVIOR: Hide under reef rubble, especially flat slabs of coral. When disturbed may secrete sulphuric acid in defense.

VISUAL ID: Shades of green, with numerous black and white speckles. Outer edges of skin flaps on back are yellow to orange with black border.

ABUNDANCE & DISTRIBUTION: Occasional Florida, Bahamas, Caribbean.

HABITAT & BEHAVIOR: Inhabit reefs and other areas where they camouflage by blending with various algae, upon which they feed.

WARTY SIDEGILL SLUG
Pleurobranchus areolatus
SUBCLASS:
Opisthobranchia
ORDER:
Sidegill Slugs
Notaspidea
FAMILY:
Pleurobranchidae

SIZE: 2 - 4 in.,
6½ in. max.
DEPTH: 0 - 80 ft.

APRICOT SIDEGILL SLUG
Berthellina engeli
SUBCLASS:
Opisthobranchia
ORDER:
Sidegill Slugs
Notaspidea
FAMILY:
Pleurobranchidae

SIZE: 1 - 2 ½ in.,
3¼ in. max.
DEPTH: 0 - 100 ft.

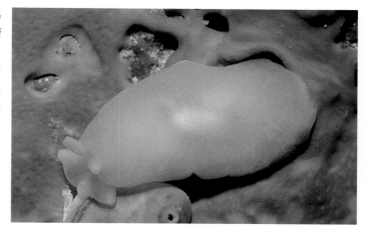

ORNATE ELYSIA
Elysia ornata
SUBCLASS:
Opisthobranchia
ORDER:
Sea Slugs
Sacoglossa
FAMILY:
Elysiidae

SIZE: 1 - 1½ in.,
2 in. max.
DEPTH: 0 - 100 ft.

VISUAL ID: Brown line along outer edge of skin ruffles. Color varies from green to orange to yellow.

ABUNDANCE & DISTRIBUTION: Occasional Florida, Bahamas, Caribbean.

HABITAT & BEHAVIOR: Inhabit reefs and other areas where they camouflage by blending with *Caulerpa* species of algae, upon which they feed.

VISUAL ID: Brilliant stripes and bands of red, blue, green and yellow. White "Y"-shaped mark on head between rhinophores.

ABUNDANCE & DISTRIBUTION: Rare Florida, Bahamas, Jamaica.

HABITAT & BEHAVIOR: Inhabit areas of reef rubble and sand near shallow patch reefs.

VISUAL ID: Thin black lines and a few iridescent blue spots on shell. Body and shell are shades of green to brown.

ABUNDANCE & DISTRIBUTION: Occasional Caribbean. Circumtropical.

HABITAT & BEHAVIOR: Inhabit bays and other calm water areas, often under docks. Found blending in with Sea Grape Alga, *Caulerpa racemosa*, upon which they feed. Secrete milky white liquid when disturbed.

BROWN-LINED ELYSIA

Elysia subornata

SUBCLASS:
Opisthobranchia
ORDER:
Sea Slugs
Sacoglossa
FAMILY:
Elysiidae

SIZE: ³/₄ - 1¹/₄ in.,
1¹/₂ in. max.
DEPTH: 1 - 100 ft.

PAINTED ELYSIA

Elysia picta

SUBCLASS:
Opisthobranchia
ORDER:
Sea Slugs
Sacoglossa
FAMILY:
Elysiidae

SIZE: ¹/₂ - 1 in.,
1¹/₄ in. max.
DEPTH: 0 - 20 ft.

LINED-SHELL SEA SLUG

Lobiger souverbiei

SUBCLASS:
Opisthobranchia
ORDER:
Sea Slugs
Sacoglossa
FAMILY:
Oxynoidae

SIZE: ³/₄ - 1 in.,
1¹/₂ in. max.
DEPTH: 0 - 35 ft.

VISUAL ID: Numerous skin ruffles on back resemble leaf lettuce. Color extremely variable, generally shades of green [opposite], occasionally blue [below right]. May be marked with yellow and red [below]. Large white spots along side.

ABUNDANCE & DISTRIBUTION: Common Florida, Bahamas, Caribbean.

HABITAT & BEHAVIOR: Inhabit reefs and other areas where they camouflage by blending with various algae, upon which they feed.

Yellow & Red Marked Variety

VISUAL ID: Shades of light green to brown with darker, fine, net-like pattern. Rhinophores and skin flap borders are whitish. Scattered small, pointed skin papillae. Have smooth, thin external shell that is often covered with folds of skin.

ABUNDANCE & DISTRIBUTION: Occasional Florida, Bahamas, Caribbean.

HABITAT & BEHAVIOR: Inhabit bays and other calm water areas, often under docks. Found blending in with Sea Grape Alga, *Caulerpa racemosa*, upon which they feed. Secrete milky white liquid when disturbed.

LETTUCE SEA SLUG
Tridachia crispata
SUBCLASS:
Opisthobranchia
ORDER:
Sea Slugs
Sacoglossa
FAMILY:
Elysiidae

SIZE: 1 - 2 in.,
4 in. max.
DEPTH: 0 - 40 ft.

Blue Variety

RETICULATED SEA SLUG
Oxynoe antillarum
SUBCLASS:
Opisthobranchia
ORDER:
Sea Slugs
Sacoglossa
FAMILY:
Oxynoidae

SIZE: $^1/_2$ - $^3/_4$ in.,
$1^1/_2$ in. max.
DEPTH: 0 - 35 ft.

VISUAL ID: Numerous large, leaf-like cerata on back. Translucent with burgundy and white spots and markings.Cerata often bordered with white.

ABUNDANCE & DISTRIBUTION: Rare Florida, Bahamas, Caribbean.

HABITAT & BEHAVIOR: Found in a variety of habitats where algae is present. Can drop cerata when disturbed.

VISUAL ID: Tentacles transparent to translucent white. Head is opaque white to base of white-tipped rhinophores. Numerous translucent, fringe-like cerata on back; color varies with color of food consumed.

ABUNDANCE & DISTRIBUTION: Rare Florida, Bahamas, Caribbean.

HABITAT & BEHAVIOR: Feed on opisthobranch eggs. Found in varied habitats where eggs are seasonally present. Most striking in coloration after consuming the scarlet eggs of the Caribbean Spanish Dancer.

VISUAL ID: Numerous translucent, fringe-like cerata on back with brown and white markings. Tentacles and rhinophores white-tipped.

ABUNDANCE & DISTRIBUTION: Occasional Florida, Bahamas, Caribbean. Can be abundant in localized areas.

HABITAT & BEHAVIOR: Inhabit rocky intertidal areas.

HARLEQUIN GLASS-SLUG
Cyerce cristallina
SUBCLASS:
Opisthobranchia
ORDER:
Sea Slugs
Sacoglossa
FAMILY:
Caliphyllidae

SIZE: 1 - 1¹/₂ in.,
3 in. max.
DEPTH: 3 - 45 ft.

LONG-EARED NUDIBRANCH
Favorinus auritulus
SUBCLASS:
Opisthobranchia
ORDER:
Nudibranchs
Nudibranchia
FAMILY:
Facelinidae

SIZE: ¹/₄ - ¹/₂ in.,
³/₄ in. max.
DEPTH: 0 - 45 ft.

LYNX NUDIBRANCH
Phidiana lynceus
SUBCLASS:
Opisthobranchia
ORDER:
Nudibranchs
Nudibranchia
FAMILY:
Facelinidae

SIZE: ¹/₂ - ³/₄ in.,
1¹/₄ in. max.
DEPTH: 0 - 8 ft.

VISUAL ID: Numerous fringe-like cerata on back vary from black to gray to white. Body translucent cream to white. Head often flushed with red or orange.

ABUNDANCE & DISTRIBUTION: Occasional Florida, Bahamas, Caribbean. Can be locally abundant.

HABITAT & BEHAVIOR: Inhabit live and dead reef areas around Christmas Tree Hydroids [Pg. 71] upon which they feed. Undischarged stinging nematocysts of prey are engulfed but not digested; instead, they are transported to the cerata for use in their own defense.

VISUAL ID: Numerous fringe-like cerata on back. Color patterns as well as the forms of their bodies vary greatly.

ABUNDANCE & DISTRIBUTION: Uncommon Florida, Bahamas, Caribbean. Also in Brazil.

HABITAT & BEHAVIOR: Varied habitats including mangrove estuaries, areas of reef rubble and living reefs. Feed on wide range of cnidarians including tentacles of Upside-Down Jellyfish [pg. 87] and hydroids. Undischarged stinging nematocysts of prey are engulfed but not digested; instead, they are transported to the cerata for use in their own defense.

NOTE: Positive visual identification is nearly impossible; internal examination is usually required.

VISUAL ID: Numerous fringe-like cerata with white speckles. Most commonly orange, also bluish and gray.

ABUNDANCE & DISTRIBUTION: Occasional Caribbean.

HABITAT & BEHAVIOR: Inhabit living reefs. Feed on sea rods of the genus *Plexaurella*.

NOTE: At publication, this nudibranch has not yet been scientifically described.

CHRISTMAS TREE HYDROID NUDIBRANCH
Learchis poica
SUBCLASS:
Opisthobranchia
ORDER:
Nudibranchs
Nudibranchia
FAMILY:
Facelinidae

SIZE: ³/₄ - 1 in.,
1¹/₄ in. max.
DEPTH: 1 - 60 ft.

FRINGE-BACK NUDIBRANCH
Dondice occidentalis
SUBCLASS:
Opisthobranchia
ORDER:
Nudibranchs
Nudibranchia
FAMILY:
Facelinidae

SIZE: 1 - 1¹/₄ in.,
1³/₄ in. max.
DEPTH: 0 - 100 ft.

WHITE-SPECKLED NUDIBRANCH
Paleo jubatus
SUBCLASS:
Opisthobranchia
ORDER:
Nudibranchs
Nudibranchia
FAMILY:
Facelinidae

SIZE: 1¹/₂ - 2 in.,
2¹/₂ in. max.
DEPTH: 10 - 100 ft.

Nudibranchs

VISUAL ID: Foremost tentacles are very long, about half the length of the body. Along either side of back are tufts of cerata. Shades of brown with white markings.
ABUNDANCE & DISTRIBUTION: Occasional Bahamas, Caribbean.
HABITAT & BEHAVIOR: Inhabit living reefs. Feed on hydroids.
NOTE: At publication, this nudibranch has not yet been scientifically described.

VISUAL ID: Navy blue to deep purple with brilliant yellow-gold stripes and markings. Large crown of feather-like anal gills.
ABUNDANCE & DISTRIBUTION: Occasional to common Florida.
HABITAT & BEHAVIOR: Inhabit reefs, feed upon sponges.

VISUAL ID: Yellow-gold anal gills, purple rhinophores. Yellow-gold body with numerous purple spots. Mantle border of white skin ruffles.
ABUNDANCE & DISTRIBUTION: Rare Caribbean.
HABITAT & BEHAVIOR: Inhabit shallow rocky areas and reefs, feed on sponges.

LONG-HORN NUDIBRANCH

Facelina sp.

SUBCLASS:
Opisthobranchia
ORDER:
Nudibranchs
Nudibranchia
FAMILY:
Facelinidae

SIZE: ³/₄ - 1¹/₄ in.,
1³/₄ in. max.
DEPTH: 30 - 100 ft.

FLORIDA REGAL SEA GODDESS

Hypselodoris edenticulata

SUBCLASS:
Opisthobranchia
ORDER:
Nudibranchs
Nudibranchia
FAMILY:
Chromodoridae

SIZE: 1¹/₂ - 2¹/₂ in.,
4³/₄ in. max.
DEPTH: 20 - 130 ft.

GOLD-CROWNED SEA GODDESS

Hypselodoris acriba

SUBCLASS:
Opisthobranchia
ORDER:
Nudibranchs
Nudibranchia
FAMILY:
Chromodoridae

SIZE: 1¹/₄ - 1³/₄ in.,
2¹/₂ in. max.
DEPTH: 10 - 35 ft.

VISUAL ID: Thin gold lines down black back, whitish mantle border with gold line trim. Occasional blue spots on back.

ABUNDANCE & DISTRIBUTION: Occasional Caribbean; rare Bahamas.

HABITAT & BEHAVIOR: Inhabit living reefs, prefer areas of moderate current. Feed on Blue Sponge, *Dysidea janiae.*

VISUAL ID: Black spots on white mantle border. Yellow-gold stripes on back and sides.

ABUNDANCE & DISTRIBUTION: Uncommon, known only from South Florida. Most numerous in Miami's Biscayne Bay.

HABITAT & BEHAVIOR: Live in association with sponges of the genus *Dysidea* .

VISUAL ID: Purple spots scattered over brown back and sides, white mantle border.

ABUNDANCE & DISTRIBUTION: Uncommon, known only from Jamaica, Cayman Islands, Belize and Bay Islands.

HABITAT & BEHAVIOR: Inhabit reef in areas where algae overgrows dead corals, especially branches of Staghorn Coral, *Acropora cervicornis.*

NOTE: This species and another similar appearing species found in the Caribbean have yet to be described.

GOLD-LINE SEA GODDESS

Hypselodoris ruthae

SUBCLASS:
Opisthobranchia
ORDER:
Nudibranchs
Nudibranchia
FAMILY:
Chromodoridae

SIZE: ³/₄ - 1 in.,
1¹/₂ in. max.
DEPTH: 1 - 65 ft.

BLACK-SPOTTED SEA GODDESS

Hypselodoris bayeri

SUBCLASS:
Opisthobranchia
ORDER:
Nudibranchs
Nudibranchia
FAMILY:
Chromodoridae

SIZE: 1 - 1¹/₂ in.,
2 in. max.
DEPTH: 1 - 50 ft.

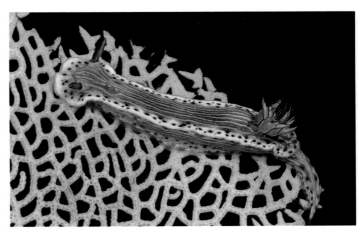

PURPLE-SPOTTED SEA GODDESS

Hypselodoris sp.

SUBCLASS:
Opisthobranchia
ORDER:
Nudibranchs
Nudibranchia
FAMILY:
Chromodoridae

SIZE: 1 - 1¹/₂ in.,
2 in. max.
DEPTH: 12 - 45 ft.

VISUAL ID: Purple anal gills and rhinophores. White with black markings on back, yellow mantle border.
ABUNDANCE & DISTRIBUTION: Uncommon Florida Keys, Bahamas, Caribbean.
HABITAT & BEHAVIOR: Inhabit living reefs. Feed on sponges.

VISUAL ID: Blue with red mantle border.
ABUNDANCE & DISTRIBUTION: Uncommon Florida, Bahamas.
HABITAT & BEHAVIOR: Prefer areas of moderate current. Found on sponges of the genus *Dysidea*, sometimes in large numbers.

VISUAL ID: Reddish-brown, white mantle border with gold stripe around edge.
ABUNDANCE & DISTRIBUTION: Rare Caribbean.
HABITAT & BEHAVIOR: Hide under coral slabs in calm, protected areas.

PURPLE-CROWNED SEA GODDESS
Chromodoris kempfi
SUBCLASS:
Opisthobranchia
ORDER:
Nudibranchs
Nudibranchia
FAMILY:
Chromodoridae

SIZE: $^1/_2$ - $^3/_4$ in.,
1 in. max.
DEPTH: 25 - 75 ft.

RED-LINE BLUE SEA GODDESS
Chromodoris nyalya
SUBCLASS:
Opisthobranchia
ORDER:
Nudibranchs
Nudibranchia
FAMILY:
Chromodoridae

SIZE: $^1/_2$ - $^3/_4$ in.,
$1^1/_2$ in. max.
DEPTH: 6 - 30 ft.

BROWN SEA GODDESS
Chromodoris grahami
SUBCLASS:
Opisthobranchia
ORDER:
Nudibranchs
Nudibranchia
FAMILY:
Chromodoridae

SIZE: $^3/_4$ - 1 in.,
$1^1/_2$ in. max.
DEPTH: 1 - 10 ft.

VISUAL ID: Back reddish-brown with two white blotches between rhinophores and anal gills, white mantle border. Numerous, scattered bluish spots of different sizes. Overall pattern of colored areas and spots extremely variable.

ABUNDANCE & DISTRIBUTION: Occasional Florida, Bahamas, Caribbean.

HABITAT & BEHAVIOR: Hide under coral slabs and rubble in calm, protected rocky and sandy areas.

VISUAL ID: Rhinophores and anal gills tipped with red. White body, red mantle border with yellow edge.

ABUNDANCE & DISTRIBUTION: Uncommon, known only from South Florida and northeastern Bahamas. Most numerous in Miami's Biscayne Bay. Also in eastern tropical and subtropical Pacific.

HABITAT & BEHAVIOR: Inhabit reefs and rocky areas. Feed on sponges.

NOTE: This nudibranch probably became established in South Florida by passing through the Panama Canal on a ship bottom or in a ballast tank.

VISUAL ID: Cream to tan, covered with reddish-brown spots and blotches.

ABUNDANCE & DISTRIBUTION: Occasional Florida, Bahamas, Caribbean.

HABITAT & BEHAVIOR: Hide under coral slabs in live reef areas. If disturbed can swim with an undulating head-to-tail motion.

HARLEQUIN BLUE SEA GODDESS
Chromodoris clenchi
SUBCLASS:
Opisthobranchia
ORDER:
Nudibranchs
Nudibranchia
FAMILY:
Chromodoridae

SIZE: ³/₄ - 1 in.,
1¹/₂ in. max.
DEPTH: 1 - 14 ft.

RED-TIPPED SEA GODDESS
Glossodoris sedna
SUBCLASS:
Opisthobranchia
ORDER:
Nudibranchs
Nudibranchia
FAMILY:
Chromodoridae

SIZE: 1 - 1³/₄ in.,
3 in. max.
DEPTH: 10 - 50 ft.

BROWN-SPECKLED DORIS
Aphelodoris antillensis
SUBCLASS:
Opisthobranchia
ORDER:
Nudibranchs
Nudibranchia
FAMILY:
Asteronitidae

SIZE: ¹/₂ - 1 in.,
1¹/₄ in. max.
DEPTH: 6 - 12 ft.

VISUAL ID: Distinctive dome shape. Patterns and color variable, ranging from white [below] to orange [below right] to black [opposite]. Vein-like markings usually in mantle border. Soft and slimy to the touch.

ABUNDANCE & DISTRIBUTION: Occasional Florida, Bahamas, Caribbean.

HABITAT & BEHAVIOR: Hide under coral slabs in shallow water habitats. Feed on sponges.

White Variety

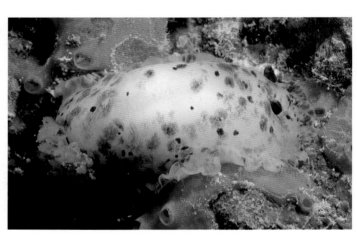

VISUAL ID: Color variable, cream or beige with dark brown spots to almost solid dark brown.

ABUNDANCE & DISTRIBUTION: Occasional Florida, Bahamas, Caribbean.

HABITAT & BEHAVIOR: Hide under coral slabs in many habitats, usually shallow, but occasionally to 100 feet. Small individuals can swim with undulating head-to-tail motion. Large individuals shed pieces of mantle when disturbed.

SLIMY DORIS
Dendrodoris krebsii
SUBCLASS:
Opisthobranchia
ORDER:
Nudibranchs
Nudibranchia
FAMILY:
Dendrodorididae

SIZE: 1¹/₂ - 2¹/₂ in.,
6 in. max.
DEPTH: 3 - 15 ft.

Orange Variety

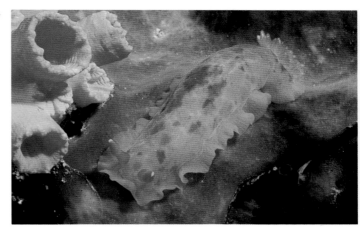

BROWN DORIS
Discodoris evelinae
SUBCLASS:
Opisthobranchia
ORDER:
Nudibranchs
Nudibranchia
FAMILY:
Discodorididae

SIZE: 1¹/₄ - 1³/₄ in.,
4 in. max.
DEPTH: 12 - 30 ft.

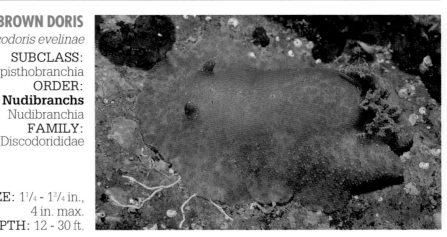

Nudibranchs

VISUAL ID: Red to orange to yellow, speckled with white.
ABUNDANCE & DISTRIBUTION: Occasional Bahamas, Caribbean.
HABITAT & BEHAVIOR: Inhabit living reefs. Feed on red sponges.

VISUAL ID: White body with black spots of varying size. Numerous, short cerata.
ABUNDANCE & DISTRIBUTION: Uncommon Florida, Bahamas, Caribbean, West Africa.
HABITAT & BEHAVIOR: Inhabit living reefs.

VISUAL ID: Mottled, varies from almost totally white to orange, red and dark purple. When disturbed, rolls out mantle border skin-folds to reveal bright red band.
ABUNDANCE & DISTRIBUTION: Uncommon Caribbean.
HABITAT & BEHAVIOR: Inhabit living reefs. When disturbed, can swim with undulating movement of mantle border skin-folds.
NOTE: Closely related to the Spanish Dancer, *H.sanguineus*, found in the Indo-Pacific.

LEATHER-BACKED DORIS

Platydoris angustipes

SUBCLASS:
Opisthobranchia
ORDER:
Nudibranchs
Nudibranchia
FAMILY:
Platydorididae

SIZE: 1 - 2 in.,
4¹/₂ in. max.
DEPTH: 0 - 35 ft.

BLACK-SPOTTED NUDIBRANCH

Phyllidiopsis papilligera

SUBCLASS:
Opisthobranchia
ORDER:
Nudibranchs
Nudibranchia
FAMILY:
Phyllidiidae

SIZE: 1 - 2 in.,
4¹/₂ in. max.
DEPTH: 50 - 100 ft.

CARIBBEAN SPANISH DANCER

Hexabranchus morsomus

SUBCLASS:
Opisthobranchia
ORDER:
Nudibranchs
Nudibranchia
FAMILY:
Hexabranchidae

SIZE: 2 - 3 in.,
4³/₄ in. max.
DEPTH: 20 - 100 ft.

VISUAL ID: Two or more paired, large, flattened cerata on each side. Rhinophores large and paddle-like. Translucent, light olive-brown to orangish-brown.

ABUNDANCE & DISTRIBUTION: Seasonally common Florida, Bahamas.

HABITAT & BEHAVIOR: Inhabit floats of Sargasso weed. Feed on hydroids that grow on Sargasso branches.

VISUAL ID: Rows of light brown cerata down each side, covered with clusters of whitish hemispherical bumps. Dark brown body.

ABUNDANCE & DISTRIBUTION: Occasional Florida, Bahamas, Caribbean. Also in Brazil.

HABITAT & BEHAVIOR: Live in association with hydroids of the genus *Dentitheca* [pg. 73] upon which they feed. Color and size make them difficult to spot, presence is often given away by more obvious creamy yellow spiral egg case deposited on hydroid branches.

VISUAL ID: Tips of cerata highly branched. Varies from red to orange to yellow with darker net pattern, occasionally spotted with white.

ABUNDANCE & DISTRIBUTION: Occasional Caribbean.

HABITAT & BEHAVIOR: Inhabit areas of moderate current with reef rubble bottoms that are populated by hydroids, upon which they feed.

SARGASSUM NUDIBRANCH

Scyllaea pelagica

SUBCLASS:
Opisthobranchia
ORDER:
Nudibranchs
Nudibranchia
FAMILY:
Scyllaeidae

SIZE: $^1/_2$ - $^3/_4$ in.,
2 in. max.
DEPTH: 0 - 2 ft.

GRAPE-CLUSTER NUDIBRANCH

Doto uva

SUBCLASS:
Opisthobranchia
ORDER:
Nudibranchs
Nudibranchia
FAMILY:
Dotoidae

SIZE: $^1/_4$ - $^1/_2$ in. max.
DEPTH: 15 - 60 ft.

TASSELED NUDIBRANCH

Bornella calcarata

SUBCLASS:
Opisthobranchia
ORDER:
Nudibranchs
Nudibranchia
FAMILY:
Bornellidae

SIZE: $^3/_4$ - $1^1/_2$ in.,
$4^3/_4$ in. max.
DEPTH: 30 - 120 ft.

VISUAL ID: Cerata highly branched. Varies from grayish white to orange (note colors of three individuals in picture).

ABUNDANCE & DISTRIBUTION: Uncommon Florida, Bahamas, Caribbean. Can be locally common.

HABITAT & BEHAVIOR: Inhabit living reefs. Feed on sea rod gorgonians of the genus *Plexaurella*, commonly found under colonies that have fallen over.

VISUAL ID: Numerous scattered spines, to two inches in length, cover surface. Color varies, including white, yellow, orange, red and purple. Mantle patterned in brown, gold and white [below right].

ABUNDANCE & DISTRIBUTION: Common Florida, Bahamas, Caribbean.

HABITAT & BEHAVIOR: Inhabit reefs, often attach under ledge overhangs. Well camouflaged, often overgrown by a variety of organisms [below right].

REACTION TO DIVERS: Snap valves shut when approached. With slow, patient approach, valves may remain open, allowing close observation of mantle.

TUFTED NUDIBRANCH
Tritoniopsis frydis
SUBCLASS:
Opisthobranchia
ORDER:
Nudibranchs
Nudibranchia
FAMILY:
Tritoniidae

SIZE: ¹/₂ - 1¹/₄ in.,
1³/₄ in. max.
DEPTH: 30 - 120 ft.

ATLANTIC THORNY-OYSTER
Spondylus americanus
CLASS:
Oysters
Bivalvia

SIZE: 3 - 4 in.,
5¹/₂ in. max.
DEPTH: 50 - 130 ft.

**Open Valves
With Exposed Mantle**

Fileclams

VISUAL ID: Brilliant red to orange-red mantle. Tentacles often reddish-orange [right], especially in shallow water and white [below right] in deeper water. Whitish to brownish valves sculptured with many fine, radiating ribs.

ABUNDANCE & DISTRIBUTION: Common Florida, Bahamas, Caribbean.

HABITAT & BEHAVIOR: Inhabit narrow cracks, crevices and recesses. Valves usually hidden with only mantle and tentacles exposed. Often attach to substrate by byssal threads. Can swim with jerky movements by repeatedly snapping valves open and shut.

REACTION TO DIVERS: Snap valves shut and retreat into recesses if threatened.

VISUAL ID: White to lavender mantle and tentacles. White to tan valves deeply sculptured with many radiating, sharply spined ribs.

ABUNDANCE & DISTRIBUTION: Common Florida, Bahamas, Caribbean.

HABITAT & BEHAVIOR: Hide under stones in shallow water. Can swim with jerky movements by repeatedly snapping valves open and shut.

REACTION TO DIVERS: Snap valves shut and retreat into dark, protected areas if threatened.

ROUGH FILECLAM
Lima scabra
CLASS:
Fileclams
Bivalvia
FAMILY:
Limidae

SIZE: 2 - 3¹/₂ in.
DEPTH: 3 - 130 ft.

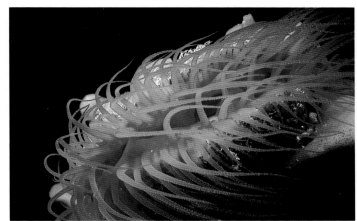

White Tentacles

SPINY FILECLAM
Lima lima
CLASS:
Fileclams
Bivalvia
FAMILY:
Limidae

SIZE: 2 - 3¹/₂ in.
DEPTH: 3 - 25 ft.

VISUAL ID: Numerous raised rings encircle white to pinkish tentacles; mantle red, orange or occasionally white. White valves of unequal size are sculptured with small, uneven, radiating ribs.

ABUNDANCE & DISTRIBUTION: Occasional Florida, Bahamas, Caribbean.

HABITAT & BEHAVIOR: Inhabit shallow waters, often under rocks. Can swim with jerky movements by repeatedly snapping valves open and shut.

REACTION TO DIVERS: Snap valves shut and retreat to dark, protected areas if threatened.

VISUAL ID: Irregular rows of short, scaly spines project from around outer border of valves. Valves flattish and sculptured with concentric growth plates radiating from the hinge. Small wings at end of hinge. Shades of brown, often mottled.

ABUNDANCE & DISTRIBUTION: Common South Florida, Bahamas, Caribbean.

HABITAT & BEHAVIOR: Attach to rocks, wrecks and, occasionally, sea fans. Well camouflaged, often overgrown by a variety of organisms.

REACTION TO DIVERS: Snap shut when approached. This movement often attracts attention to oyster.

NOTE: Member of famous pearl-oyster family. Occasionally produce small pearls, rarely of value from Florida waters, occasionally of value from southern Caribbean. Interiors are covered with lustrous mother-of-pearl.

VISUAL ID: Long, wing-like structure extends along valve hinge. Dark brown to black.

ABUNDANCE & DISTRIBUTION: Common Florida, Bahamas, Caribbean.

HABITAT & BEHAVIOR: Attach to stalks of gorgonians, most commonly sea plumes. Well camouflaged, often overgrown by a variety of organisms (note two individuals are in picture).

ANTILLEAN FILECLAM
Lima pellucida
CLASS:
Fileclams
Bivalvia
FAMILY:
Limidae

SIZE: ³/₄ - 1 in.
DEPTH: 5 - 25 ft.

ATLANTIC PEARL-OYSTER
Pinctada radiata
CLASS:
Oysters
Bivalvia
FAMILY:
Pteriidae

SIZE: 2 - 3 in.
DEPTH: 6 - 65 ft.

ATLANTIC WING-OYSTER
Pteria colymbus
CLASS:
Oysters
Bivalvia
FAMILY:
Pteriidae

SIZE: 2 - 3 in.
DEPTH: 10 - 100 ft.

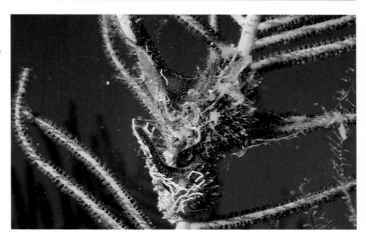

VISUAL ID: Fan-shaped valves with eight to ten heavy ribs, some lined with short knobs. White-speckled tentacles are translucent to reddish.

ABUNDANCE & DISTRIBUTION: Occasional Florida, Bahamas, Caribbean.

HABITAT & BEHAVIOR: Hide under rocks and in recesses. Often attach to substrate by byssal threads. Can swim with jerky movements by repeatedly snapping valves open and shut.

REACTION TO DIVERS: Snap valves shut and retreat into recesses if threatened.

VISUAL ID: Valves interlock in zig-zag pattern.

ABUNDANCE & DISTRIBUTION: Common Florida, Bahamas, Caribbean.

HABITAT & BEHAVIOR: Attach to gorgonians, dead corals and substrate. Well camouflaged, often overgrown by a variety of organisms, especially encrusting sponge [pictured], hydroids and algae.

REACTION TO DIVERS: Close valves when disturbed.

NOTE: Formerly classified as *Lopha frons*.

VISUAL ID: Valve opening is long, irregular and often twisted. Yellowish, with a few light radial rays.

ABUNDANCE & DISTRIBUTION: Common to occasional Florida, Bahamas, Caribbean.

HABITAT & BEHAVIOR: Attach to rocks, under ledge overhangs, wrecks and other substrata. Prefer habitats with high sedimentation. Hundreds of individuals often encrust a large area. Usually covered with sediment, other debris and encrusting sponge.

SIMILAR SPECIES: Bicolor Purse-Oyster, *I. bicolor*, heavy, irregular growth plates form concentric pattern; most commonly attach to rocks in tidal areas, occasionally found on shallow reefs.

KNOBBY SCALLOP

Chlamys imbricata

CLASS:
Scallops
Bivalvia
FAMILY:
Pectinidae

SIZE: 1 - 1³/₄ in.
DEPTH: 10 - 25 ft.

FROND OYSTER

Dendostrea frons

CLASS:
Oysters
Bivalvia
FAMILY:
Ostreidae

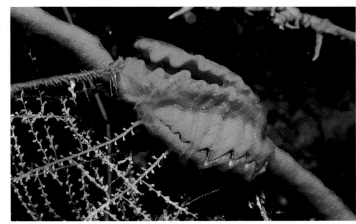

SIZE: 1¹/₂ - 2¹/₂ in.
DEPTH: 20 - 130 ft.

LISTER PURSE-OYSTER

Isognomon radiatus

CLASS:
Oysters
Bivalvia
FAMILY:
Isognomonidae

SIZE: 1 - 2¹/₂ in.
DEPTH: 10 - 60 ft.

VISUAL ID: Flat and thin with smooth, rounded valve openings. Interior stained with brown, purple or black.

ABUNDANCE & DISTRIBUTION: Common to occasional Florida, Bahamas, Caribbean.

HABITAT & BEHAVIOR: Grow in clusters on mangrove roots, dock pilings, ship-wrecks and rocks. Prefer areas with high sedimentation. Usually covered with encrusting sponge and sediment. Occasionally on reefs; may attach to gorgonians.

NOTE: Also commonly known as "Mangrove Oyster."

VISUAL ID: Thin, fan-shaped valves. Amber to gray, somewhat translucent. Rows of short projections radiate from base.

ABUNDANCE & DISTRIBUTION: Common Caribbean, occasional Bahamas, rare Florida.

HABITAT & BEHAVIOR: Wide variety of habitats. Bury in mud or sand, or inhabit narrow openings in reefs, with valves only slightly exposed.

REACTION TO DIVERS: Close when disturbed.

VISUAL ID: Smooth, highly polished valves vary in color and pattern. Most commonly white with a yellowish tint and rays of pink. May have concentric markings of yellow, pink or lavender, with or without rays, or may be one solid color. Slight incurve of valves' central lips are distinctive.

ABUNDANCE & DISTRIBUTION: Common Caribbean, rare Florida, Bahamas.

HABITAT & BEHAVIOR: Inhabit shallow sand flats, where they bury beneath the surface. Valves of non-living specimens are often found in great numbers.

FLAT TREE-OYSTER
Isognomon alatus
CLASS:
Oysters
Bivalvia
FAMILY:
Isognomonidae

SIZE: 1 - 3 in.
DEPTH: 0 - 40 ft.

AMBER PENSHELL
Pinna carnea
CLASS:
Penshells
Bivalvia
FAMILY:
Pinnidae

SIZE: 4 - 6 in.,
10 in. max.
DEPTH: 6 - 50 ft.

SUNRISE TELLIN
Tellina radiata
CLASS:
Tellins
Bivalvia
FAMILY:
Tellinidae

SIZE: 1$\frac{1}{2}$ - 2$\frac{1}{2}$ in.,
3 in. max.
DEPTH: 0 - 25 ft.

VISUAL ID: Girdle is gray with bands of black, and covered with short, coarse, hair-like spines. Plates are brown when not eroded or encrusted.

ABUNDANCE & DISTRIBUTION: Abundant Caribbean.

HABITAT & BEHAVIOR: Inhabit rocky shorelines; attach to rocks and solid substrate.

NOTE: Often used by natives as bait, and on some islands as food.

VISUAL ID: Girdle is marbled in bluish-gray, covered with round scales. Plates gray, often with tints or markings of green and olive. Elongated oval shape.

ABUNDANCE & DISTRIBUTION: Common to uncommon Caribbean, except off coast of Central America. This and two similar species are visually indistinguishable, positive identification requires microscopic examination. However, they can often be identified by their distribution.

HABITAT & BEHAVIOR: Inhabit rocky shorelines and reefs. Attach to rocks and solid substrata.

SIMILAR SPECIES: Florida Slender Chiton, *S. floridana,* Florida and Central American Coast to Panama. Slender Chiton, *S. bahamensis,* only member of genus in Bahamas, also in Florida Keys and Yucatan to Honduras.

VISUAL ID: Girdle is crimson to greenish yellow to orange, with lighter spots and occasional bands, and is textured like granular sugar. Plates are ornately sculptured and patterned in gray, greenish-brown and, often, crimson.

ABUNDANCE & DISTRIBUTION: Uncommon Florida, Bahamas, Caribbean.

HABITAT & BEHAVIOR: Inhabit shallow, rocky inshore areas and reefs. Attach to rocks and solid substrate.

FUZZY CHITON
Acanthopleura granulata
CLASS:
Chitons
Amphineura

SIZE: 1¹/₂ - 3¹/₂ in.
DEPTH: Intertidal

CARIBBEAN SLENDER CHITON
Stenoplax purpurascens
CLASS:
Chitons
Amphineura

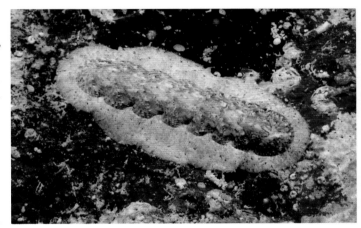

SIZE: 1 - 2 in.
DEPTH: 0 - 20 ft.

ORNATE CHITON
Tonicia schrammi
CLASS:
Chitons
Amphineura

SIZE: ¹/₂ - ³/₄ in.
DEPTH: 10 - 45 ft.

VISUAL ID: Entire length of oblong body is bordered by a thin fin which forms a point at the rear. Color varies: during day often shades of gray with white spots on back; at night, generally mottled and spotted in shades of white, brown, green and lavender, may be iridescent. Arms are shorter than body.

ABUNDANCE & DISTRIBUTION: Common South Florida, Bahamas, Caribbean.

HABITAT & BEHAVIOR: Inhabit shallow waters, often swim over reefs and turtle grass beds.

REACTION TO DIVERS: Wary; generally retreat slowly, but will jet away rapidly if chased. May allow close approach with slow, non-threatening movements.

NOTE: This is the only squid commonly encountered over Caribbean reefs.

VISUAL ID: Triangular-shaped fins extend from rear half of body. Adult males can be distinguished by red, flame-like markings on side of body. Juveniles [pictured] have short arms and tentacles of about equal length, large eyes and elongated body.

ABUNDANCE & DISTRIBUTION: Common Florida, Bahamas, Caribbean.

HABITAT & BEHAVIOR: An inshore, open-water species, rarely found over reefs. Egg clusters attach to reefs. After hatching, young may remain around reefs for a few weeks or months.

NOTE: This identification is probable, but cannot be confirmed without a specimen. The fin's shape, location and body length confirm that it is an arrow squid, Family Loliginidae. The juveniles of several squid species (less than 4 inches in total length) may be observed over a reef and adjacent areas. Their color patterns are not distinctive, making juveniles difficult to distinguish from pictures alone.

VISUAL ID: A blue ring creates a false eye marking, called an ocellus, below the true eye. Skin texture forms a reticulated pattern of patches and thin grooves. Color extremely variable, often mottled. Eggs small, less than $1/4$ inch.

ABUNDANCE & DISTRIBUTION: Occasional Florida, Bahamas, Caribbean. Very common Haiti.

HABITAT & BEHAVIOR: Inhabit shallow coral reefs.

NOTE: This species was formerlly known as *Octopus hummelinki.*

SIMILAR SPECIES: Mexican Four-Eyed Octopus, *O. maya*, distinguished by false eye that does not have a blue ring. Distribution restricted to southern Gulf of Mexico, including Isla Mujeres off northeastern Yucatan.

CARIBBEAN REEF SQUID

Sepioteuthis sepioidea

CLASS:
Cephalopoda
SUBORDER:
Squid
Teuthoidea

SIZE: 6 - 12 in.
DEPTH: 0 - 60 ft.

INSHORE ARROW SQUID
Juvenile

Doryteuthis plei

CLASS:
Cephalopoda
SUBORDER:
Squid
Teuthoidea

SIZE: 8 - 18 in.
DEPTH: 0 - 130 ft.

CARIBBEAN TWO-SPOT OCTOPUS

Octopus filosus

CLASS:
Cephalopoda
ORDER:
Octopuses
Octopoda

SIZE: 8 - 10 in.
DEPTH: 15 - 35 ft.

VISUAL ID: Red to orangish-brown, coloration relatively uniform, rarely mottled. Small size helps distinguish this octopus. Skin texture is smooth. Eggs are small, less than ¼ inch and number up to 2,000.

ABUNDANCE & DISTRIBUTION: Rare Florida, Bahamas, Caribbean.

HABITAT & BEHAVIOR: Inhabit sand or mud bottoms and areas adjacent to reefs. Often reside in empty shells and bottles.

SIMILAR SPECIES: There is a common, yet undescribed and easily confused species in South and Gulf Coast Florida, along the Central American coast to Venezuela. Inhabit shallow grass beds. Can be distinguished by its dark brown to brownish-gray color. The egg size of brooding females that measure up to ½ inch are distinctive from the eggs of *O. joubini* eggs that are less than ¼ inch.

VISUAL ID: Frequently display pale to intense iridescent blue-green cast, often with brown mottling. Dark ring around eye is generally evident [below], no dark edges around suckers (compare with similar Common Octopus [next]). Skin relatively smooth with small, scattered wart-like skin papillae. Arms 4-6 times body length. Eggs large, up to ⅝ inch long, and usually number less than 1000.

ABUNDANCE & DISTRIBUTION: Common Florida, Bahamas, Caribbean.

HABITAT & BEHAVIOR: Inhabit coral reefs, reside in recesses or sponges. Most common octopus found in the open on reefs at night, never out in daytime. Often spread bodies in distinctive parachute pattern to attack and engulf prey [note juvenile below right].

ATLANTIC PYGMY OCTOPUS

Octopus joubini

CLASS:
Octopuses
Cephalopoda
ORDER:
Octopoda

SIZE: 2 - 4 in.,
6 in. max.
DEPTH: 3 - 35 ft.

CARIBBEAN REEF OCTOPUS

Octopus briareus

CLASS:
Octopuses
Cephalopoda
ORDER:
Octopoda

SIZE: 12 - 20 in.
DEPTH: 15 - 75 ft.

Juvenile

VISUAL ID: Edges of suckers dark, no dark ring around eye (compare with similar Caribbean Reef Octopus [previous]). Skin texture is a reticulated pattern of patches and thin grooves. Color and patterns highly variable, often mottled reddish-brown with frontal white spots. Arms 3 - 4 times body length. Eggs very small, less than $\frac{1}{8}$ inch and numbering over 100,000.

ABUNDANCE & DISTRIBUTION: Occasional Florida, Bahamas, Caribbean.

HABITAT & BEHAVIOR: Inhabit sea grass beds, areas of sand and rubble, and coral reefs. Reside in holes in hard substrata. Area around hole littered with shells and debris. This is the only octopus commonly found in the open on reefs during the day.

VISUAL ID: Numerous white oval spots, on brick red or bright red to brownish-gray background. Usually display large, wart-like skin papillae on mantle. Arms 4-6 times body length. Eggs small, less than $\frac{1}{8}$ inch.

ABUNDANCE & DISTRIBUTION: Uncommon Florida, Bahamas, Caribbean. Also circum-tropical and sub-tropical.

HABITAT & BEHAVIOR: Inhabit sand flats and rubble areas adjacent to reefs. Forage along reef edge for shrimp and crabs. When threatened turn bright red and display bold white spots.

VISUAL ID: A dark stripe running down each arm is usually visible. White frontal spots and white streak on mantle. Skin texture forms a reticulated pattern of patches in thin grooves. Color and patterns variable, often mottled reddish-brown to brownish-gray. May display wart-like skin papillae on mantle. Eggs small, less than $\frac{1}{8}$ inch, are carried by female in her arms.

ABUNDANCE & DISTRIBUTION: Rare Florida, Bahamas, Caribbean.

HABITAT & BEHAVIOR: Inhabit sea grass beds, muddy bottoms and sand flats adjacent to reefs. Forage in open for crustaceans. Can rapidly bury themselves by diving into mud or sand.

COMMON OCTOPUS
Octopus vulgaris
CLASS:
Cephalopoda
ORDER:
Octopuses
Octopoda

SIZE: 15 - 28 in.,
3 ft. max.
DEPTH: 15 - 75 ft.

WHITE SPOTTED OCTOPUS
Octopus macropus
CLASS:
Cephalopoda
ORDER:
Octopuses
Octopoda

SIZE: 12 - 20 in.
DEPTH: 15 - 75 ft.

BROWNSTRIPE OCTOPUS
Octopus burryi
CLASS:
Cephalopoda
ORDER:
Octopuses
Octopoda

SIZE: 6 - 12 in.
DEPTH: 15 - 75 ft.

Phylum Echinodermata

(Ee-KINE-oh-DER-ma-tuh / Gr. spiny skin)

Sea Stars, Sea Urchins & Sea Cucumbers

All echinoderms are marine and have a hard, internal skeleton composed of small calcareous plates called ossicles. Often, the ossicles have projections that give the body surface a spiny appearance. Members of the phylum have five body sections of equal size that are arranged around a central axis. Most have hundreds of small tube feet, called podia, that work in unison, either to move the animal over the bottom, or to capture food.

FEATHER STARS

Class Crinoidea (Cry-noy-DEE-uh / L. a lily)

Feather stars, also known as crinoids, are the most ancient of echinoderms. These animals have changed little according to fossil records, and are sometimes referred to as "living fossils." They have small, flattened pentagon-shaped bodies with five **arms** that immediately fork one or more times, giving them a total of ten or more long arms in multiples of five. Numerous short appendages extend along both sides of each arm creating a structure that resembles a feather. Skeletal ossicles give the arms a jointed appearance. Arms are used to sweep the water for particles of food. They adhere tightly, like Velcro, to anything that comes into contact with them and break easily. Fortunately, broken arms can be regenerated. Some crinoids can move short distances by swimming with coordinated arm movements, but most walk on jointed legs called cirri. Some species anchor inside narrow crevices with only their arms visible; others position themselves high atop coral heads and other reef structures.

SEA STARS

Class Asteroidea (Ass-ter-OY-dee-uh / Gr. star form)

Asteroids have long been known as starfish, but a more modern and appropriate common name is sea stars. They usually have **five arms**, although a few species have more. The arms are triangular, merging at the base into the central disc. Broken arms can be regenerated, and in some species a new animal can form from a severed member. The mouth is located centrally on the undersurface, with anus on the top. Two or four rows of podia, tipped with suction discs, extend from the mouth down each arm. They are used both for movement and capturing prey. Some sea stars can evert their stomachs through their mouths to envelop and consume prey.

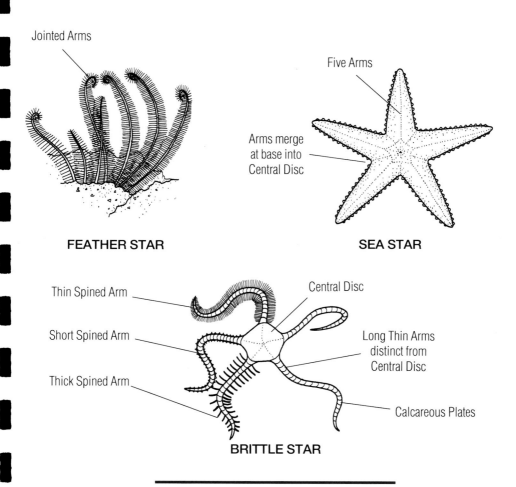

Jointed Arms

FEATHER STAR

Five Arms

Arms merge at base into Central Disc

SEA STAR

Thin Spined Arm

Short Spined Arm

Thick Spined Arm

Central Disc

Long Thin Arms distinct from Central Disc

Calcareous Plates

BRITTLE STAR

BRITTLE & BASKET STARS

Class Ophiuroidea (Oh-fee-ER-OY-dee-uh / Gr. serpent tail in appearance)

Both orders in this class have long, thin arms that, unlike sea stars, do not widen as they approach the central disc. The central disc is a flattened, smooth and somewhat rounded pentagon. The mouth, centrally located on the underside, opens into the stomach; there is no intestine or anus.

Brittle stars, Order Ophiurae, have a small **central disc** that rarely exceeds one inch in diameter, and five arms with numerous **spines** arranged in rows. The spines of different species can be distinct: they can be short or long, thin or thick, pointed or blunt. The tops of the arms are lined with large **calcareous plates** that allow only lateral movement. This armor results in arms that break off easily, giving rise to the common name. Severed arms, however, can be regenerated. In spite of their brittleness and restricted mobility, the arms allow the animal to move more rapidly than other members of the phylum. During the day brittle stars are occasionally seen clinging to sponges and gorgonian, but they generally hide under rocks and inside crevices, waiting for night before moving into the open to feed.

Basket stars, Order Euryalae, have five arms that repeatedly subdivide into numerous branches, resembling coiling tentacles. Unlike brittle stars, basket stars lack heavy arm shields and therefore can move their arms in all directions. During the day, the animals commonly cling to gorgonians, curling their network of arms into a tight ball. At night, they climb to the tops of gorgonians or other reef outcroppings, and spread their arms into the current to form a plankton net. Tiny, fine spines and tube feet work to transfer captured food to the mouth.

BASKET STAR

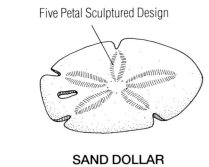

Anus

Spine

Mouth

SEA URCHIN

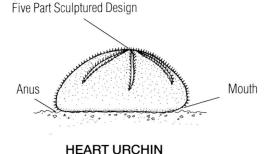

Five Part Sculptured Design

Anus

Mouth

HEART URCHIN

Five Petal Sculptured Design

SAND DOLLAR

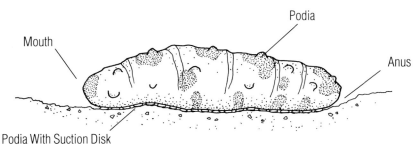

Podia

Mouth

Anus

Podia With Suction Disk

SEA CUCUMBER

SEA URCHINS, HEART URCHINS, SAND DOLLARS & SEA BISCUITS

Class Echinoidea (Eck-ih-NOY-dee-uh / L. spiny)

A skeleton of ten fused calcareous plates, covered with numerous spines, encases the body of echinoids. They are characterized into two basic groups, regular and irregular.

Sea urchins, regular echinoids, typically have spherical bodies with long protective **spines** and tube feet. The **mouth** is centrally located on the underside and the **anus** on the top. The mouth is a complicated arrangement of five teeth, called Aristotle's Lantern, used for scraping algae and other organic food from rocks. The spines of some species are long, sharp and needle-like, while others are stubby and blunt. Long, pointed spines easily puncture the skin, and are difficult to remove because the shaft is covered with recurved spinelets that function as miniature fish hooks. This causes a rather painful wound which should be treated to prevent infection.

Heart urchins, Order Spatangoida, are irregular echinoids. Their bodies are non-spherical, shaped more like an oval dome. The **mouth**, which lacks Aristotle's Lantern, is in front, the **anus** at the rear. On top is a distinct **five-part sculptured design.** The body is covered with short, tightly packed spines well-adapted for burrowing; tube feet are degenerate or absent. They spend most of their lives buried in sand or mud where they feed on organic material. Although common, heart urchins are seldom seen. If the animal is spotted in the open at all, it is usually at night. Skeletal remains are occasionally found on the sand.

Sand dollars and sea biscuits, Order Clypeasteroida, are also irregular echinoids. Their bodies are disc-shaped, with a **five-petal sculptured design** on the back. The mouth, which has an Aristotle's Lantern, is centered on the underside, with the anus toward the rear. The very short, compacted spines that cover the body appear as fuzz, and are well adapted for burrowing. Like heart urchins, they live under the sand and are rarely sighted in the open. Their skeletal remains, rather than the living animals, are usually found.

SEA CUCUMBERS

Class Holothuroidea (Hoe-low-ther-OY-dee-uh / Gr. plant-like in appearance)

Sea cucumbers have sausage-shaped bodies, with a **mouth** in front and **anus** at the rear. The five body-sections common to all echinoderms are not visible in these animals, but are part of their internal structure. They also have no external spines or arms, and the skeletal plates are reduced to microscopic size and buried in the leathery body wall. The shape of these hidden plates is the key to scientific classification, and thus many species cannot be positively identified underwater. **Podia** on the underside are tipped with suction discs; those on the back have been modified into a variety of shapes and sizes. These are often the visual clue to underwater identification. Sea cucumbers are usually sighted slowly crawling across sand or reef, scooping up organic debris.

Feather Stars

VISUAL ID: Twenty arms, most commonly orange, occasionally greenish or black with yellow-or orange-tipped side branches.

ABUNDANCE & DISTRIBUTION: Abundant to common Caribbean; occasional Bahamas. Not reported Florida.

HABITAT & BEHAVIOR: Inhabit coral reefs. Hide bodies in recesses, exposing only arms.

NOTE: Formerly classified in genus *Nemaster*.

Greenish Variety

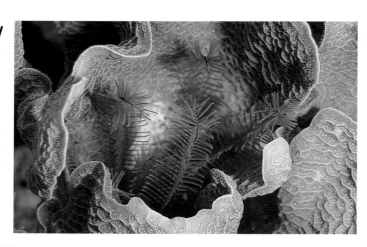

VISUAL ID: Side branches appear to be beaded. Twenty arms, color widely variable. Side branches are most commonly silver-gray, occasionally with black tips.

ABUNDANCE & DISTRIBUTION: Occasional Caribbean, Bahamas. Not reported Florida.

HABITAT & BEHAVIOR: Inhabit deeper coral reefs. Hide bodies in recesses, exposing only arms.

NOTE: Formerly classified in genus *Nemaster*.

GOLDEN CRINOID
Davidaster rubiginosa
CLASS:
Feather Stars
Crinoidea

SIZE: Arms 7-10 in.
DEPTH: 30-130 ft.

**Black With
Yellow-Tip Variety**

BEADED CRINOID
Davidaster discoidea
CLASS:
Feather Stars
Crinoidea

SIZE: Arms 5-8 in.
DEPTH: 60-130 ft.

VISUAL ID: Forty black arms, with white-tipped side branches.

ABUNDANCE & DISTRIBUTION: Common southern Caribbean; occasional to uncommon central Caribbean; rare northern Caribbean. Not reported Florida, Bahamas.

HABITAT & BEHAVIOR: Inhabit coral reefs. Attach to tops of tall sponges, coral heads and other pinnacles, where they are completely exposed.

VISUAL ID: Ten red and white banded arms and side arms.

ABUNDANCE & DISTRIBUTION: Common Caribbean, occasional Bahamas. Not reported Florida.

HABITAT & BEHAVIOR: Inhabit coral reefs. Commonly attach to branches of sea plumes, sea rods and sea whips. Unique ability to coordinate arm movements enables this species to swim in open water.

VISUAL ID: Thick, short arms, heavy body. Knobby spines form net-like geometric design of contrasting color. Orangish-brown to tan. Juveniles are green.

ABUNDANCE & DISTRIBUTION: Common to occasional Florida, Bahamas, Caribbean.

HABITAT & BEHAVIOR: Inhabit shallow sea grass beds and sand flats.

BLACK & WHITE CRINOID
Nemaster grandis
CLASS:
Feather Stars
Crinoidea

SIZE: Arms 7-10 in.
DEPTH: 30-130 ft.

SWIMMING CRINOID
Analcidometra armata
CLASS:
Feather Stars
Crinoidea

SIZE: Arms 2$^1/_2$-3$^1/_2$ in.
DEPTH: 45-130 ft.

CUSHION SEA STAR
Oreaster reticulatus
CLASS:
Sea Stars
Asteroidea

SIZE: 8-14 in.
DEPTH: 5-35 ft.

Sea Stars

VISUAL ID: Nine long, tapered arms. Bluish-gray to purple to tan, darker at central disc and center of arms.

ABUNDANCE & DISTRIBUTION: Uncommon Caribbean; rare Florida.

HABITAT & BEHAVIOR: Inhabit shallow sand or sandy mud bottoms. Burrow to feed, rarely seen in the open on bottom.

VISUAL ID: Cream to yellow, with brown, purplish, greenish, gray or black bands. Five long, tapered, limp arms. Numerous spines create velvet-like appearance.

ABUNDANCE & DISTRIBUTION: Occasional Florida, Bahamas, Caribbean.

HABITAT & BEHAVIOR: Inhabit sand or sandy mud bottoms. Burrow beneath surface, but often forage in the open at night.

VISUAL ID: Conspicuous border of whitish spines on five long, tapered arms. White, cream, gray or brown with darker central stripe that is occasionally indistinct. Covered with a beaded or net-like pattern.

ABUNDANCE & DISTRIBUTION: Common Florida; occasional Bahamas, Caribbean.

HABITAT & BEHAVIOR: Inhabit sand bottoms around reefs. Burrow beneath surface, but occasionally forage in the open.

NINE-ARMED SEA STAR
Luidia senegalensis
CLASS:
Sea Stars
Asteroidea

SIZE: 6-12 in.
DEPTH: 5-35 ft.

BANDED SEA STAR
Luidia alternata
CLASS:
Sea Stars
Asteroidea

SIZE: 6-12 in.
DEPTH: 10-130 ft.

STRIPED SEA STAR
Luidia clathrata
CLASS:
Sea Stars
Asteroidea

SIZE: 6-10 in.
DEPTH: 10-130 ft.

VISUAL ID: Four to seven slender, tubular arms with rounded tips. Rounded nodules on surface are distributed randomly. Arms often of unequal length. Orangish-brown to tan, occasionally dull red to purple.

ABUNDANCE & DISTRIBUTION: Common Florida; occasional to uncommon Bahamas, Caribbean.

HABITAT & BEHAVIOR: Inhabit reefs. An arm that is broken off will regenerate another sea star by forming a new disc and arms. The buds of new arms form a star-like pattern at the trailing end of a regenerating arm, giving rise to the common name.

SIMILAR SPECIES: Comet Star, *Ophidiaster guildingii*, has only five arms and is difficult to distinguish under water from similar appearing five-armed Common Comet Star.

**Five-armed Variety;
One Arm Lost**

VISUAL ID: Mottled red with long tubular arms.

ABUNDANCE & DISTRIBUTION: Rare Florida Keys; occasional east coast Central America. Distribution of this species is not well documented, possibly in other locations.

HABITAT & BEHAVIOR: Inhabit areas of coral rubble and shallow patch reefs. Hide under rubble.

COMMON COMET STAR
Linckia guildingii
CLASS:
Sea Stars
Asteroidea

SIZE: 5-8 in.
DEPTH: 20-130 ft.

**New Individual
Regenerating from
a Severed Arm**

MOTTLED RED
SEA STAR
Copidaster lymani
CLASS:
Sea Stars
Asteroidea

SIZE: 4-8 in.,
12 3/4 in. max.
DEPTH: 0-25 ft.

Sea Stars

VISUAL ID: Five arms bordered with marginal plates have short, outward-pointing spines. At base between arms, two, or occasionally four spines, are turned distinctively inward. Uniformly reddish-brown to brown or gray.
ABUNDANCE & DISTRIBUTION: Uncommon Florida Keys, Bahamas, Caribbean.
HABITAT & BEHAVIOR: Inhabit sandy bottoms. Often burrow into sand.

VISUAL ID: Five arms are bordered with bead-like marginal plates which, when viewed from above, appear to be spineless. Brown, purple or maroon, with contrasting marginal plates of light yellow or tan.
ABUNDANCE & DISTRIBUTION: Common Florida; occasional to uncommon Bahamas, Caribbean.
HABITAT & BEHAVIOR: Inhabit sand and mud bottoms. Often burrow beneath surface.

VISUAL ID: Reddish-orange to orangish-yellow spines form irregular ridges running arms' length, valleys (papular areas) bluish-white.
ABUNDANCE & DISTRIBUTION: Common to occasional both Florida coasts; uncommon southern Caribbean. Not reported central or northern Caribbean.
HABITAT & BEHAVIOR: Inhabit rocky reefs and sand flats. Occasionally on dock pilings and other similar structures.

TWO-SPINED SEA STAR
Astropecten duplicatus
CLASS:
Sea Stars
Asteroidea

SIZE: 5-8 in.
DEPTH: 10-35 ft.

BEADED SEA STAR
Astropecten articulatus
CLASS:
Sea Stars
Asteroidea

SIZE: 4-6 in.
DEPTH: 20-100 ft.

ORANGE-RIDGED SEA STAR
Echinaster spinulosus
CLASS:
Sea Stars
Asteroidea

SIZE: 4-5 in.
DEPTH: 0-130 ft.

VISUAL ID: Five wide, short, triangular arms emerge from central disc. Color widely variable, including white, tan, yellow, red, blue and olive.

ABUNDANCE & DISTRIBUTION: Occasional Florida, Bahamas, Caribbean.

HABITAT & BEHAVIOR: Inhabit reefs. Secretive; hide under rocks, coral rubble or in crevices. Can burrow into sand.

SIMILAR SPECIES: Tiny Blunt-Armed Star, *A. hartmeyeri*, grow to only one-half inch. Have somewhat longer, more distinct, arms. White to pinkish-white. Caribbean only.

VISUAL ID: Bright red, may have white markings near center of disc and black markings around tips of arms.

ABUNDANCE & DISTRIBUTION: Rare Florida, Bahamas, Caribbean.

HABITAT & BEHAVIOR: Hide under corals and reef rubble near deep drop-offs.

VISUAL ID: Thick, stud-like spines on tubular arms and small central disc. Brownish-white with wide brown band on each arm.

ABUNDANCE & DISTRIBUTION: Rare Belize.

HABITAT & BEHAVIOR: Inhabit shallow areas of coral rubble.

NOTE: Species of the genus *Mithrodia* are known primarily from deep water, well below safe scuba diving depths and are rarely reported in the Caribbean. This specimen, photographed in shallow water, at night, off Belize, cannot be identified to species from the picture alone and may be a rare undescribed species. If observed, a sighting report should be made to R.E.E.F.

BLUNT-ARMED SEA STAR

Asterina folium

CLASS:
Sea Stars
Asteroidea

SIZE: ½-1 in.
DEPTH: 20-100 ft.

RED MINIATURE SEA STAR

Porania regularis

CLASS:
Sea Stars
Asteroidea

SIZE: ½-1¼ in.
DEPTH: 35-130 ft.

STUDDED SEA STAR

Mithrodia sp.

CLASS:
Sea Stars
Asteroidea

SIZE: 5 in.
DEPTH: 15-25 ft.

Brittle Stars

VISUAL ID: Numerous long, thin glassy spines cover arms. Distinct dark central line runs the length of arms. Yellow, brown, gray or black; color of arms and spines may be different.

ABUNDANCE & DISTRIBUTION: Common Caribbean, Bahamas; occasional to uncommon Florida.

HABITAT & BEHAVIOR: Live on sponges, fire coral and occasionally gorgonians.

Black & Gray Juvenile

VISUAL ID: Reticulated network of fine dark lines on bone white to bluish disc. Arms whitish to pale yellow with brownish bands and short spines.

ABUNDANCE & DISTRIBUTION: Common Florida, Bahamas, Caribbean.

HABITAT & BEHAVIOR: Inhabit sandy areas around reefs. Hide under slabs of coral and rubble.

SPONGE BRITTLE STAR
Ophiothrix suensonii

CLASS:
Brittle Stars
Ophiuroidea
ORDER:
Ophiurae

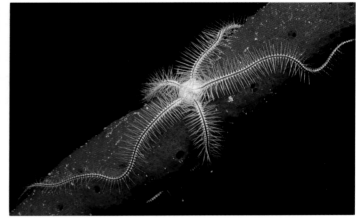

SIZE: Disc ½ - ¾ in.
Arms 2½ -3½ in.
DEPTH: 10-130 ft.

On Fire Coral

RETICULATED BRITTLE STAR
Ophionereis reticulata

CLASS:
Brittle Stars
Ophiuroidea
ORDER:
Ophiurae

SIZE: Disc ½ -¾ in.
DEPTH: 10-130 ft.

VISUAL ID: Numerous long, pointed spines cover arms. Distinctive, thin central stripe of pale pigment extends down arm, becoming more conspicuous near tip. Shades of brown.

ABUNDANCE & DISTRIBUTION: Uncommon Florida Keys, Bahamas, Northwest Caribbean.

HABITAT & BEHAVIOR: Inhabit fore reefs. Associate with living corals.

VISUAL ID: Heavy, blunt dorsal spines on arms, especially near disc. Mottled to banded brown, gray and black. Never show reddish hues.

ABUNDANCE & DISTRIBUTION: Common Florida, Bahamas, Caribbean.

HABITAT & BEHAVIOR: Inhabit reefs and areas of coral rubble. Hide under rocks and in dark recesses.

SIMILAR SPECIES: Red Brittle Star, *O. wendti*, dorsal spines long, thin and pointed. Usually has rust or reddish hues, occasionally bright red.

VISUAL ID: Red and cream bands on smooth arms. Disc may be solid, patterned or mottled with the same colors.

ABUNDANCE & DISTRIBUTION: Occasional Florida, Bahamas, Caribbean.

HABITAT & BEHAVIOR: Inhabit deeper areas of fore reef. Forage about bottom in open at night. Have been observed, on rare occasions, climbing sea fans.

SPINY BRITTLE STAR
*Ophiocoma
paucigranulata*
CLASS:
Brittle Stars
Ophiuroidea
ORDER:
Ophiurae

SIZE: Disc ³/₄ -1 in.
Arms 4-6 in.
DEPTH: 5-80 ft.

BLUNT-SPINED BRITTLE STAR
Ophiocoma echinata
CLASS:
Brittle Stars
Ophiuroidea
ORDER:
Ophiurae

SIZE: Disc ³/₄ -1¹/₄ in.
Arms 4-6 in.
DEPTH: 10-80 ft.

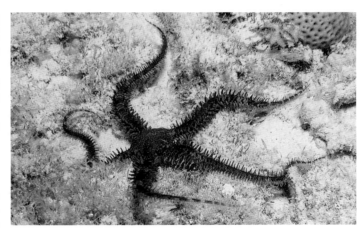

RUBY BRITTLE STAR
*Ophioderma
rubicundum*
CLASS:
Brittle Stars
Ophiuroidea
ORDER:
Ophiurae

SIZE: Disc ¹/₂ -³/₄ in.
Arms 3-4 in.
DEPTH: 35-80 ft.

VISUAL ID: Arms usually banded gray and white, occasionally green or brown and white. Disc color variable, olive-green, gray, brown or white, often with white and/or black spots. Short spines give arms serrated appearance.

ABUNDANCE & DISTRIBUTION: Common Florida, Bahamas, Caribbean.

HABITAT & BEHAVIOR: Inhabit shallow to mid-range reefs. Hide under rocks, coral heads and in recesses.

SIMILAR SPECIES: Short-Armed Brittle Star, *O. brevicaudum*, relatively short, lightly banded arms, inhabit very shallow water areas of rubble. Short-Spined Brittle Star, *O. brevispinum*, disc shades of green, often green with banded arms, inhabit sea grass beds. Chocolate Brittle Star, *O. cinereum*, color variable, often brown, arms indistinctly banded and smooth in appearance.

VISUAL ID: Pink disc, yellow arms. Colors may be bright and intense or pale.

ABUNDANCE & DISTRIBUTION: Occasional to rare Belize, Cayman Islands and Grand Turk.

HABITAT & BEHAVIOR: Inhabit deeper reefs and sloping drop-offs. Hide under rocks, coral heads and in recesses. Have been observed climbing sea plumes.

NOTE: This is a recently described species and its geographical distribution is not well-known. It is apparently rare or absent in most locations. Sightings should be reported to R.E.E.F.

VISUAL ID: Reddish arms are finely banded and branch only once or twice.

ABUNDANCE & DISTRIBUTION: Occasional South Florida, Bahamas, Caribbean.

HABITAT & BEHAVIOR: Inhabit steep, deeper fore reefs. Large groups cling to gorgonians, especially sea rods. Wrap tightly around gorgonian during day, unfurling at night to feed.

BANDED-ARM BRITTLE STAR

Ophioderma appressum

CLASS:
Brittle Stars
Ophiuroidea
ORDER:
Ophiurae

SIZE: Disc ¾ -1 in.
Arms 4-6 in.
DEPTH: 10-60 ft.

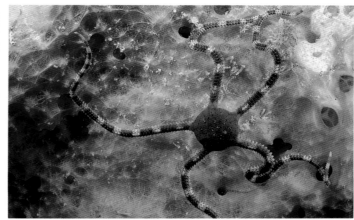

GAUDY BRITTLE STAR

Ophioderma ensiferum

CLASS:
Brittle Stars
Ophiuroidea
ORDER:
Ophiurae

SIZE: Disc ½ -¾ in.
Arms 3-4 in.
DEPTH: 50-100 ft.

SEA ROD BASKET STAR

Schizostella bifurcata

CLASS:
Basket Stars
Ophiuroidea
ORDER:
Euryalae

SIZE: Disc ½ -1 in.
Arms 1-2 in.
DEPTH: 40-100 ft.

Basket Stars – Sea Urchins

VISUAL ID: Numerous thin, branched arms which, when extended, form a fan-shaped plankton net. Orange to tan to dark brown. Juveniles are usually tan and lavender [below right], but can also be black.

ABUNDANCE & DISTRIBUTION: Common South Florida, Bahamas, Caribbean.

HABITAT & BEHAVIOR: Inhabit reefs. Coil into a tight ball during day, and hide in dark recesses or attach to sea plumes [below left]. Feed at night by orienting to face current and spreading arms to filter planktonic animals.

Coiled Daytime Appearance

VISUAL ID: Numerous long, thin, sharp spines. Usually all black, occasionally have some grayish-white spines. Young have black and white banded spines.

ABUNDANCE & DISTRIBUTION: Abundant to common Florida, Bahamas, Caribbean.

HABITAT & BEHAVIOR: Found in all habitats. Hide during day in sheltered locations. Feed in the open on algae at night.

EFFECT ON DIVERS: Spines easily puncture the skin and break off in the flesh, causing a painful wound. The embedded spines give off a purple dye, causing a slight discoloration under the skin. Treat area for infection; embedded spines will dissolve within a few days. Victim with numerous wounds may need treatment for shock.

GIANT BASKET STAR
Astrophyton muricatum
CLASS:
Basket Stars
Ophiuroidea
ORDER:
Euryalae

SIZE: Disc 1-1³/₄ in.
Arms 1-1¹/₂ ft.
DEPTH: 20-90 ft.

Juvenile

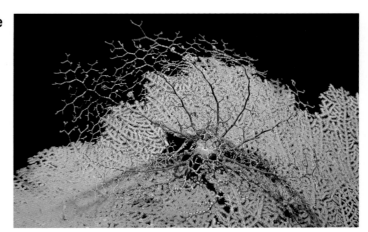

LONG-SPINED URCHIN
Diadema antillarum
CLASS:
Sea Urchins
Echinoidea

SIZE: Body 2-3 in.
Spines 4-8 in.
DEPTH: 0-130 ft.

Sea Urchins

VISUAL ID: Adults uniform dark purple or black. Spines much shorter and more slender than similar appearing Long Spine Urchin [previous]. Gaps between spines at joints of major plates. Juvenile [pictured] body is pinkish cream to tan, with spines of greenish-tan, banded in reddish-brown hues. Rows of brilliant blue spots near base of spines.

ABUNDANCE & DISTRIBUTION: Rare South Florida, Caribbean.

HABITAT & BEHAVIOR: Prefer deep-water habitats, rarely within depth range of scuba.

EFFECT ON DIVERS: Spines easily puncture the skin and break off in the flesh, causing a painful wound.

VISUAL ID: Short, thick, pointed spines. Black to reddish-brown. Usually some reddishness on body or spines.

ABUNDANCE & DISTRIBUTION: Common to uncommon Florida, Bahamas, Caribbean.

HABITAT & BEHAVIOR: Most common in shallow rocky and tidal areas, but occasionally much deeper. Bore holes in substrate, which they occupy during day. Feed on algae in the open (near their holes) at night.

EFFECT ON DIVERS: Spines can produce a puncture wound.

NOTE: Individuals in Caribbean tend to be much smaller than those in Florida.

VISUAL ID: Pointed spines have violet to dark brown tips, greenish shaft and white ring around base. Body reddish to maroon.

ABUNDANCE & DISTRIBUTION: Occasional to uncommon Florida, Bahamas, Caribbean. Not reported in extreme eastern Caribbean.

HABITAT & BEHAVIOR: Inhabit shallower reefs. Hide during day in sheltered locations, often in Lettuce Coral, *Agaricia tenuifolia*. Feed on algae, in the open at night.

EFFECT ON DIVERS: Spines can produce puncture wound.

MAGNIFICENT URCHIN
Astropyga magnifica
CLASS:
Sea Urchins
Echinoidea

SIZE: Body 2-5³/₄ in.
Spines 2¹/₂ -4¹/₂ in.
DEPTH: 65-130 ft.

ROCK-BORING URCHIN
Echinometra lucunter
CLASS:
Sea Urchins
Echinoidea

SIZE: Body 1¹/₄ -3 in.
Spines ³/₄ -1¹/₄ in.
DEPTH: 0-15 ft.

REEF URCHIN
Echinometra viridis
CLASS:
Sea Urchins
Echinoidea

SIZE: Body 1¹/₄ -2 in.
Spines 1-1¹/₂ in.
DEPTH: 15-45 ft.

289

Sea Urchins

VISUAL ID: Mixed in with spines are podia, and stalked, jaw-like structures that appear as purple balls. Body and spines usually white, occasionally green to brown.

ABUNDANCE & DISTRIBUTION: Occasional Caribbean. Not reported Florida, Bahamas.

HABITAT & BEHAVIOR: Inhabit shallower reefs. Hide in sheltered locations, often around Staghorn Coral, *Acropora cervicornis*, and Lettuce Coral, *Agaricia tenuifolia*.

EFFECT ON DIVERS: Spines can produce puncture wound.

VISUAL ID: Densely covered with short spines, which part somewhat to form grooves at joints of major plates. Body and spines commonly white to green in Caribbean. May be red, purple, green or white in Florida and Bahamas. Podia white.

ABUNDANCE & DISTRIBUTION: Common to occasional Florida, Bahamas, Caribbean.

HABITAT & BEHAVIOR: Inhabit sea grass beds and reefs. Often camouflage by covering themselves with sea grass and other debris.

EFFECT ON DIVERS: Spines can produce puncture wound.

VISUAL ID: Thick, cylindrical, blunt spines. Body light to dark reddish-brown. Spines often covered with various organisms and algae.

ABUNDANCE & DISTRIBUTION: Common to uncommon Florida, Bahamas, Caribbean.

HABITAT & BEHAVIOR: Inhabit sea grass beds, areas of reef rubble and reefs. Often hide in sheltered locations.

JEWEL URCHIN
Lytechinus williamsi
CLASS:
Sea Urchins
Echinoidea

SIZE: Body 1-2 in.
Spines $1/2$ -$1^1/4$ in.
DEPTH: 15-50 ft.

VARIEGATED URCHIN
Lytechinus variegatus
CLASS:
Sea Urchins
Echinoidea

SIZE: Body 2-3 in.
Spines $1/2$ - $3/4$ in.
DEPTH: 3-50 ft.

SLATE-PENCIL URCHIN
Eucidaris tribuloides
CLASS:
Sea Urchins
Echinoidea

SIZE: Body $1^1/2$ -2 in.
Spines $1^1/2$ -2 in.
DEPTH: 10-75 ft.

VISUAL ID: Densely covered with short, white spines. Body usually black, but can be dark purple or reddish brown.

ABUNDANCE & DISTRIBUTION: Abundant to uncommon Florida, Bahamas, Caribbean.

HABITAT & BEHAVIOR: Inhabit sea grass beds, occasionally on shallow reefs. Often camouflage by covering themselves with sea grass and other debris.

NOTE: Numbers greatly reduced in some locations by natives who harvest them and eat their roe.

VISUAL ID: Densely covered with short, brown spines. Pentagonal petal design on back.

ABUNDANCE & DISTRIBUTION: Common Florida, Bahamas, Caribbean.

HABITAT & BEHAVIOR: Inhabit sandy areas, often around reefs. Burrow beneath sand during day, may emerge at night. Heart Urchin Crab [pg. 175] lives within the protection of its spines. Broken remains are often on sand.

VISUAL ID: Disc-shaped. (Unlike similar species, has no notches in disc margin and no holes in body.) Densely covered with fine spines. Pentagonal petal design on back. Living specimens are shades of brown; shells of dead specimens are gray.

ABUNDANCE & DISTRIBUTION: Occasional Caribbean.

HABITAT & BEHAVIOR: Inhabit shallow, sandy areas around reefs. Burrow beneath sand during day, occasionally come out at night. Broken remains are often on sand.

SIMILAR SPECIES: Four-Notched Sand Dollar, *Encope michelini*, has four notches in disc around margin, and a single oval hole through body; South Florida and Gulf coast. Five-Notched Sand Dollar, *Encope emarginata*, has five notches in disc around margin, and a single oval hole through body; Caribbean.

WEST INDIAN SEA EGG

Tripneustes ventricosus
CLASS:
Sea Urchins
Echinoidea

SIZE: Body 4-5 in.
Spines ¹/₂ -³/₄ in.
DEPTH: 0-30 feet.

RED HEART URCHIN

Meoma ventricosa
CLASS:
Echinoidea
ORDER:
Heart Urchins
Spatangoida

SIZE: 4-6 in.
DEPTH: 3-130 ft.

SAND DOLLAR

Clypeaster subdepressus
CLASS:
Echinoidea
ORDER:
Sand Dollars
Clypeasteroida

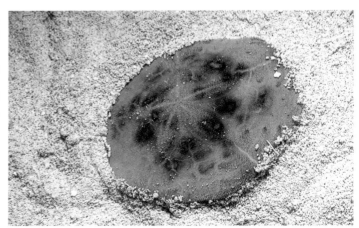

SIZE: 3-4 in.,
6 in. max.
DEPTH: 0-40 ft.

VISUAL ID: Disc-shaped with six, elongated oval holes in body. Densely covered with fine spines. Pentagonal petal design on back. Living specimens are shades of brown; young silvery gray; dead specimens are gray.

ABUNDANCE & DISTRIBUTION: Occasional Florida, Bahamas, Caribbean.

HABITAT & BEHAVIOR: Inhabit shallow sandy areas around reefs. Burrow beneath sand during day, occasionally in open at night. Broken remains are often on sand.

SIMILAR SPECIES: Five-Keyhole Sand Dollar, *M. quinquiesperforata*, has five elongated oval holes in body; Florida, Bahamas, Caribbean.

VISUAL ID: Back covered with half-inch long, spike-like podia. Chocolate brown to gray, often with scattered spots and blotches of white.

ABUNDANCE & DISTRIBUTION: Occasional Florida, Bahamas, Caribbean.

HABITAT & BEHAVIOR: Inhabit sandy areas around reefs. Can be quite active, and may be observed crawling or even rolling over and over.

VISUAL ID: Five conspicuous, squarish, calcareous teeth around anus. Mottled yellow-brown to brown or cream, sole is lighter. Podia on back are small and knobby.

ABUNDANCE & DISTRIBUTION: Occasional Florida, Bahamas, Caribbean.

HABITAT & BEHAVIOR: Inhabit sea grass beds and sandy areas around reefs.

SIX-KEYHOLE SAND DOLLAR

Mellita sexiesperforata

CLASS:
Echinoidea
ORDER
Sand Dollars
Clypeasteroida

SIZE: 2-3½ in.,
4 in max.
DEPTH: 0-35 ft.

FURRY SEA CUCUMBER

Astichopus multifidus

CLASS:
Sea Cucumbers
Holothuroidea

SIZE: 10-16 in.
DEPTH: 40-100 ft.

FIVE-TOOTHED SEA CUCUMBER

Actinopygia agassizii

CLASS:
Sea Cucumbers
Holothuroidea

SIZE: 8-10 in.
DEPTH: 10-80 ft.

Sea Cucumbers

VISUAL ID: Three rows of podia on sole, the center row is wider and split by a seam. Earth-tone colors and patterns highly variable. Small, knob-like podia on back are often a contrasting shade or color.

ABUNDANCE & DISTRIBUTION: Occasional Florida, Bahamas, Caribbean.

HABITAT & BEHAVIOR: Inhabit sea grass beds, shallow reef rubble patches, and sandy areas around reefs.

VISUAL ID: Large cone-like podia on back. Reddish-brown to tan, podia often a lighter shade.

ABUNDANCE & DISTRIBUTION: Uncommon Caribbean.

HABITAT & BEHAVIOR: Inhabit reef rubble patches and sandy areas around reefs.

VISUAL ID: Dark gray to black, with deep, conspicuous creases. Sole is rose to white with scattered, small brown podia.

ABUNDANCE & DISTRIBUTION: Common Caribbean; occasional Bahamas. Not reported Florida.

HABITAT & BEHAVIOR: Inhabit sea grass beds and sandy areas around reefs.

THREE-ROWED SEA CUCUMBER

Isostichopus badionotus

CLASS:
Sea Cucumbers
Holothuroidea

SIZE: 10-16 in.
DEPTH: 10-60 ft.

CONICAL SEA CUCUMBER

Eostichopus arnesoni

CLASS:
Sea Cucumbers
Holothuroidea

SIZE: 10-16 in.
DEPTH: 25-75 ft.

DONKEY DUNG SEA CUCUMBER

Holothuria mexicana

CLASS:
Sea Cucumbers
Holothuroidea

SIZE: 10-14 in.
DEPTH: 10-60 ft.

Sea Cucumbers

VISUAL ID: Thin, elongated body, often somewhat flask-shaped. Thin podia on back, and long, disc-tipped podia on sole. Variable coloration, may be yellow, reddish-orange, brown, gray or purplish.

ABUNDANCE & DISTRIBUTION: Uncommon Florida, Bahamas, Caribbean, also circumtropical.

HABITAT & BEHAVIOR: Inhabit reefs and areas of reef rubble.

VISUAL ID: Long, thin body extends from recess in reef. Mouth, on underside, has short, ruffled tentacles. Mottled brown to cream. Scattered, pointed podia.

ABUNDANCE & DISTRIBUTION: Occasional Florida, Bahamas, Caribbean.

HABITAT & BEHAVIOR: Inhabit coral reefs. Posterior firmly attaches in recess, while oral end of elongated body extends out, sweeping the reef for food, primarily at night. When disturbed, rapidly retracts body into recess.

VISUAL ID: Long, worm-like, body appears to be segmented with three large bead-like knobs on each. A mop-like crown of long, thick, feathery tentacles usually extends from around mouth. Shades of gray, brown, green or yellow, often with light and/or dark stripes and, occasionally, variegated with small white blotches. Body soft and fragile, skin sticky. They have no tube feet.

ABUNDANCE & DISTRIBUTION: Occasional South Florida, Bahamas, Caribbean.

HABITAT & BEHAVIOR: Hide under coral slabs, rubble and in recesses during the day. Often in open at night.

REACTION TO DIVERS: Highly contractile, when disturbed constrict dramatically. Will stick if touched.

SLENDER SEA CUCUMBER

Holothuria impatiens

CLASS:
Sea Cucumbers
Holothuroidea

SIZE: 8-12 in.
DEPTH: 25-130 ft.

TIGER TAIL SEA CUCUMBER

Holothuria thomasi

CLASS:
Sea Cucumbers
Holothuroidea

SIZE: 3-6 ft.
DEPTH: 20-100 ft.

BEADED SEA CUCUMBER

Euapta lappa

CLASS:
Sea Cucumbers
Holothuroidea

SIZE: 10-15 in.,
max 3 ft.
DEPTH: 20-100 ft.

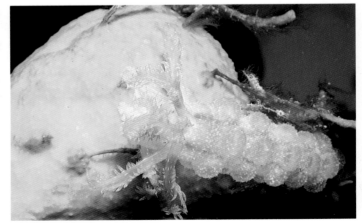

IDENTIFICATION GROUP 10

Phylum Chordata
Subphylum Urochordata

(Core-DOT-uḥ / Gr. string / Your-oh-CORE-dot-uh / Gr. tail string)

Tunicates

Most chordates have backbones and are called vertebrates; urochordates do not have backbones, but are included because they have four important characteristics that are shared by all members of the phylum — at some point in their life cycle all have a tail, dorsal central nerve cord, pharyngeal gill clefts and notochord. The latter functions as a support system for the dorsal nerve cord and is replaced by bone in vertebrates. The subphylum's common name, tunicate, comes from a body covering of cellulose material called a **tunic**.

TUNICATES

Class Ascidiacea (Ah-sid-EE-aa-see-uh / Gr. little bottle)

Although tunicates are among the most common marine invertebrates, they are probably the least recognized. In most cases, they are simply overlooked, ignored or mistaken for sponges. They are attached to the substrate at one end; at the opposite end they have two siphons. Water is drawn in through the **incurrent** or buccal **siphon**, pumped through a **gill net** in the body, where food and oxygen are extracted, and then discharged through an **excurrent** or atrial **siphon**. Body shape, as well as size, varies considerably among species; some are only a quarter inch in length while others may exceed five inches. Tunicates come in a dazzling array of colors that is often enhanced by a translucent quality of the tunic.

When the animal is disturbed, muscular bands rapidly close the siphons. This ability easily distinguishes tunicates from sponges, which either cannot close their openings, or do so very slowly. In spite of their sponge-like appearance, tunicates are complicated animals with nervous, digestive, reproductive and circulatory systems.

Solitary tunicates are called **simple ascidians**, and include most of the larger species. Many of the smaller species grow in varying degrees of colonialism and are called **compound tunicates**. In some species individuals are joined only at their bases, while in more intimate associations, numerous individuals are completely embedded in a **common tunic** and the individuals are recognizable only by their two siphons. The most specialized colonies are those in which the individuals are not only imbedded in a common tunic, but their excurrent siphons open into a large common chamber or cloaca. Some of these colonies form geometric designs with the **incurrent siphons** evenly spaced around a **central outflow opening** or cloacal orifice. Others have incurrent siphons scattered randomly around larger **outflow openings**. Compound colonies often cover an area, appearing much like an encrusting sponge.

PELAGIC TUNICATES

Class Thaliacea (Thal-ee-AA-see-uh / Gr. to flourish or bloom)

Members of this class are pelagic, free-swimming tunicates found in open water that occasionally swim over reefs. They are translucent-to-transparent animals that resemble a jet engine pod in both appearance and function. The **incurrent** or buccal and **excurrent** or atrial **siphons** are at opposite ends of the pod. Water is pushed through the body by muscular contractions, moving the animal by water jet propulsion. Orange **cerebral ganglions** can usually be seen at the top, near the buccal siphon.

Members of the genera Salpa and Doliolumn are solitary adults that reproduce by asexual budding. Occasionally, buds are seen connected in long chains or other patterns. When mature, an individual detaches and swims free.

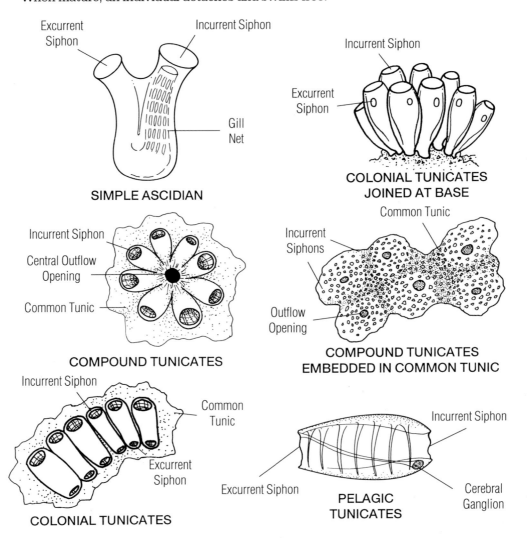

Excurrent Siphon · Incurrent Siphon · Gill Net
SIMPLE ASCIDIAN

Incurrent Siphon · Excurrent Siphon
COLONIAL TUNICATES JOINED AT BASE

Incurrent Siphon · Central Outflow Opening · Common Tunic
COMPOUND TUNICATES

Common Tunic · Incurrent Siphons · Outflow Opening
COMPOUND TUNICATES EMBEDDED IN COMMON TUNIC

Incurrent Siphon · Common Tunic · Excurrent Siphon
COLONIAL TUNICATES

Excurrent Siphon · Incurrent Siphon · Cerebral Ganglion
PELAGIC TUNICATES

Tunicates

VISUAL ID: Lavender to dark purple or brown, may appear black at depth. Heavy, thick, gelatinous body. Solitary.

ABUNDANCE & DISTRIBUTION: Occasional South Florida, Bahamas, Caribbean.

HABITAT & BEHAVIOR: Inhabit coral reefs. Hide most of body in tight crevice or hole, exposing only small part of upper body and siphons.

REACTION TO DIVERS: Relatively unafraid; close siphons only when closely approached or molested.

VISUAL ID: Body globular, with two large protruding siphons. Just inside the incurrent siphon is a ring of bristle-like, unbranched tentacles. Mottled in shades of brown.

ABUNDANCE & DISTRIBUTION: Occasional South Florida, Bahamas, Caribbean.

HABITAT & BEHAVIOR: Inhabit coral reefs. Their bodies are often covered and camouflaged by algae.

REACTION TO DIVERS: Shy; close siphons and contract body when approached.

SIMILAR SPECIES: Two species, without common names, *Microcosmus exasperatus* and *Pyura vittata*, can be distinguished from the Giant Tunicate by the branched tentacles inside their incurrent siphon.

VISUAL ID: Long tubular incurrent siphon extends from crevice or recess in reef. Yellow to yellow-green to green to gray-green.

ABUNDANCE & DISTRIBUTION: Occasional Caribbean.

HABITAT & BEHAVIOR: Inhabit reefs. Hide bodies and excurrent siphons in crevices or recesses.

REACTION TO DIVERS: Somewhat shy; close incurrent siphon when approached, but rarely retract it unless molested.

REEF TUNICATE
Rhopalaea abdominalis
CLASS:
Tunicates
Ascidiacea

SIZE: ³/₄ - 1¹/₂ in.
DEPTH: 25 - 75 ft.

GIANT TUNICATE
Polycarpa spongiabilis
CLASS:
Tunicates
Ascidiacea

SIZE: 3 - 4 in.
DEPTH: 25 - 100 ft.

GREEN TUBE TUNICATE
Ascidia sydneiensis
CLASS:
Tunicates
Ascidiacea

SIZE: Siphon
length 2 - 4 in.,
width ³/₄ - 1¹/₂ in.
DEPTH: 30 - 130 ft.

VISUAL ID: Bodies transparent and often shaded with white, red or purple. Occasionally translucent. Siphon rims and internal body parts are typically carmine to purple, although there may be some variations.

ABUNDANCE & DISTRIBUTION: Common to occasional Florida, Bahamas, Caribbean.

HABITAT & BEHAVIOR: Inhabit reefs and walls. Grow in clusters ranging from a few to nearly 1,000 individuals. Often attach to gorgonians, black coral trees and sponges.

REACTION TO DIVERS: Relatively unafraid; close siphons only when closely approached or molested.

NOTE: May have other color phases not reported in scientific literature.

 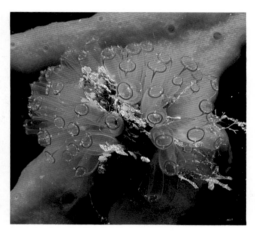

VISUAL ID: Bodies dense blue, siphon rims white. Smallest member of this genus in Caribbean.

ABUNDANCE & DISTRIBUTION: Occasional Caribbean.

HABITAT & BEHAVIOR: Inhabit reefs.

REACTION TO DIVERS: Relatively unafraid; close siphons only when closely approached or molested.

NOTE: May have other color phases not reported in scientific literature; for example, the first picture on next page appears to be a greenish-yellow variety of this species.

PAINTED TUNICATE
Clavelina picta
CLASS:
Tunicates
Ascidiacea

SIZE: ¹/₂ - ³/₄ in.
DEPTH: 15 - 100 ft.

Color Varieties

BLUE BELL TUNICATE
Clavelina puerto-
secensis
CLASS:
Tunicates
Ascidiacea

SIZE: ¹/₄ - ¹/₂ in.
DEPTH: 20 - 100 ft.

VISUAL ID: Members of this genus can generally be identified by their shape, location of siphons, and trait of growing in clusters. Colors and markings of many species, however, are neither consistent or well established in scientific literature. Positive identification requires microscopic examination of internal body parts.

ABUNDANCE & DISTRIBUTION: Common Florida, Bahamas, Caribbean.

HABITAT & BEHAVIOR: Inhabit reefs and attach to a variety of substrate.

NOTE: Pictured specimens, opposite, are possibly a color variety of Blue Bell Tunicate [pg. 305]; and specimens, on right page below, are probably a color variety of Painted Tunicate [pg. 305].

 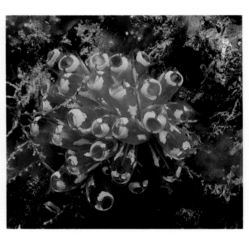

VISUAL ID: Bodies and internal parts transparent to translucent orange, occasionally yellow or pink. Both siphons protrude from top. Grow in clusters ranging from several to hundreds of individuals.

ABUNDANCE & DISTRIBUTION: Common Florida, Bahamas, Caribbean.

HABITAT & BEHAVIOR: Inhabit areas of mangrove and turtle grass, occasionally on shallow reefs. Attach to roots of mangroves, stems of turtle grass. On reefs they attach to gorgonians, sponges and areas of dead coral.

REACTION TO DIVERS: Relatively unafraid; close siphons only when closely approached or molested.

NOTE: A few Painted Tunicates [pg. 305] in shades of red and lavender are also in photograph.

BULB TUNICATES
Clavelina sp.
CLASS:
Tunicates
Ascidiacea

SIZE: $^1/_4$ - $^3/_4$ in.
DEPTH: 15 - 130 ft.

MANGROVE TUNICATE
Ecteinascidia turbinata
CLASS:
Tunicates
Ascidiacea

SIZE: $^1/_2$ - 1 in.
DEPTH: 1 - 40 ft.

VISUAL ID: Tiny individuals grow in clusters, their tunics joining at the bases to form a common tunic that encrusts areas of the substrate. Reported to be yellow-green, green, orange and purple. May have other color varieties. Interiors of siphons are often contrasting shades or colors.

ABUNDANCE & DISTRIBUTION: Common Florida, Bahamas, Caribbean.

HABITAT & BEHAVIOR: Inhabit reefs and walls. Often encrust areas of dead coral and the surface of large sponges.

REACTION TO DIVERS: Unafraid; close siphons only when molested.

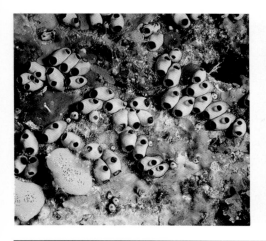 

VISUAL ID: Small individuals with thick tunics growing in close association are distinctive of this species. Usually brown upper body, paler below, any intervening tunic tissue also pale. Occasionally pale siphons and mottled.

ABUNDANCE & DISTRIBUTION: Occasional Florida, Bahamas, Caribbean.

HABITAT & BEHAVIOR: Inhabit reefs. Often attach in areas of dead coral and shipwrecks. Frequently covered and camouflaged by algae.

REACTION TO DIVERS: Relatively unafraid; close siphons only when closely approached or molested.

NOTE: Identification is tentative. Because there are several similar appearing genera and species, positive identification requires microscopic examination of internal body parts.

ENCRUSTING SOCIAL TUNICATE
Symplegma viride
CLASS:
Tunicates
Ascidiacea

SIZE: ¹/₄ in.
DEPTH: 15 - 100 ft.

Color Varieties

MOTTLED SOCIAL TUNICATE
Polyandrocarpa tumida
CLASS:
Tunicates
Ascidiacea

SIZE: ¹/₄ - ¹/₂ in.
DEPTH: 25 - 75 ft.

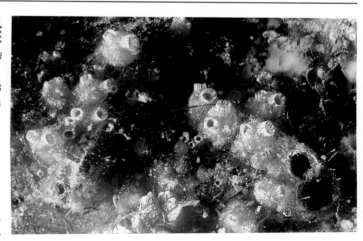

Tunicates

VISUAL ID: Numerous small individuals embedded in a firm, common berry-like, tunic that attaches to the substrate by a short stalk. Vary from violet to red to orange. Individuals are recognizable only by their two siphon openings that are often outlined in a darker shade.

ABUNDANCE & DISTRIBUTION: Occasional Florida, Bahamas, Caribbean.

HABITAT & BEHAVIOR: Inhabit reefs. Often grow in areas of dead coral and algae.

REACTION TO DIVERS: Unafraid; close siphons only when molested.

NOTE: This growth form of the genus is probably an undescribed species. It is closely related and could possibly be the same as an Indo-Pacific species.

VISUAL ID: Numerous small individuals embedded in a black, firm, globular common tunic. Individuals are recognizable only by their two siphon openings that protrude slightly from the surface, and are outlined with white.

ABUNDANCE & DISTRIBUTION: Occasional Florida, Bahamas, Caribbean.

HABITAT & BEHAVIOR: Inhabit reefs. Often grow in areas of dead coral and algae.

REACTION TO DIVERS: Unafraid; close siphons only when molested.

NOTE: Identification is tentative. Because there are several similar appearing genera and species, positive identification requires microscopic examination of internal body parts.

VISUAL ID: Numerous small tunicates embedded in a white, firm, globular common tunic. Each individual forms slight depression in the surface of the colony and can be recognized by the two siphon openings that protrude slightly.

ABUNDANCE & DISTRIBUTION: Occasional Florida, Bahamas, Caribbean.

HABITAT & BEHAVIOR: Inhabit reefs. Often grow in areas of dead coral and algae.

REACTION TO DIVERS: Unafraid; close siphons only when molested.

NOTE: Identification of genus is tentative, could also be *Polycitor* or *Stomozoa*. Because of the similarity in appearance of these genera and many similar species, positive identification requires microscopic examination of internal body parts.

STRAWBERRY TUNICATE

Eudistoma sp.

CLASS:
Tunicates
Ascidiacea

SIZE: Colony 1 - 1½ in.
DEPTH: 20 - 100 ft.

BLACK CONDOMINIUM TUNICATE

Eudistoma obscuratum

CLASS:
Tunicates
Ascidiacea

SIZE: Colony 1 - 4 in.
DEPTH: 25 - 75 ft.

WHITE CONDOMINIUM TUNICATES

Eudistoma sp.

CLASS:
Tunicates
Ascidiacea

SIZE: Colony 1 - 4 in.
DEPTH: 25 - 75 ft.

VISUAL ID: Brick red with yellow markings is characteristic of this species, although they are also reported in a wide range of colors, from black to bright orange. Tiny, elongated individuals growing in a common tunic cluster around central outflow openings. Each individual can be recognized by the small opening of its incurrent siphon.

ABUNDANCE & DISTRIBUTION: Occasional Florida, Bahamas, Caribbean.

HABITAT & BEHAVIOR: Colonies encrust areas of dead coral, shipwrecks, dock pilings and even turtle grass blades.

REACTION TO DIVERS: Unafraid; close siphons only when molested.

VISUAL ID: Several species of this genus can be recognized by their long, curved and meandering rows of individuals on either side of hallway-like central chambers that have occasional outflow openings. These rows often form circular patterns with centers composed of translucent tunic. Usually brightly colored, often orange or green. In the margin of the colony tiny, finger-shaped blood vessels may be discernable, radiating toward the edge.

ABUNDANCE & DISTRIBUTION: Occasional Florida, Bahamas, Caribbean.

HABITAT & BEHAVIOR: Colonies encrust areas of dead coral, shipwrecks, dock pilings and gorgonian stalks.

REACTION TO DIVERS: Generally unafraid; close siphons only when molested.

NOTE: Because there are several similar appearing species in a variety of colors and patterns, positive identification requires microscopic examination of internal body parts.

VISUAL ID: Members of this genus are somewhat elongated, grow in a common tunic, and cluster in circular patterns around central outflow openings. Each individual can be recognized by the small opening of its incurrent siphon. The arrangement of individuals in the tunic and their color patterns often form geometric designs. Colors and markings of many species are not consistent or well established in scientific literature. Positive identification requires microscopic examination of internal body parts.

ABUNDANCE & DISTRIBUTION: Occasional Florida, Bahamas, Caribbean.

HABITAT & BEHAVIOR: Colonies encrust areas of dead coral, shipwrecks, dock pilings and gorgonian stalks.

REACTION TO DIVERS: Generally unafraid; close siphons only when molested.

FLAT TUNICATE
Botrylloides nigrum
CLASS:
Tunicates
Ascidiacea

SIZE: ¹/₄ in. or less
DEPTH: 3 - 100 ft.

ROW ENCRUSTING TUNICATES
Botrylloides sp.
CLASS:
Tunicates
Ascidiacea

SIZE: ¹/₄ in. or less
DEPTH: 5 - 100 ft.

GEOMETRIC ENCRUSTING TUNICATES
Botryllus sp.
CLASS:
Tunicates
Ascidiacea

SIZE: ¹/₄ in. or less
DEPTH: 5 - 100 ft.

VISUAL ID: Mottled in a variety of colors including shades of brown, pink, red, and even blue. The colonies form cushions that are soft, not firm like those of *Eudistoma* [pg. 311]. Tiny individuals, growing in a common tunic, form circular or ovular patterns around central outflow openings. Each individual can be recognized by the small opening of its incurrent siphon.

ABUNDANCE & DISTRIBUTION: Occasional Florida, Bahamas, Caribbean.

HABITAT & BEHAVIOR: Colonies encrust areas of dead coral, shipwrecks, some species of living coral and gorgonian stalks.

REACTION TO DIVERS: Unafraid; close siphons only when molested.

VISUAL ID: Tiny individuals, in a common tunic, form circular or ovular patterns around a single outflow opening. These orange or purple button-like colonies usually grow in small clusters.

ABUNDANCE & DISTRIBUTION: Occasional Florida, Bahamas, Caribbean.

HABITAT & BEHAVIOR: Inhabit reefs. Encrust areas of dead coral, often between encrusting colonies of sponge.

REACTION TO DIVERS: Relatively unafraid; close siphons only when closely approached or molested.

VISUAL ID: Numerous tiny individuals are embedded in a soft, thin, globular tunic. Their excurrent siphons empty into a swollen, interior chamber that has random, large, outflow openings. Has many color varieties including yellow, orange, green, brown, and gray. Other unreported color varieties are possible. Usually has white outlines around the tiny incurrent siphons. Only this genus of the Family Didemnidae [pg. 319] lacks spicules in their tunic which accounts for the soft structure. May appear, at first glance, as an encrusting sponge; note the visual similarity to red encrusting sponge in the photograph.

ABUNDANCE & DISTRIBUTION: Common Caribbean.

HABITAT & BEHAVIOR: Inhabit reefs. Encrust in protected areas, often under ledge overhangs and in shallow depressions on walls.

REACTION TO DIVERS: Unafraid; when molested, close siphons and dramatically deflate and retract.

MOTTLED ENCRUSTING TUNICATE
Distaplia bermudensis
CLASS:
Tunicates
Ascidiacea

SIZE: ¹/₄ in. or less
DEPTH: 25 - 65 ft.

BUTTON TUNICATE
Distaplia corolla
CLASS:
Tunicates
Ascidiacea

SIZE: ¹/₄ in. or less
DEPTH: 25 - 75 ft.

GLOBULAR ENCRUSTING TUNICATE
Diplosoma glandulosum
CLASS:
Tunicates
Ascidiacea

SIZE: Colonies 1 - 4 in.
DEPTH: 25 - 100 ft.

VISUAL ID: Distinguished from many similar appearing species by dense spicules embedded in the tunic that appear as tiny, white specks over the surface. Commonly orange, occasionally white. Numerous individuals are embedded in the thin, encrusting tunic. Their excurrent siphons empty into an interior chamber that has one or several outflow openings. Those with multiple outflow openings often form meandering chains. May appear, at first glance, as an encrusting sponge.

ABUNDANCE & DISTRIBUTION: Common Caribbean; occasional South Florida, Bahamas.

HABITAT & BEHAVIOR: Inhabit coral reefs. Attach to a variety of substrate, especially common on Orange Elephant Ear Sponges [pg. 53].

REACTION TO DIVERS: Unafraid; when molested, close siphons and dramatically deflate and retract.

VISUAL ID: Dark gray. Numerous tiny individuals are embedded in a soft, thin tunic. Their excurrent siphons empty into an inflated internal chamber that has random, large outflow openings. Dark, tiny incurrent siphons are scattered over the surface of the tunic. May appear, at first glance, as an encrusting sponge.

ABUNDANCE & DISTRIBUTION: Occasional Caribbean.

HABITAT & BEHAVIOR: Inhabit reefs. Encrust protected areas, often under ledge overhangs and in shallow depressions on walls. Occasionally overgrow live areas of reefs.

REACTION TO DIVERS: Unafraid; when molested, close siphons and dramatically deflate and retract.

VISUAL ID: Numerous tiny individuals are embedded in a tough, leathery tunic. Their excurrent siphons empty into thin internal chambers that have relatively small outflow openings. Tiny incurrent siphons are scattered over the surface of the tunic. At first glance, they appear to be encrusting sponges. Usually shades of gray, but can be blue-green, green or white.

ABUNDANCE & DISTRIBUTION: Common Florida, Bahamas, Caribbean.

HABITAT & BEHAVIOR: Inhabit shallow reefs. Encrust and often overgrow living corals.

REACTION TO DIVERS: Unafraid; close siphons only when molested.

WHITE SPECK TUNICATE
Didemnum conchyliatum
CLASS:
Tunicates
Ascidiacea
FAMILY:
Didemnidae

SIZE: Colony ¼ - 2 in.
DEPTH: 20 - 100 ft.

BLACK OVERGROWING TUNICATE
Didemnum vanderhorsti
CLASS:
Tunicates
Ascidiacea
FAMILY:
Didemnidae

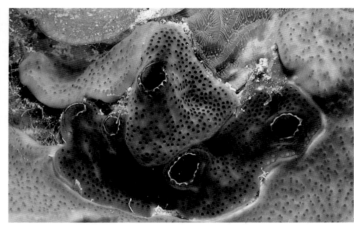

SIZE: Colony 1 - 4 in.
DEPTH: 20 - 75 ft.

OVERGROWING MAT TUNICATE
Trididemum solidum
CLASS:
Tunicates
Ascidiacea
FAMILY:
Didemnidae

SIZE: Colony 3 - 12 in.
DEPTH: 10 - 40 ft.

Tunicates – Pelagic Tunicates

VISUAL ID: Members of the Family Didemnidae are generally typified by numerous tiny individuals embedded in a thin tunic that is usually firm and opaque. Their incurrent siphons are scattered over the tunic's surface. The excurrent siphons empty into an internal chamber that has large outflow openings. Colors, markings and physical appearance of genera and species, however, are neither consistent or well established in scientific literature. Positive identification requires microscopic examination. There are five Caribbean genera, *Trididemnum*, *Didemnum*, *Leptoclinides*, *Lissoclinum*, and *Diplosoma*. At first glance, they often appear as an encrusting sponge.

ABUNDANCE & DISTRIBUTION: Common Florida, Bahamas, Caribbean.

HABITAT & BEHAVIOR: Inhabit reefs. Encrust and occasionally overgrow living parts of reefs.

REACTION TO DIVERS: Unafraid; when molested, close siphons and dramatically deflate and retract.

VISUAL ID: Transparent individuals that resemble a jet engine pod. Often joined in chains and other formations [see next page].

ABUNDANCE & DISTRIBUTION: Occasional worldwide.

HABITAT & BEHAVIOR: Swim in open water by water-jet action. Many species reproduce by budding, forming long chains and other formations of individuals.

REACTION TO DIVERS: None.

NOTE: Pictured individual, opposite, is a salp. Members of the genus *Salpa* can be distinguished by transparent muscular bands that do not completely encircle the body, while the bands of the genus *Doliolumn* encircle the body.

OVERGROWING TUNICATES

CLASS:
Tunicates
Ascidiacea
FAMILY:
Didemnidae

SIZE: Colonies 1 - 4 in.
DEPTH: 20 - 100 ft.

PELAGIC TUNICATES

Salpa sp.
CLASS:
Pelagic Tunicates
Thaliacea

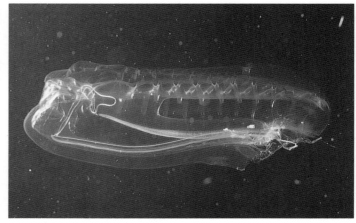

SIZE: 1 - 2 in.
DEPTH: 10 - 130 ft.

Pelagic Tunicates

Pelagic Tunicates; chains and other formations

Budding reproduction in process
[middle left]

Circular formation
[middle right]

Chain formations [right, bottom left and right]

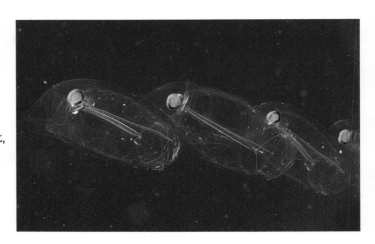

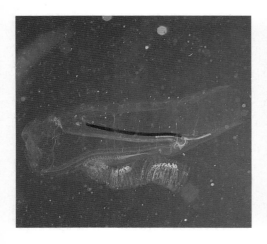

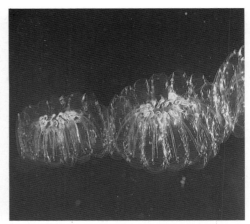

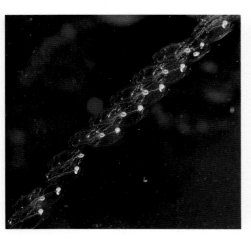

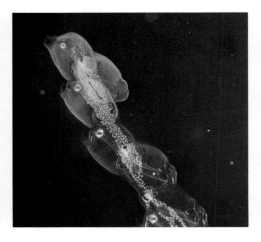

1. PORIFERA
Sponges

No.	Name	Page	Date	Location
	Branching Tube Sponge *Pseudoceratina crassa*	17		
	Rough Tube Sponge *Oceanapia bartschi*	19		
	Stove-pipe Sponge *Aplysina archeri*	19		
	Yellow Tube Sponge *Aplysina fistularis*	21		
	Convoluted Barrel Sponge *Aplysina lacunosa*	21		
	Brown Tube Sponge *Agelas conifera*	23		
	Brown Clustered Tube Sponge *Agelas wiedenmyeri*	23		
	Branching Vase Sponge *Callyspongia vaginalis*	25		
	Azure Vase Sponge *Callyspongia plicifera*	25		
	Strawberry Vase Sponge *Mycale laxissima*	27		
	Pink Vase Sponge *Niphates digitalis*	27		
	Brown Bowl Sponge *Cribrochalina vasculum*	27		
	Netted Barrel Sponge *Verongula gigantea*	29		
	Giant Barrel Sponge *Xestospongia muta*	29		
	Leathery Barrel Sponge *Geodia neptuni*	29		
	Loggerhead Sponge *Spheciospongia vesparium*	31		
	Black-ball Sponge *Ircinia strobilina*	31		
	Stinker Sponge *Ircinia felix*	31		
	Orange Ball Sponge *Cinachyra alloclad*	33		
	Dark Volcano Sponge *Calyx podatypa*	33		
	Pitted Sponge *Verongula rigida*	33		
	Pink Lumpy Sponge *Monanchora unguifera*	35		
	Lumpy Overgrowing Sponge *Holopsamma helwigi*	35		
	Fire Sponge *Tedania ignis*	35		
	Touch-Me-Not Sponge *Neofibularia nolitangere*	37		
	Brown Encrusting Octopus Sponge *Ectyoplasia ferox*	37		
	Lavender Rope Sponge *Niphates erecta*	39		
	Row Pore Rope Sponge *Aplysina cauliformis*	39		

2. CNIDARIA
Hydroids, Siphonophores, True Jellyfish, Box Jellies, Sea Anemones, Zoanthids,
Corallimorphs, Tube-dwelling Anemones

No.	Name	Page	Date	Location
	Feather Hydroid *Gymnangium longicauda*	69		
	Slender Feather Hydroid *Gymnangium speciosum*	69		
	Feather Plume Hydroid *Aglaophenia latecarinata*	69		
	Branching Hydroid *Sertularella speciosa*	71		
	Christmas Tree Hydroid *Halocordyle disticha*	71		
	Algae Hydroid *Thyroscyphus ramosus*	71		
	Unbranched Hydroid *Cnidoscyphus marginatus*	73		
	Feather Bush Hydroid *Dentitheca dendritica*	73		
	Stinging Hydroid *Macrorhynchia allmani*	73		
	Stinging Bush Hydroid *Macrorhynchia robusta*	75		
	Thread Hydroid *Halopteris carinata*	75		
	Seafan Hydroid *Solanderia gracilis*	75		
	Solitary Gorgonian Hydroid *Ralpharia gorgoniae*	77		
	Solitary Sponge Hydroid *Zyzzyzus warreni*	77		
	Club Hydromedusa *Orchistoma pileus*	77		
	Jelly Hydromedusa *Aequorea aequorea*	79		
	Portuguese Man-Of-War *Physalia physalis*	79		
	Floating Siphonophore *Rhizophysa* sp.	79		
	Paired-bell Siphonophore *Agalma okeni*	81		
	Red-spotted Siphonophore *Forskalia edwardsi*	81		
	Warty Jellyfish *Pelagia noctiluca*	81		
	Blue-tinted Jellyfish *Phyllorhiza punctata*	83		
	Moon Jelly *Aurelia aurita*	83		
	Cannonball Jelly *Stomolophus meleagris*	83		
	Marbled Jelly *Lychnorhiza* sp.	85		
	Stinging Cauliflower *Drymonema dalmatinum*	85		
	Sea Thimble *Linuche unguiculata*	85		
	Upsidedown Jelly *Cassiopea frondosa*	87		

No.	Name	Page	Date	Location
	Forked Tentacle Corallimorph *Discosoma carlgreni*	105		
	Umbrella Corallimorph *Discosoma neglecta*	107		
	Orange Ball Corallimorph *Pseudocorynactis caribbeorum*	107		
	Banded Tube-dwelling Anemone *Arachnanthus nocturnus*	107		

3. CTENOPHORA
Comb Jellies

No.	Name	Page	Date	Location
	Sea Walnut *Mnemiopsis mccradyi*	111		
	Warty Comb Jelly *Leucothea multicornis*	111		
	Winged Comb Jelly *Ocyropsis crystallina*	111		
	Spot-winged Comb Jelly *Ocyropsis maculata*	113		
	Red-spot Comb Jelly *Eurhamphaea vexilligera*	113		
	Sea Gooseberry *Euplakamis* sp.	113		
	Venus' Girdle *Cestum veneris*	115		
	Small Venus' Girdle *Velamen parallelum*	115		
	Flattened Helmet Comb Jelly *Beroe ovata*	115		

4. PLATYHELMENTHES - RHYNCHOCOELA
Flatworms - Ribbon Worms

No.	Name	Page	Date	Location
	Leopard Flatworm *Pseudoceros pardalis*	119		
	Lined Flatworm *Pseudoceros crozieri*	119		
	Netted Flatworm *Pseudoceros texarus*	119		
	Bicolored Flatworm *Pseudoceros bicolor*	121		
	Splendid Flatworm *Pseudoceros splendidus*	121		
	Red & White Striped Ribbon Worm	121		

5. ANNELIDA
Fireworms, Feather Duster Worms, Calcareous Tube Worms, Spaghetti Worms

No.	Name	Page	Date	Location
	Bearded Fireworm *Hermodice carunculata*	125		
	Red-tipped Fireworm *Chloeia viridis*	125		
	Scale Worms	127		
	Sponge Worms *Haplosyllis* sp.	127		
	Southern Lugworm *Arenicola cristata*	127		

No.	Name	Page	Date	Location
	Magnificent Feather Duster *Sabellastarte magnifica*	129		
	Social Feather Duster *Bispira brunnea*	129		
	Variegated Feather Duster *Bispira variegata*	131		
	Ghost Feather Duster *Anamobaea* sp.	131		
	Yellow Fanworm *Notaulax occidentalis*	133		
	Brown Fanworm *Notaulax nudicollis*	133		
	Ruffled Feather Duster *Hypsicomus* sp.	133		
	Split-crown Feather Duster *Anamobaea orstedii*	135		
	Black-spotted Feather Duster *Branchiomma nigromaculata*	135		
	Shy Feather Duster *Megalomma* sp.	135		
	Christmas Tree Worm *Spirobranchus giganteus*	137		
	Star Horseshoe Worm *Pomatostegus stellatus*	137		
	Red-spotted Horseshoe Worm *Protula* sp.	139		
	Touch-Me-Not Fanworm *Hydroides spongicola*	139		
	Sea Frost *Filograna huxleyi*	139		
	Blushing Star Coral Fanworm *Vermiliopsis* n. sp.	141		
	Spaghetti Worm *Eupolymnia crassicornis*	141		
	Medusa Worm *Loimia medusa*	141		

6. ARTHROPODA

Shrimp, Lobsters, Hermit Crabs, Porcelain Crabs, True Crabs, Mantis Shrimp, Isopods, Mysid Shrimp, Barnacles, Horseshoe Crab

No.	Name	Page	Date	Location
	Two Claw Shrimp *Brachycarpus biunguiculatus*	147		
	Banded Coral Shrimp *Stenopus hispidus*	147		
	Golden Coral Shrimp *Stenopus scutellatus*	147		
	Peppermint Shrimp *Lysmata wurdemanni*	149		
	Scarlet-striped Cleaning Shrimp *Lysmata grabhami*	149		
	Squat Anemone Shrimp *Thor amboinensis*	149		
	Arrow Shrimp *Tozeuma carolinense*	151		
	Pederson Cleaner Shrimp *Periclimenes pedersoni*	151		
	Spotted Cleaner Shrimp *Periclimenes yucatanicus*	151		
	Red Snapping Shrimp *Alpheaus armatus*	153		

No.	Name	Page	Date	Location
	Large-claw Snapping Shrimp *Synalpheus* sp.	153		
	Red Night Shrimp *Rhynchocinetes rigens*	153		
	Caribbean Spiny Lobster *Panulirus argus*	155		
	Spotted Spiny Lobster *Panulirus guttatus*	155		
	Smoothtail Spiny Lobster *Panlirus laevicauda*	154		
	Red Banded Lobster *Justitia longimanus*	157		
	Copper Lobster *Palinurellus gundlachi*	157		
	Spanish Lobster *Scyllarides aequinoctialis*	157		
	Regal Slipper Lobster *Arctides Guinaensis*	159		
	Sculptured Slipper Lobster *Parribacus antarcticus*	159		
	Giant Hermit *Petrochirus diogenes*	159		
	Stareye Hermit *Dardanus venosus*	161		
	Bareye Hermit *Dardanus fucosus*	160		
	White Speckled Hermit *Paguristes punticeps*	161		
	Red Banded Hermit *Paguristes erythrops*	161		
	Red Reef Hermit *Paguristes cadenati*	163		
	Orangeclaw Hermit *Calcinus tibicen*	163		
	Red-stripe Hermit *Phimochirus holthuisi*	163		
	Polkadotted Hermit *Phimochirus operculatus*	165		
	Spotted Porcelain Crab *Porcellana sayana*	165		
	Green Porcelain Crab *Petrolisthes armatus*	165		
	Batwing Coral Crab *Carpilius corallinus*	167		
	Black Coral Crab *Paraliomera dispar*	167		
	Eroded Mud Crab *Glyptoxanthus erosus*	167		
	Florida Stone Crab *Menippe mercenaria*	169		
	Green Clinging Crab *Mithrax sculptus*	169		
	Banded Clinging Crab *Mithrax cinctimanus*	169		
	Red-ridged Clinging Crab *Mithrax forceps*	171		
	Channel Clinging Crab *Mithrax spinosissimus*	171		
	Hairy Clinging Crab *Mithrax pilosus*	171		

No.	Name	Page	Date	Location
	Gaudy Clown Crab *Platypodiella spectabilis*	173		
	Rough Box Crab *Calappa gallus*	173		
	Flame Box Crab *Calappa flammea*	172		
	Nimble Spray Crab *Percnon gibbesi*	173		
	Heart Urchin Pea Crab *Dissodactylus primitives*	175		
	Ocellate Swimming Crab *Portunus sebae*	175		
	Redhair Swimming Crab *Portunus ordwayi*	174		
	Sargassum Swimming Crab *Portunus soyi*	175		
	Blue Crabs *Callinectes* sp.	177		
	Yellowline Arrow Crab *Stenorhynchus seticornis*	177		
	Cryptic Teardrop Crab *Pelia mutical*	177		
	Neck Crab *Podochela* sp.	179		
	Scaly-tailed Mantis *Lysiosquilla scabricauda*	179		
	Reef Mantis *Lysiosquilla glabriuscular*	181		
	Swollen-claw Mantis *Gonodactylus oerstedii*	181		
	Dark Mantis *Gonodactylus curacaoensis*	181		
	Soldierfish Isopod *Anilocra laticaudata*	183		
	Mysid Shrimp *Mysidium* sp.	183		
	Sessile Barnacles	183		
	Smooth Goose-Neck Barnacle *Lepas anatifera*	185		
	Grooved Goose-Neck Barnacle *Lepas anserifera*	184		
	Scaled Goose-Neck Barnacle *Lepas pectinata*	184		
	Black Coral Barnacle *Oxynaspis gracilis*	185		
	Horseshoe Crab *Limulus polyphemus*	185		

7. ECTOPROCTA
Bryozoans

No.	Name	Page	Date	Location
	White Fan Bryozoan *Reteporellina evelinae*	189		
	Brown Fan Bryozoan *Canda simplex*	189		
	Tan Fan Bryozoan *Scrupocellaria* sp.	189		
	Purple Reef Fan *Bugula minima*	191		

No.	Name	Page	Date	Location
	White Tangled Bryozoan *Bracebridgia subsulcata*	191		
	Tangled Ribbon Bryozoan *Membranipora* sp.	191		
	Spiral-tufted Bryozoan *Bugula turrita*	193		
	Seaweed Bryozoan *Caulibugula dendrograpta*	193		
	Tubular-horn Bryozoan *Schizoporella violacea*	193		
	Bleeding Teeth Bryozoan *Trematooecia aviculifera*	195		
	Pearly Orange Encrusting Bryozoan *Hippopodina feegeensis*	195		
	Purple Encrusting Bryozoan *Schizoporella* sp.	195		
	Pearly Red Encrusting Bryozoan *Steginoporella magnilabris*	195		

8. MOLLUSCA
Snails, Shell-less Snails, Chitons, Bivalves, Squid, Octopuses

No.	Name	Page	Date	Location
	Queen Conch *Strombus gigas*	201		
	Milk Conch *Strombus costatus*	201		
	Hawkwing Conch *Strombus raninus*	201		
	Florida Fighting Conch *Strombus alatus*	203		
	Roostertail Conch *Strombus gallus*	203		
	West Indian Fighting Conch *Strombus pugilis*	202		
	Roostertail Conch *Strombus gallus*	203		
	Florida Horse Conch *Pleuroploca gigantea*	203		
	True Tulip *Fasciolaria tulipa*	205		
	Atlantic Triton's Trumpet *Charonia variegata*	205		
	Atlantic Hairy Triton *Cymatium pileare*	205		
	King Helmet *Cassis tuberosa*	207		
	Flame Helmet *Cassis flammea*	206		
	Emperor Helmet, Queen Helmet *Cassis madagascariensis*	206		
	Netted Olive *Oliva reticularis*	207		
	Lettered Olive *Oliva sayana*	206		
	Glowing Marginella *Marginella pruniosum*	207		
	White-Spotted Marginella *Marginella guttata*	206		
	West Indian Starsnail *Lithopoma tectum*	209		

No.	Name	Page	Date	Location
	American Starsnail *Lithopoma americanaum*	208		
	Stocky Cerith *Cerithium litteratum*	209		
	Chocolate-lined Topsnail *Calliostoma javanicum*	209		
	Coffee Bean Trivia *Trivia pediculus*	211		
	Atlantic Deer Cowrie *Cypraea cervus*	211		
	Measled Cowrie *Cypraea zebra*	211		
	Atlantic Gray Cowrie *Cypraea cinerea*	213		
	Atlantic Yellow Cowrie *Cypraea spurca acicularis*	213		
	Spotted Cyphoma *Cyphoma macgintyi*	213		
	Flamingo Tongue *Cyphoma gibbosm*	215		
	Fingerprint Cyphoma *Cyphoma signatum*	215		
	West Indian Simnia *Cymbovula acicularis*	215		
	Florida Wormsnail *Vermicularia knorrii*	217		
	Miniature Melo *Micromela undata*	217		
	Striate Bubble *Bulla striata*	217		
	Mysterious Headshield Slug *Navanax Aenigmaticus*	219		
	Leech Headshield Slug *Chelidonura hirundinina*	219		
	Blue-ring Sea Hare *Stylocheilus longicauda*	219		
	White-spotted Sea Hare *Aplysia parvula*	221		
	Spotted Sea Hare *Aplysia dactylomela*	221		
	Ragged Sea Hare *Bursatella leach*	221		
	Warty Sidegill Slug *Pleurobranchus areolatus*	223		
	Apricot Sidegill Slug *Berthellina engeli*	223		
	Ornate Elysia *Elysia ornata*	223		
	Brown-lined Elysia *Elysia subornata*	225		
	Painted Elysia *Elysia picta*	225		
	Lined-shell Sea Slug *Lobiger souverbiei*	225		
	Lettuce Sea Slug *Tridachia crispata*	227		
	Reticulated Sea Slug *Oxynoe antillarum*	227		
	Harlequin Glass-slug *Cyerce cristallina*	229		

No.	Name	Page	Date	Location
	Atlantic Pearl-oyster *Pinctada radiata*	251		
	Atlantic Wing-oyster *Pteria colymbus*	251		
	Knobby Scallop *Chlamys imbricata*	253		
	Frons Oyster *Lopha frons*	253		
	Lister Purse-oyster *Isognomon radiatus*	253		
	Bicolor Purse-oyster *Isognomon bicolor*	252		
	Flat Tree-oyster *Isognomon alatus*	255		
	Amber Penshell *Pinna carnea*	255		
	Sunrise Tellin *Tellina radiata*	255		
	Fuzzy Chiton *Acanthopleura granulata*	257		
	Florida Slender Chiton *Stenoplax floridana*	257		
	Ornate Goddess Chiton *Calloplax janeirensis*	257		
	Caribbean Reef Squid *Sepioteuthis sepioidea*	259		
	Inshore Arrow Squid *Doryteuthis plei*	259		
	Caribbean Two-spot Octopus *Octopus filosus*	259		
	Mexican Four-eyed Octopus *Octopus maya*	258		
	Atlantic Pygmy Octopus *Octopus joubini*	261		
	Caribbean Reef Octopus *Octopus briareus*	261		
	Common Octopus *Octopus vulgaris*	263		
	White-spotted Octopus *Octopus macropus*	263		
	Brownstripe Octopus *Octopus burryi*	263		

9. ECHINODERMATA
Feather Stars, Sea Stars, Brittle Stars, Basket Stars, Sea Urchins,
Heart Urchins, Sand Dollars, Sea Cucumbers

No.	Name	Page	Date	Location
	Golden Crinoid *Davidaster rubiginosa*	269		
	Beaded Crinoid *Davidaster discoidea*	269		
	Black & White Crinoid *Nemaster grandis*	271		
	Swimming Crinoid *Analcidometra armata*	271		
	Cushion Sea Star *Oreaster reticulatus*	271		
	Nine-armed Sea Star *Luidia senegalensis*	273		
	Banded Sea Star *Luidia alternata*	273		

No.	Name	Page	Date	Location
	Slate-pencil Urchin *Eucidaris tribuloidesï*	291		
	West Indian Sea Egg *Tripneustes ventricosus*	293		
	Red Heart Urchin *Meoma ventricosa*	293		
	Sand Dollar *Clypeaster subdepressus*	293		
	Four-Notched Sand Dollar *Encope michelini*	292		
	Five-Notched Sand Dollar *Encope emarginata*	292		
	Six-Keyhole Sand Dollar *Mellita sexiesperforata*	295		
	Five-Keyhole Sand Dollar *Mellita quinquiesperforata*	295		
	Furry Sea Cucumber *Astichopus multifidus*	295		
	Five-toothed Sea Cucumber *Actinopyga agassizii*	295		
	Three-rowed Sea Cucumber *Isostichopus badionotus*	297		
	Conical Sea Cucumber *Eostichopus arnesoni*	297		
	Donkey Dung Sea Cucumber *Holothuria mexicana*	297		
	Slender Sea Cucumber *Holothuria impatiens*	299		
	Tiger Tail Sea Cucumber *Holothuria thomasi*	299		
	Beaded Sea Cucumber *Euapta lappa*	299		

10. CHORDATA
Tunicates, Pelagic Tunicates

No.	Name	Page	Date	Location
	Reef Tunicate *Rhopalaea abdominalis*	303		
	Giant Tunicate *Polycarpa spongiabilis*	303		
	Green Tube Tunicate *Ascidia sydneiensis*	303		
	Painted Tunicate *Clavelina picta*	305		
	Blue Bell Tunicate *Clavelina puerto-secensis*	305		
	Bulb Tunicates *Clavelina sp.*	307		
	Mangrove Tunicate *Ecteinascidia turbinata*	307		
	Encrusting Social Tunicate *Symplegma viride*	309		
	Mottled Social Tunicate *Polyandrocarpa tumida*	309		
	Strawberry Tunicate *Eudistoma sp.*	311		
	Black Condominium Tunicate *Eudistoma obscuratum*	311		
	White Condominium Tunicates *Eudistoma sp.*	311		

No.	Name	Page	Date	Location
	Flat Tunicate *Botrylloides nigrum*	313		
	Row Encrusting Tunicates *Botrylloides* sp.	313		
	Geometric Encrusting Tunicates *Botryllus* sp.	313		
	Mottled Encrusting Tunicate *Distaplia bermudensis*	315		
	Button Tunicate *Distaplia corolla*	315		
	Globular Encrusting Tunicate *Diplosoma glandulosum*	315		
	White Speck Tunicate *Didemnum conchyliatum*	317		
	Black Overgrowing Tunicate *Didemnum vanderhorsti*	317		
	Overgrowing Mat Tunicate *Trididemum solidum*	317		
	Overgrowing Tunicates *Didemnidae*	319		
	Pelagic Tunicates *Thaliacea*	319 320		

ADDITIONAL SPECIES